CONTEMPORARY
APPROACHES TO
IBSEN

VOL. IV

*Reports from
the Fourth International Ibsen Seminar,
Skien 1978*

UNIVERSITETSFORLAGET
OSLO – BERGEN – TROMSØ

© The Norwegian Research Council for Science and the Humanities 1979
(Norges almenvitenskapelige forskningsråd)

Section: A. 68. T. 4

ISBN: 82-00-01937-3

Distribution offices:

NORWAY
Universitetsforlaget
Boks 2977 Tøyen
Oslo 6

UNITED KINGDOM
Global Book Resources Ltd.
109 Great Russel Street
London WC 3ND

UNITED STATES and CANADA
Columbia University Press
136 South Broadway
Irvington-on-Hudson
New York 10533

Printed in Norway by
H. Lyche & Co., Drammen

CONTEMPORARY
APPROACHES TO
IBSEN

IBSEN YEARBOOK [IBSENÅRBOKEN] 1978

HEAD EDITOR
DANIEL HAAKONSEN
Professor of Scandinavian Literature
University of Oslo

EDITORIAL BOARD
ELSE HÖST
EINAR ÖSTVEDT
JOHN NORTHAM

CONTENTS

Foreword

This volume of the Ibsen Yearbook gathers the papers delivered at The Fourth International Ibsen Seminar, held in Skien between the 22nd and the 28th of May 1978. One of the contributors does not want his paper to be printed for the time being.

The main topic of the seminar was «Henrik Ibsen's drama – psychological, social or existential?», and the discussions were centered on three plays: *Ghosts, Rosmersholm* and *John Gabriel Borkman.*

The Skien seminar was part of the celebration of the 150th anniversary of Ibsen's birth. In the U.S.A. another seminar, celebrating the same event, inspired the formation of a new «Ibsenforbund»: *Ibsen Society of America.* An announcement from this new society is printed at the end of the present volume.

D. H.

Social themes and issues in
Ghosts, Rosmersholm and John Gabriel Borkman[1]

EDVARD BEYER

It is usual to group Ibsen's modern plays chronologically – four plays in each group. The first one – from *Pillars* of *Society* to *An Enemy of the People* – is labelled social drama, the second – from *The Wild Duck* to *Hedda Gabler* – psychological plays, and the third – from *The Masterbuilder* to *Wen We Dead Awaken* –, Ibsen's «late», more or less symbolic plays, presenting existential problems, the old dramatist passing retrospective judgement on his own life and work.

This neat arrangement may be useful from a teacher's point of view, but it is unduely schematic. The three plays that are to be the theme of this seminar, belong to the three groups respectively, *Ghosts* to the first, the social plays, *Rosmersholm* to the psychological and *John Gabriel Borkman* to the group of «late» plays. But they are all psychological, they all raise ethical and existential issues, and they are all social plays. In opposition to the traditional scheme I suggest that *Rosmersholm* and *John Gabriel Borkman* are social plays to the same extent as *Ghosts* – or even more. Of course I then use the word 'social' in a wide sense, implying that the play under consideration reflects or interprets essential characteristics of the society of its time, that the *dramatis personae* are stamped or destined by their social surroundings, and that the action is conditioned by the society in which it takes place.

The scene of *Ghosts* is a landed property in a rainy landscape on a fiord of Western Norway, not far from what Mrs. Alving calls 'en halvstor by', a medium sized town – Bergen has been suggested. The main characters belong to the class of government officials. The late Mr. Alving was an officer, not beyond the rank of captain, it is true, but rich enough to be a profitable match and to buy a rural estate, and he has had the honorary title of chamberlain bestowed on him. As a minister

[1] Quotations from *Rosmersholm* are taken from J. W. McFarlane's translation (The Oxford Ibsen, vol. VI, 1960). *John Gabriel Borkman* is quoted from the translations by Rolf Fjelde (Ibsen. Four Major Plays, 1970) and Michael Meyer (When We Dead Awaken and three other plays, 1960).

9

in the state church pastor Manders is also a government official, a civil servant of the king. They both represent the aristocracy of officialdom that had governed the country ever since 1814, but was now – about 1880 – fighting stubbornly against the advancing forces of democracy – the lower middle classes, the bulk of the peasantry, and the liberal professions – , a fight that resulted in a total defeat a few years later, in 1883—84. The late chamberlain belongs to the past in every sense of the word, and he did so when he was still alive; it is significant that he preferred to lie on the sofa reading «an *old* government yearbook» (my italics). The clergy had more and more taken over the ideological warfare and self-justification of the civil servants, the final argument being that according to the Bible the authorities hold their might from God. In the year 1876 a prominent cleric declared that modern liberalism came from the Devil, as revolt against the authorities was revolt against God. The modern ideas of the time – positivism, utilitarianism, feminism, darwinism, criticism of the Bible were regarded as threats not only to Christianity but to the existing order of society. In this context pastor Manders may be best understood. He is not a mere charicature, but a type of his time. He does not only fight for his own cause, but he is defending the moral, social and – by implication – political authority of his class. When he so bluntly condemns the books and periodicals he has not read, he can do so blindly confiding in the judgement of his more well-read colleagues.

Against all this Mrs. Alving has risen, and she has been for a long time struggling for her own liberation. She has seen the seamy side of the existing social order. Pastor Manders himself first made her doubt the traditional doctrines. Since then she has gradually adopted an independent way of thinking. But she has also experienced that the imbibed ideology is more deeply rooted in the mind than what people really «think and believe» but dare not confess whether to others nor to themselves. «Over the whole country there must be ghosts, as numerous as the sands of the sea.»

The existing Norwegian society is regarded as backward and confined. This is most directly expressed through Osvald, who has seen a freer and happier life abroad, but who is also well aware that if he tried to live the same kind of life here, it would still not be the same, but turn into ugliness. These words call forth Mrs. Alving's final understanding of her husband's tragedy, and the plight of the «joy-of-life» in this constricted, censorious society. They also point to the implied criticism of the moral double-dealing that is symbolized by the close alliance between Manders and Engstrand.

10

In a social and historical perspective *Ghosts* depicts what a modern historican, Jens Arup Seip, has called «a regime on the eve of its ruin». But it also shows how the old order survives in the minds of people.

Rosmersholm takes place after the fall of the old dominion. Some words about «the rulers of the moment» in rektor Kroll's conservative paper nearly gives the exact date: the action must be taking place after 1884. The play is more coloured by contemporary Norwegian politics than any other of Ibsen's plays. (We also know from his letters that he to a great extent built on what he had seen and experienced of Norwegian politics during his visit in the summer of 1885.)

The play has obvious points of similarity with *Ghosts*. This applies to dramatic structure as well as to theme and social surroundings. The manor of Rosmersholm reminds us of Mrs. Alving's Rosenvold. But Rosmersholm is much more closely identified with the power of the past and, in particular, of «l'ancien régime». In this manor one and the same family is said to have been living as government officials – mostly parsons and military officers – for about two hundred years, in other words since about 1660, when absolute monarchy was established in Denmark-Norway. From an historical point of view it is unthinkable. Official servants were not appointed that way; they were a migratory race. Ibsen has, however, with open eyes broken the rules of realism, obviously for the purpose of assembling as much as possible of traditional, economic, physical and spiritual power and authority in one place. The manor has become a symbol. As Kroll puts it: «Since time immemorial Rosmersholm has been like a stronghold of order and high thinking of respect [---] and esteem for all those things which are accepted and acknowledged by the best people in our society.» Rosmer, on the other hand, regrets that from this place the Rosmers have «spread gloom and depression all these long years». Kroll speaks as a civil servant, a headmaster, not a cleric, but a spiritual kinsman of Manders all the same. Kroll is a typical exponent of the defeated class – stubborn, embittered, uncompromising. Mortensgård, the newspaper editor, belongs to the victorious party, although not to the «Pure Left» that was soon to emerge, but the cautious, tactical, calculating, right wing of the party. Rebekka West, on the other hand, is a child of the free-thinking, individualistic opposition against all traditional norms and values, carried to extremes.

In the middle of all this Rosmer tries to find his way. He used to be a parson, but has resigned from his position; he has abandoned his faith, and he now breaks with his friends and colleagues. He has untied himself from the family traditions and is intending to atone for its illdoings during «the long, long ages». The ruthlessnes of the political struggle appals him, and he confronts it with his dream or vision of reconciliation, harmony and collaboration in a nation of «free and happy, noble human beeings». It is a dream of a synthesis, a union on a higher level of Christian ethics and radical, human emancipation, a renewed version of what Maximos in *Emperor and Galilean* called «the third empire».

Rosmer's vision is the only glimpse we get in any of Ibsen's social plays of a balanced harmony between the unhampered selfrealisation of the individual and the demands of society and human solidarity. Ibsen himself had – in a letter to Bjørnson 1884 – hoped for a new and resolute party that could rally the unprivileged classes in a struggle for radical democratic reforms. Rosmer, on the other hand, believes in reconciliation and cooperation of the classes. But he is never allowed to work for his ideas. He is overtaken and paralyzed by his own past.

Ghosts and *Rosmersholm* reflect and interpret – in our perspective – the dissolution and ruin of the old social order. *John Gabriel Borkman,* written ten years after *Rosmersholm,* is set in a fullblown capitalist society. It was written during the hectic boom and «Gründerzeit» of the second half of the eighteen-nineties. Borkman's activity, it is true, came to an end long before, and could chronologically be placed in the seventies, during the first industrial revolution on a larger scale in Norway. But his gigantic dreams and visions – «Drilling new shafts, endlessly! Waterfalls! Stone quarries! Trade routes and shipping lines, girdling the globe. [---] That entire enormous stock pool [---]» – rather belong to the eighteen-nineties after all.

Early capitalism in Norway was the background of *Pillars of Society,* written nineteen years before. There are evident thematic similarities between the two plays, but there is an enormous difference between Bernick modernizing his shipyard and speculating in the new railway and Borkman giving himself away to his fantastic projects. *John Gabriel Borkman* is in about the same proportion to Bjørnson's *Beyond our Powers – Part Two* published the year before, as *Pillars of Society* is to Bjørnson's *A Bankruptcy* (1875). In both cases Bjørnson dramatized the social problems, the clash of the forces, whereas Ibsen concentrates on ethical and psychological themes. In *Beyond our Powers* the working masses are confronted by allmighty capitalistic employers. In *John Gabriel Borkman* we meet a representative of this new upper class at close quarters. Borkman is a former bank director who long ago dreamed of liberating the powers of the ore «that wants to come up into daylight and serve mankind.» – «All the sources of power in this country I wanted at my command. The earth, the mountains, the forests, the sea – I wanted to subjugate all the riches they held, and carve out a kingdom for myself, and use it to further the well-being of so many thousands of others.» It is not my task to analyze Borkman's secret motives and decide how much he was from the beginning inspired by honest altruism, and how much he was fascinated and tempted by «the kingdom and the power and the glory». In any case he sold his beloved for a bank directorship, stole large sums in the vaults of the bank and ruined innumerable customs, treated his wife and son with frightful chill, and entrenched himself behind an obstinate self-righteousness, unapproachable for any kind of human warmth, doomed – without the slightest glimpse of a redeeming recognition. His way of thinking is completely reified, «But in the last analysis, any woman can be repleaced by another.» The only thing he has always loved are the veins of ore and the «chained millions». «I love you, all the treasures longing to be born, with your luminous blessings of power and of glory! I love you, love you, love you!»

John Gabriel Borkman is – from a social and historical point of view – a tragedy of the alluring, devastating power of capitalism that does not only destroy its most obvious, defenceless victims, but enslaves and annihilates all human feelings in the man who longed to be its master. «A hand of ice that gripped my heart,» he says in the last moment of his life. But he corrects himself, «No. Not a hand of ice. A hand of iron.» There are good reasons for calling it the iron hand of capitalism.

A psychological aspect

OTTO HAGEBERG

It is a pleasure to see Ibsen scholars from so many countries assembled here, to begin a seminar in which, once again, we shall be asking what it is that particularly distinguishes Ibsen's writing, and considering different approaches to the analysis of his work. I am sure we all agree that Ibsen's drama can be studied from many angles, and that the light shed on the works varies according to the questions we ask. No-one here believes that Ibsen was either a social or a psychological or an existential writer. We would agree that all these aspects are reflected in his works at the same time; but no doubt we may disagree about which questions bring us closest to the distinctive quality of his writing.

No one would dispute that a comprehensive study of Ibsen's drama must include the sociological perspective, particularly where his realistic plays on contemporary society are concerned. His characters, with their relationships and conflicts, are to a large extent determined by historical and social forces, by a particular social structure and organization, and by their social class. Although Ibsen wrote most of hes realistic social dramas a long way away from Norway, they give an interesting and, I believe, largely true picture of important aspects of Norwegian society towards the end of the nineteenth century. It will therefore always be an important aim of Ibsen research to identify and define the forces that condition the characters and their relationships.

This implies that we also need to go on asking in what ways the characters' own insight is restricted by the ways of thinking and the ideological pressures of the society they live in. Not only sociologically but also ideologically orientated criticism is indispensable to Ibsen research.

It is equally clear that such an approach will not satisfy all those who are interested in Ibsen's drama. The society he lived in lies behind us, and besides he arouses just as much interest in distant countries as here at home. This suggests that his depictions are generally valid, that through his *creative imagination* he finds and communicates images of life in which people from different societies, cultures, and periods can recognize themselves. It is tempting to let the remark that great art always is universal suffice as a comment on this; but the researcher will feel unhappy with that cliché, and will go on to ask what it is that creates this universality. One answer is that Ibsen's intense dramatic situations present images of life in which people discover that life has consisted, and consists, of fundamental *choices,* choices involving values and requiring the destruction of something, whatever choice is made. Ibsen shows, as few other dramatists have, how longing and dreams of liberation, self-fullfillment, the release of imprisoned forces – and one's commitment to one's longing and dreams, – can carry within them their own opposites: destruction, despair, coldness, death. And it is a basic human experience, expressed in images in all cultures, that human existence is placed in a magnetic field between poles of values that can not be reconciled. Thus we find an existential aspect in Ibsen's drama; and we can add that some of his major characters are bearers of a kind of idealism.

My task in this introductory session is to say a little about a third aspect of Ibsen's drama, the psychological. I do so with pleasure and conviction, believing that this aspect is basic to at least parts of Ibsen's realist drama. But it does not belong in a separate compartment from the social or existential, being closely interwoven with both. In my view the nature of the social forces in Ibsen's plays can only be revealed by analysis of the characters and their inter-relationships, including analysis of their language and what it reveals of their secret inner lives. Similarly I believe that the particular quality of Ibsen's idealism can only be closely defined by taking into account his brilliant and acute psychological insight. It could also be argued that the universal quality of his drama is intimately linked with his penetration to the soul's hidden depths.

My words have been consciously chosen to point in a particular direction, towards depth psychology. A short introductory talk leaves little scope for anything but assertions, unsupported by thorough analysis. Among my assertions – which may be questioned later – is the claim that Ibsen's dramatic genius consists not least in his having been able with his creative imagination to grasp or indeed to anticipate, without any theoretical frame of reference, methods of interpretation that have been fundamental in depth psychology and particularly in psychoanalysis in this century, long before Freud and others had provided them with scientific foundations. Let me repeat, for emphasis, that it was with his creative imagination that Ibsen achieved this understanding. Ibsen sees – as others had not seen – fundamental realities in human life, regardless of historical period. And by means of his creative vision he builds up a system. His psychological studies, and his descriptions of the dynamic relationships between people, appear familiar to scholars acquainted with depth psychology, but when other readers and spectators also respond to them, it must be from the depths of their own souls.

One might lose heart, however, from reading some of the applications of depth psychology to Ibsen's plays. There are, admittedly, honourable exceptions, such as Gunnar Brandell's discussion, of *The Lady from the Sea* in particular, in the article «Freud och hans tid» in *Vid säklets källor*. I also admire Derek Russell Davis's «A Reappraisal of Ibsen's Ghosts», which makes expert use of modern psychodynamic theories. In his book *Sjelelige kriser i menneskets liv*. Ingjald Nissen gives us valuable, Adler-inspired studies of individual psychology in *The Wild Duck, Rosmersholm*, and *Hedda Gabler*, though he pays little attention to the texts as literature. Arne Duve's atomistic and sometimes highly speculative studies provoke opposition rather than inspire imitation. Nevertheless, I would venture the claim that there is a particular need in Ibsen research to-day for scholars who can combine knowledge of depth psychology with respect for the literary qualities of the writing, and so can set in order for us the signs in the texts of Ibsen's insight into the unconscious.

I remarked earlier that Ibsen constructs a *system*. We all know that one of the hallmarks of Ibsen's drama is the retrospective technique. But this technique is more than a dramaturgic device. Increasingly, it also expresses a particular view of human nature. The retrospective technique implies that the characters gradually come to realize that their lives are different from what they had believed them to be, and are governed by forces of which they are not fully conscious. The dialogue is an analytical process, with a constant interplay between surface and depth, the realized and the unrealized, the conscious and the unconscious. Speeches have a *manifest* and a *latent* content. The characters conceal facts from others and from themselves. It can, of course, be maintained that the play as a unified whole reveals the latent content, and that the characters finally attain full awareness of their natures and their situations. Such an argument implies that Ibsen as creator is in complete conscious control and knows all the time what the characters do not know. This is to some extent true, and particularly of certain plays, but is hardly the whole truth. As readers or spectators, we know that there is often something enigmatic at the end of an Ibsen play. The

16

closing scenes allow for at least two interpretations, presenting on the one hand the clarification and establishment of values, and on the other a confrontation with new riddles. Exactly what awareness is it that the characters have achieved? What sets of values do they reveal in the catastrophe? Are they presented as tragic heroes or heroines, or are they exposed as self-betrayed and life-denying characters who reject life's demands and escape into the catastrophe? This is *the* central problem in Ibsen research, and the answer has usually been an «either-or» where a «not only but also» might in fact be preferable. Ibsen's image of man is double, part of a double view of life. His point of departure is idealism, and an image of man as free and free to make real choices among real and possibly irreconcilable values. This is a driving force throughout all his plays. But Ibsen's creative imagination comes into conflict with his idealism, when it exposes the unconscious and presents it as a system and as a controlling force in the personality. His drama can be seen as a kind of research into the human which brings this force to light.

To talk about the unconscious as a system is not easy for a layman, nor indeed for the specialists, to judge from the theory of depth psychology. On this occasion, at any rate, we shall have to make do with some over-simplification. The unconscious is a force that creates *transformations,* and in fact makes compulsive transformation a part of man's nature and mode of existence. The secret, personal, and socially unacceptable forces in human life, not least the instinctive drives, disguise themselves and appear in masks. This is what psychoanalysis designates with concepts like conversion, repression, compensation, rationalization, and sublimation or, in connection with dream theory, compression, displacement, and manifest and latent content.

I think it is useful and perhaps even necessary to bring this frame of reference to bear on Ibsen research, though at present I shall merely be touching on a few points. Ibsen's language, his dialogue, has recently been attracting some attention. Both Inga Stina Ewbank and John Northam, among others, have shown how characters undergo linguistec change in the course of a play, and this is important. But in my opinion one of the theoretical premises for an understanding of Ibsen's language must be that the speeches often consist of emotions transformed so as to appear in verbal disguises, under false names. So we cannot rest content with the surface meaning of the speeches, but must consider and interpret them as emotional role-playing. This gives rise to an important methodological problem: how can one decode the underlying meaning? I certainly have no set answer. Although they may not be found illuminating by everyone, let me quote a few words from the well-known French psychoanalyst and literary scolar André Green's article «La déliaison» in *Littérature* (1971); concerning the relation between reader and text he remarks that «He listens to it in the manner that is typical of psychoanalystic listening. That is the paradox: closely attentive reading is accompanied by relaxed listening, a floating kind of reading. The latter is not careless, on the contrary. It notices anything that may be thought to seduce the reader's attention».

At this point I would have liked to illustrate generously, instead of simply making a few more assertions. An application of one's «floating» reading to an analysis of the dialogue between Rebekka West and Johannes Rosmer in the third act of *Rosmersholm*, would show that when they talk about the joy they used to experience together in their former conversations about his dreams of creating the noble man, «noble man» is a disguised concept. The language of this dialogue is loaded in a very special way. It puts a transformed and spiritualized sexuality in the place of dangerous hidden emotion.

This kind of approach to the analysis of dialogue gives access to a new understanding of the relationship between the characters in the play. While on the subject of *Rosmersholm*, let me make another claim. If we extend Freud's Rebekka West analysis, we can show how her rejection of Johannes Rosmer is connected with the overdetermination for both of them of word and conceptions relating to passion and sexuality. They are part of a complex that at the same time triggers off *fear*. That is why Rebekka has to «put her hands to her ears as if terrified» when Johannes in the proposal scene says *And let us smother all memories in freedom, joy, and passion*. This sets me off on a new track. Ibsen's genius as a psychologist resides particularly in his ability to show systematically how different aspects of the life of the psyche are joined together organically in a *complex*. That brings us to a new concept from psychoanalytical theory, which I have already mentioned and which can be a useful tool, namely *overdetermination*. The term is applied to the fact that a concept can represent several meanings and several emotional poles at the same time. Let me use Ellida Wangel's attidute to the sea in *The Lady from the Sea* as an illustration. The sea attracts and frightens her at the same time; she calls it «fascinating» and «horrifying». To understand this, we have to remember that the sea has from the start been for her the element of freedom in which she has mirrored all her vague longings. In her first meeting with the stranger, her longing for freedom and her erotic fantasies become bound together. But the erotic idyll ends when the man commits a mysterious murder, and at the me time the two of them wed themselves (passively, on her part) to the sea and throw their linked rings into it. We see that, in Ellida's fantasy, initiation into erotic life is made dependent on violence, death, and murder. The sea in her experience therefore stands for both sexuality, the longing for freedom, and violence. And the child of her voluntary forced marriage with Dr. Wangel has eyes that change colour according to the weather and the sea, and becomes bound up with the stranger and their lovers' meeting and their separation out by Bratthammeren. From this point of view Ellida's fear of sex becomes comprehensible − not only as a result of her human degradation in the marriage she has sold herself into, but also in relation to the horrifying pattern of eroticism, violence, and death in the first wedding by the sea. Her complicated relationship to the sea and to sexuality can thus be seen as part of an *overdetermined* complex.

What I have·said is very fragmentary and may seem atomistic. But I am convinced that it is fruitful to apply a frame of reference from psychoanalysis to Ibsen's plays. A great deal remains undone, especially the *collection* of observations. I have tried to present more systematic analyses from this angle in my commentaries on *The Wild Duck, Rosmersholm, The Lady from the Sea,* and *Hedda Gabler* in volume five of the one hundred and fiftieth anniversary edition of Ibsen's collected works, but these, too, were limited by shortage of space.

Finally I would like to say a little about how this perspective need not exclude consideration of the social or existential aspects of Ibsen's drama. It appears that in Ibsen as in life, the forces that create linguistic and symbolic transformations and idealistic superstructures are often social. An analysis of psychological patterns will thus automatically lead to an analysis of the socially conditioned forces that cause traumas, complexes, and transformations of the instinctive drives. With regard to the existential aspect, it can be said on the one hand that the unconscious as part of the psychological make-up is timeless and general. But Ibsen's own brand of idealism, on the other hand, is historically linked to a view of man that is earlier than Freud. And even though Ibsen's creative imagination is able to grasp the new image of man, he does not abandon the other view. Despite his voyage of discovery to the unconscious depths of the human soul, an exploration that forces him to expose the hidden forces, he does not give up his vision of the whole human being. It could in a sense thus be argued that all Ibsen's drama is *overdetermined.* The presence at the same time of both views of man is what to my mind gives to Ibsen's drama its very individual life, making of his writing something unique which continues to fascinate. But in order to grasp this characteristic of his writing, we must take the depth psychology perspective seriously in our research, just as we take his idealism seriously. Western European culture, at least, still reflects the tension between these two diverging ways of understanding man.

«Existential»

DANIEL HAAKONSEN

Nobody is likely to-day to deny that Ibsen can be read and understood in the light of modern psychology or sociology. Some critics will contend, however, that the full meaning of his plays cannot be disentangled merely by psychological or social considerations. We need, in fact, to consider alternative ideas about Ibsen's dramatic art, and the word «existential» could well suit our purpose. In using the word here I do not associate it too closely with any particular existentialist philosophy, that of Søren Kierkegaard, say, or that of Jean-Paul Sartre. We must in fact keep the concept «existential» and «existentialist» apart. This does not imply that Ibsen was not greatly influenced by Søren Kierkegaard – he undoubtably was – but that «existential» is a more comprehensive and more general term than «existentialist».

In an existential perspective we aknowledge a dramatic character's relationship to certain values, which are not entirely conditioned by psychological or sociological factors, and which may, theoretically, compose their own independant and meaningful structure, also in a «structuralist» meaning of the word. From an existential point of view we are in fact more concerned with the relationship between men and values in themselves than with the discussion of how and why, in terms of psychological or sociological conditioning, men have come to adopt these values. From an existential perspective, in other words, not the *why* but the *what* is important: which purpose? which values implied in that purpose? what sort of commitment to the values involved?

The idea of freedom in *Ghosts, Rosmersholm,* and *John Gabriel Borkman*

ASBJØRN AARSETH

I

During the winter of 1870/71, at the time of the famous siege of Paris and the short life of the Commune, Ibsen developed some of his ideas on the concept of freedom in his correspondence with Georg Brandes. He makes it clear in these letters that he does not believe in political liberalism of the conventional kind. His attitude towards the politicians is remarkably negative. They cannot understand that the once so highly cherished ideals of the French Revolution are no longer what they were. The old concepts must be given a new meaning. Ibsen is not willing to go on eating the crumbs from the table of the 1790'ies. Political revolutions have had their day; what Ibsen is advocating is no less than the revolt of the spirit, «menneskeåndens revoltering».[1]

Brandes, a 19th century child of the 18th century revolution, could not follow Ibsen in his contempt for the political ffreedom enjoyed by the citizens of an increasing number of European states. He accused his friend of being a hater of freedom. In his answer Ibsen cuts through what he claims is a verbal dispute merely. To him freedom can never mean political freedom. Political freedom can be obtained, and it certainly can be a good thing to have free elections, tax freedom, freedom of speech, and the like. But these things concern the citizen in his relation to the state; they cannot help the human being as an individual. Indeed, the state is the curse of the individual, even the liberal state implies restrictions and limitations of various kinds.

What, then, is the meaning of freedom to Ibsen? What his views were on political matters need not be important to us. He conceived of himself as a dramatist, not as a political philosopher. Our question must therefore be how his idea of freedom was formed to meet the inherent demands of the art he was developing. This can only be studied on the basis of textual analysis. Before we go into the selected dramas, however, something should be said about the way Ibsen had acquired

---

[1] Letter to Georg Brandes, Dec., 20th, 1870.

his concept of freedom and given it a meaning which apparently had so little to do with the standard use of the word in the political rhetoric of his liberal contemporaries.

His main source, I believe, was the great German philosopher, Hegel. In the introduction to his *Philosophy of History,* Hegel contemplates the course of world history. He sees it as a manifestation of an impulse of perfectibility in the world-spirit. Historical development is seen as a function of the spirit at war with itself, striving to realize its potential being. In the sphere of nature the development of each being from a germ to its completeness is a peaceful process, an organic growth. In the sphere of the mind this process is a dramatic one, due to the conflict of the spirit with itself. With an image that must have appealed to the author of *Emperor and Galilean,* Hegel writes that the spirit has the history of the world for its «theatre».[2]

The idea that the ultimate aim of spiritual development is realization of the self, is, of course, familiar to students of Ibsen. But what is the essence of spirit, what is it that the world-spirit as well as the individual human spirit is striving to realize? The direct opposite of spirit in Hegel's philosophy is matter, and the essence of matter is gravity, the tendency toward a central point which is not in itself. Spirit, then, is that which has its center in itself; spirit is according to Hegel «self-contained existence», and this, he adds, is exactly what freedom is.[3] To realize the self is, in other Hegelian words, for the self to become free. The basic idea remains the same: The essence of spirit is freedom. We must leave the philosophy of Hegel at this point with its central term freedom unqualified and indefinite, and return to our dramatist, whose task it was not to build a system by means of abstract terms, but to create effective images of living people.

To turn from the art of the long dramatic poem to that of the prose play makes a certain change in the level of expression necessary. The solemn and imperious words uttered in the hall of the mountain king, «Man, be thyself!», would probably sound out of place in the Helmers' flat or in the garden room of Mrs. Alving. What Ibsen did to replace the slightly Hegelian touch in the rhetoric of some of his earlier dramas, was to elaborate on the freedom theme. He managed to do this not only by presenting a new dramatic language, a language which the

[2] Quoted from *Philosophy of History,* in *Great Books of the Western World,* 46. *Hegel,* Chicago, a.o., 1952, p. 178. A Danish translation of the book, by S. Kattrup, appeared in Copenhagen in 1842.

[3] *Op.cit.,* p. 160.

audience could easily recognize as closely related to the political vocabulary of the various liberal and anarchist movements of the day, but also by exploiting the possibilities for space symbolism which were at hand in terms of stage architecture. Endowed with an extraordinary dramatic instinct, Ibsen chose to concentrate on the fight for freedom, not so much on the implications of actually being free. He makes this clear in one of his letters to Brandes, who had expressed a somewhat utopian view on freedom:

Hvad De kalder frihed, kalder jeg friheder; og hvad jeg kalder kampen for friheden, er jo ikke andet end den stadige, levende tilegnelse af frihedens ide. Den, der besidder friheden anderledes end som det efterstræbte, han besidder den dødt og åndløst, thi frihedsbegrebet har jo dog det ved sig, at det stadig udvides under tilegnelsen, og hvis derfor nogen under kampen bliver stående og siger: nu har jeg den, – så viser han derved, at han netop har tabt den.[4]

The fight for freedom is everything, the possession of it means spiritual death. In this sense the true Ibsen hero is governed by the same titanic striving as Goethe's *Faust*. At the same time, however, the outcome of Ibsen's prose dramas indicates that the author for the purpose of his art has subscribed to the fateful words of God in the Prologue in Heaven: «Es irrt der Mensch, solang' er strebt.» For this and other reasons the dramatic fight for freedom in the typical Ibsen play is doomed to be a tragic fight.

II

It is now time to move closer to the text of the three plays singled out for particular attention. It is my intention to study them not as three different works from three different phases in the career of the dramatist, but as three variations on one and the same basic theme. I shall for purposes of illustration extend my argument by short remarks on some of the other prose plays as well, since it is a natural consequence of my approach that the whole series of plays from *A Doll's House* to *When We Dead Awaken* can be seen as one corpus with variables and invariables.

If we consider the stage Ibsen has chosen for his characters in the eleven plays of this series, we may notice a certain development, a gradual broadening of the sphere, as if he is experimenting to find the proper balance between a narrow, inner world and an open outer world, and he is increasingly dissatisfied with the action being limited to the con-

[4] Letter to Georg Brandes, Feb., 17th, 1871.

ventional living room of so much 19th century theatre. In *A Doll's House*, the very title suggests an extreme confinement, a world too small to a grown-up person, and as that play shows us the sudden spiritual awakening of a young woman who refuses to go on being a plaything to her husband, it is quite logical that the play ends with the heavy sound of a door being slammed – Nora's heroic self-liberating gesture as she leaves for the greater world outside. In the last play, all the acts take place in the open air, but on different levels between the sea and the snow-capped mountains to suggest the progress of the action, the fatal road to freedom. The nine plays between these two extremes present various degrees of stage enclosure, with interior scenes throughout the plays up to *Rosmersholm,* and a total balance of 50—50 as to interior and exterior scenes in the six last plays. *Ghosts, Rosmersholm,* and *John Gabriel Borkman* may serve as fairly representative instances of this development.

The implications of the stage arrangement in Ibsen's drama has of course been widely discussed by earlier critics, and much valuable insight in Ibsen's dramatic technique has resulted from this. It is my impression, however, that the basic significance of the inside as opposed to the outside world has not been studied sufficiently in the light of a general hypothesis concerning the deep structural relations in this corpus of plays. I propose to have another look at these spatial functions in the three selected plays, choosing the idea of freedom as the main theme.

In the three plays, and in several of the others, the action takes place in or near a manor-house on a country estate in the vicinity of a town. In *Ghosts,* Pastor Manders arrives at Rosenvold by boat from the nearby coastal town, in *Rosmersholm* the distance can easily be walked, in *John Gabriel Borkman* the centre of the capital can be reached by sleigh or by tram. A feature common to these plays, then, is the opposition between the country estate and the town. The things happening in the town are not presented on the stage, but related or referred to by visitors to the estate, so that the presence of the town is indirectly felt all the time. On the other hand, the existence of the characters living in the family residence is not presented as a normal way of life for a rural community or a farm with rich opportunities for a close and meaningful contact with nature. The life of Mrs. Alving is a most secluded one; she is reading a lot, but she is a lonely woman, except when her son Oswald is there to keep her company, and she is hardly ever leaving the house. Johannes Rosmer, the former clergyman, may go out for an occasional afternoon walk, but he is unable to cross the mill brook by the footbridge due to his wife's suicide by throwing herself into the mill-pond the year before. John Gabriel Borkman, the former banker, has shut himself up in the great hall on the first floor of the Rentheim residence and sees very few people. Neither is his wife, Gunhild, in the sitting-room downstairs, very keen on outdoor life. It can certainly be said about the three main characters, Mrs. Alving, Rosmer, and Borkman, that they have withdrawn from active service and have chosen a life of contemplation, study, and cultivation of more or less artificial ideals.

This impression is brought about by the dialogue between the main character and the visitor from the outside world, and it is strengthened by the use of stage directions. The interior scene is the picture of the inner life, the sphere of imagination. Through the windows we glimpse the world outside, except for the second act of *John Gabriel Borkman;* windows seem to be lacking in the empty hall where the former banker spends his days in selfimposed imprisonment, waiting for society to knock on his door and ask him to take over the management of the new bank. Instead of looking out through the window, Borkman has got a hand-mirror which he can look into, and the walls are covered with old tapestries in faded colours, showing hunting scenes, shepherds and shepherdesses, an unreal world of pastoral fiction.

In *Ghosts,* the spacious garden room of Mrs. Alving is continued at the back of the stage into a rather narrow conservatory («blomsterværelse») with large glass walls through which a part of the garden and the gloomy fjord landscape can be seen. This room with the glass walls and the flowers in need of water and care should not be interpreted as an image of the outer world making its way into the house. It rather suggests the protected sphere of the inner world as opposed to the rough weather conditions outside, characterizing Rosenvold as a greenhouse, a place for children to grow up in an atmosphere of artificial ideals. Like Borkman, pacing up and down in the hall with the faded tapestries, Mrs. Alving is not ready to realize the full consequences of her actions in the past. Mrs. Alving's conservatory and the hall of the Rentheim residence have several parallels in the scenography of the prose dramas – the artificial world of the animals in the attic of *The Wild Duck* where hunting scenes are not merely portrayed, but actually performed, the stagnant carp pond in the corner of the garden in *The Lady from the Sea,* and the inner room with the portrait of the general on the wall in *Hedda Gabler,* to mention the most conspicuous examples. They are all topologically connected with the idea of retirement from the living, real world, the open sphere of circulation and communication.

The characters dedicated to or linked with these parts of the stage, are in danger of suffering from loss of reality.

The corresponding stage element in *Rosmersholm* may seem a bit more complex. The living-room is richly decorated with flowers, which seems to be the special contribution of Rebecca – the late Mrs. Rosmer could not bear the scent of flowers, we are told. What is more, the walls are hung with portraits of clergymen, officers and officials in their uniforms, suggesting the solemn and very conservative family tradition of the Rosmers. Somehow the fresh birch twigs and the wild flowers on the stove and on the stand near the window do not mix too well with the somber gallery of ancestors; Rebecca and Rosmer have widely differing backgrounds. The complexity of the set has to do with the fact that there are two main characters in this play, mutually influencing each other, and sharing the secluded existence at Rosmersholm.

III

Our task is now to relate this basic opposition between the sphere of imagination and the sphere of circulation, between the inner world of the spirit and the outer world of public life, to the idea of freedom. But before we can do that, we must have a look at the dialogue and trace the idea in the minds of the characters. In *Ghosts,* Pastor Manders notices the books and the periodicals on Mrs. Alving's table, and it is with some aversion he refers to «the new trends of thought . . . current in the great world outside. . .» (V, 360)[5] We are not directly informed about what trends of thought he has in mind, but we may assume that it has to do with liberal ideas of various kinds. Oswald, the young artist just back from Paris, talks about «that glorious, free life out there. . .» (V, 370), and complains about the wrong impression people back home are getting of this freedom. When Manders and Mrs. Alving talk about her marriage to the late chamberlain, they tend to use words which contain the idea of being tied vs. the idea of escaping from a restricted way of life, although they have very different attitudes on this point. Manders talks about the duty of a married woman: «And your duty was to stand by the man you had chosen, and to whom you were bound by sacred ties.» (V, 371). The title of chamberlain, considered to be more honorable than that of captain, suggests that the proper sphere of Mrs Alving's husband had come to be the inner world, the chamber or even the bedroom of Rosenvold. In his earlier days, as a young lieutenant, he

---

[5] Page numbers refer to *The Oxford Ibsen,* vols. V, VI and VIII, translated and edited by James Walter McFarlane, Oxford, 1961, 1960 and 1977.

was full of «boundless energy and vitality» (V, 412), but there was no way he could find outlet for his joy of living in the little provincial town. His wife, with her devotion to duty rather than love, had no beneficial effect on him, and he died a debauched and broken man. What killed him was the narrowmindedness of the surroundings, the spiritual confinement of the little town, and his own excessive demands on life. Mrs. Alving tried to escape from this unhappy cohabitation; she talks about herself visiting Manders as «a runaway wife» (V, 374), that is, seeking freedom in another man's home. But he made her return to her husband and restore law and order.

It is the ambitious project of Mrs. Alving in the play to liberate herself from the power of the «ghosts», the dead remnants of the past, the old defunct theories and beliefs that should have no hold on the minds of living people. She realizes that she has been a coward, not telling the truth about her husband's debauchery, not revolting against the tyranny of conventions. She is still not ready to tell the truth, but she is struggling against all the ties and restrictions: «I can't stand it! I must work myself free» (V, 382). Here the original is slightly different: «Jeg må arbejde mig ud til frihed.»[6] She is standing near the window at this point, and «drumming on the window frame» (V, 382). This position clearly connects the idea of freedom with a longing to get out of the limited area of the house.

As the action proceeds, it becomes clear that her project has no chance of realization. She wants to protect her husband's memory from the unpleasant truth, and she wants her son to go on believing in a false ideal. That is why he was sent away at an early age. It is precisely Mrs. Alving's protective attitude, however, that makes spiritual freedom unattainable. In Ibsen's world, freedom can only be based on truth. Even in Paris, Oswald has not been a free man, because his mother in her letters has been hiding the truth. He describes the pains in his head in a way that evokes the idea of being tied or even chained: «It was just like having an iron band clamped tight round your neck. . .» (V, 395). Back home he is in poor health and tired, and he knows that there is no recovery for him: «Yesterday and again today, I tried to shake off these thoughts . . . fight myself free. But it's no use» (V, 394). Oswald is a prisoner of his illness. When the Orphanage is burning, he runs out to assist in putting out the fire. This physical exertion seems to be the immediate cause of the final attack of the illness. Frail plants cannot survive under rough conditions outdoors. But to live under

[6] Hundreårsutgaven, vol. IX, Oslo, 1932, p. 89.

constant care in the conservatory, is no true life. The only escape from such an artificial existence is death. The idea of freedom is a tragic one, both to Oswald and his mother.

IV

Before we proceed to *Rosmersholm,* I shall try to illustrate my interpretation of the basic relations in the deep structure of the typical Ibsen drama, of which *Ghosts* is one instance. If we apply the semiological model usually known as the logical rectangle, we should take as our point of departure the actual position of the main character, that is, the secluded life inside the house. The logical relations of opposition, negation and implication can be demonstrated like this:

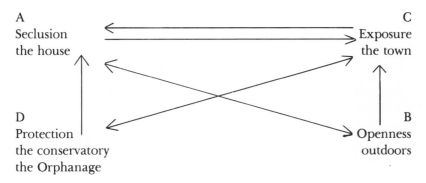

A
Seclusion
the house

C
Exposure
the town

D
Protection
the conservatory
the Orphanage

B
Openness
outdoors

This figure is, of course, like any interpretation of a complex literary work, subject to discussion. It could be developed further, for instance with Regine's garden syringe at position A as against the rain at position B, the negation manifesting itself in Regine's hostility towards the extremely wet Engstrand, the intruder from the outside. There are problems involved in this operation, it is probably not as clear-cut as it may seem. The model as it is shown here cannot explain the thematically important difference between the small town where Pastor Manders belongs and the great free world of Oswald's artist friends. They are both oppositions to the secluded and protected world of Rosenvold, but only the latter seems to represent the idea of true freedom. The small town represents rather the sphere of disillusionment. Thus in *Ghosts* there is an ambiguity on this point, but not so in *Rosmersholm.*

It is primarily in the dialogue with Kroll that Rosmer brings out his recently acquired ideas concerning the liberation of his fellow countrymen. Like the Pastor in *Ghosts,* the Headmaster in this play is a man of the town, and he is on the side of law and order, vigorously opposing the liberal ideas of the day. The great project of Rosmer is the spiritual ennoblement of his countrymen. Kroll wants to know how his former brother-in-law intends to accomplish such a task: «ROSMER. By liberating their minds and purifying their wills, I should say. KROLL. Rosmer, you are a dreamer. Are *you* going to liberate them? Are *you* going to purify them?» (VI, 314).

The scepticism of Kroll is not without our support. With Rebecca West and the housekeeper, Mrs. Helseth, looking through the window in the opening scene, we have been informed that Rosmer, returning from a walk in the vicinity of the house, is unable to come the shortest way across the footbridge. His dead wife is still with him in his thoughts. It is in fact another «ghost» play. Rebecca, who has been the encouraging force behind Rosmer's idealistic scheme, realizes that he is not spiritually free as long as he avoids crossing the bridge.

The question which is haunting his mind is whether he was responsible for his wife's suicide. What he feels he is desperately in need of, is «freedom from guilt» (VI, 349). The original term, «skyldfrihed», is used three times in the play,[7] but twice *The Oxford Ibsen* translates it into «innocence» (VI, 340, 372), thus weakening the verbal link with the idea of freedom. There is probably more talk about freedom in this play than in any of the others. The character who talks about it with the greatest pomposity is the vigorous and extremely self-confident vagabond Ulrik Brendel, once the tutor of Rosmer, who on his way to town pays his former pupil a visit. He is in great need of proper clothes and money for his planned lecture tour, but his complete lack of modesty makes him a comic figure and his rhetoric is soaring sky-high. Brendel is a caricature of Rosmer. His project is clearly a parallel to that of his pupil. For some time he has been living in seclusion, cultivating his golden dreams and ideals, but now he feels that time has come for their realization, and he has embarked on his great campaign: «I shall lay hold on life with eager hands. . . I shall step forth. . . mount up. It is the air of a tempestuous, cataclysmic age we breathe. . . I intend now to place my mite on the altar of liberty» (VI, 309). Brendel is on his way from seclusion to exposure. Rosmer will be following his former tutor before long.

Rosmer's present tutor, in a way, is Rebecca. She has established herself at Rosmersholm with the intention of forming Rosmer's mind according to the ideas of the new age. She is confessing her motive to Rosmer and Kroll towards the end of the third act:

[7] Hundreårsutgaven, vol. X, Oslo, 1932, pp. 395, 405, 429 f.

REBECCA. I wanted us to go forward together in freedom. On and on, ever further. But between you and full and complete freedom was this grim, insurmountable barrier.

ROSMER. What do you mean. . . barrier?

REBECCA. I mean, Johannes, that you could only grow to freedom in the clear light of the sun. But there you were, wilting and sickly in the gloom of a marriage like yours. (VI, 360)

Consequently, Rebecca turned against Beata and made her feel that it was her duty to remove that barrier, to make way for someone else. By this confession, Rebecca hopes that Rosmer will recover his freedom of guilt, seeing that she, and not he, was morally responsible for his wife's suicide. But he is still not able to walk accross the footbridge as he leaves for the town with Kroll shortly after.

In the last act Rosmer returns from the town, disillusioned. Kroll and his friends have convinced him that his idealistic task has no chance of success. A moment later, Ulrik Brendel pays his second visit to the house. His confrontation with the town has made it clear to him that his beautiful ideals were not worth anything in the world of practical success. What Kroll did to Rosmer, Peter Mortensgaard has done to Brendel. The idea of freedom, in its Brendel version as well as in its Rosmer version, belongs to the sphere of imagination. It has no role to play in the outside world of public life. In the town, people belong to political parties. The politicians and the newspapers fight each other with all available means; they do not fight for the truth or for freedom, but for political power. Success in this sphere depends upon the ability to live without ideals, as Peter Mortensgaard does.

After Brendel has left, Rebecca complains about the close and sultry air in the room, and opens the window. She has been a window opener from the beginning of the play, not feeling well in the old-fashioned living-room at Rosmersholm. But its atmosphere and traditions, the Rosmer philosophy of life, these qualities of the inner world have managed to transform her, to ennoble her mind, but kill her happiness. She is ready now to go where Beata went; she has sinned, and there is no freedom except through atonement. Rosmer joins her in marriage and in death. The two of them are one and there is no escape from the White Horses for the people of the house of Rosmersholm.

The deep structure of this play can be illustrated by approximately the same model that was used for *Ghosts,* except for position D, where the term Protection should be replaced by Ennoblement, suggesting the effect of Rosmersholm on its inhabitants.

V

The need for fresh air is frequently mentioned in Ibsen's realistic drama, but the difference between indoor and outdoor climate seems never more emphasized than in *John Gabriel Borkman*. Mrs. Gunhild Borkman keeps the cold winter out by means of a large, oldfashioned iron stove and heavy curtains covering the window. Her sister, Ella Rentheim, twice refers to the excessive heat. Her son, Erhart, prefers to live in town, for obvious reasons. Her husband, in many ways another version of the Chamberlain in *Ghosts,* except that this one is alive, has confined himself to the hall on the first floor. The large residence with the faded splendour is as nearly a prison as any interior scene in Ibsen's drama. The idea of freedom is particularly potent under circumstances like these.

When Erhart was a child, his father had to go to prison due to some unlawful transactions at the bank he was in charge of. Because of this disgrace, the boy was sent away from home, like Oswald in *Ghosts*. The action of the play is concerned very much with the dispute between the mother, the foster-mother (Ella Rentheim) and the father as to who has the proper claim on Erhart for his assistance in their various projects. At the same time it is a play about liberation, about the children leaving their parents' home and going out into the great wide world.

Music appeals to the imagination of Borkman in his confinement. Frida Foldal has been playing «Dance macabre» on his piano, and it reminds him of the song of the metal ore when it is 'broken free' down in the mines which he sometimes visited as a boy with his father the miner. The piano music expresses the joy of freedom, the urge to «come up into the light of day and serve mankind» (VIII, 180). This is what Borkman is longing for himself. He does not realize that his time is up. The «Dance macabre» is really a ghost song, the dancing of the dead.

In the second act, Borkman talks about the hammer-blows down in the mines loosening the ore like the strokes of the midnight bell which set it free, making it sing for joy. When the midnight bell actually sounds in the last act, however, he is unable to understand what is going on. With his wife and her sister he is standing outside the house listening to the silver bells on the harness of Mrs. Wilton's sleigh carriage, as his son, together with Mrs. Wilton and young Frida, is leaving for the South. Mrs. Borkman compares the retiring sound with funeral bells, while Ella, with her greater capacity for love, thinks it possible that they ring in life and happiness for Erhart. However fleeting his relationship with Fanny Wilton will turn out to be, Erhart is now travelling on the road to freedom − he is realizing the urge of the ore to come up into the light of day. In German, ore is called Erz, which is rather similar to his name.

Borkman refuses to accept that the bells of freedom for his son mean funeral bells for him. While old Foldal, who is run over by the sleigh with the two horses rushing down the hill carrying his daughter Frida out into the world of great opportunities, is touchingly happy on her behalf and goes limping home to comfort the poor mother, old Borkman refuses to go back into the house. He feels like «an escaped convict» (VIII, 228). He does not mind the dangerously cold air: «I will go on, and on, and on. To see if I can make my way to freedom and life and humanity again» (VIII, 228). It is a final desperate effort to realize the idea of freedom, wading through the deep snow to reach the lookout place together with Ella and enjoy the sight of his imaginary kingdom of captive millions, the hidden treasures inside the mountains.

But the prisoner is not free. His heart is clutched by a hand of ice, which is at the same time a hand of iron. The idea of freedom may be nourished in seclusion, but the climate of the outside, real world does not favour artificial ideas.

Again, the deep structure turns out to be the same as for the two former plays. There is a movement from Seclusion to Openness, an effort to follow the urge of freedom, both in the young and the old generation. Position D, the negation of C, Exposure, can in this case best be termed Imprisonment, but there is no basic difference between the three versions of this position, Protection, Ennoblement, and Imprisonment. They all suggest the fatal power of imagination, the condition required for dreaming about freedom.

We are all aware that the concept of freedom is a central one whether we consider it in social, in psychological, or in existential terms. This is why these three different approaches may all find some support in the text of Ibsen's drama. But I think that it is fair to say that interpretations along these three different lines tell us just as much, if not more, about the interpreters as about the plays. In the work of Ibsen the idea of freedom is used as an open and inclusive concept, as it is in Hegel's introduction to his *Philosophy of History*.

The confessional duologue in Ibsen

ANDREW KENNEDY

In Ibsen's later drama the dialogue of personal encounter, whereby two characters compel essential self-disclosures from one another through inter-linked sessions of talk, reaches a new intensity and dimension. The duologue becomes central to the structure of action and develops unique features of style. As a general statement this may sound familiar, especially to the Ibsen critic, although there have been few studies of the dialogue, especially of the duologue, so far as I know.[1] The achievements of Ibsen's dialogue tend to be taken for granted, or else minimised, partly through hindsight gained from post-Ibsen drama which used, developed and conventionalized its once innovatory features. It had become the dominant mode of dialogue in naturalistic drama, which later modern dramatists found it necessary to react against: to dislocate, or push towards a minimal and more implicit dialogue. If, however, our approach is from the past, through a quick 'retrospective method' – which should be acceptable in the Ibsen world – the innovatory force of Ibsen's duologues can be clearly seen.

In Sophoclean drama the relentless, ultimately destructive, quest for truth becomes a principle of action: Oedipus, for example, threatens the old Herdsman with torture for failing to disclose what he knows about the past (the guilt-laden origins of Oedipus himself). Question and answer interlock in a terrible inquisition until the Herdsman, aware that he is being asked «to speak what is dreaded»

[1] Studies of Ibsen's dramatic language:

Inga-Stina Ewbank, «Ibsen's Dramatic Language as a Link Between his 'Realism' and 'Symbolism', and «Ibsen and 'the Far More Difficult Art' of Prose», respectively in *Contemporary Approaches to Ibsen* I and II, Oslo, 1966 and 1971.

Trygve Knudsen, «Phases of Style and Language in the Works of Henrik Ibsen» in *Skrifttradisjon og litteraturmål,* Festkrift, Universitetsforlaget, Oslo, 1967, pp. 143—71. (See also: n. 13.)

John Northam, *Ibsen, A Critical Study,* Cambridge University Press 1973, and «A note on the language of *Rosmersholm», Ibsenårbok,* Oslo, 1977, (See also: n. 9)

Oedipus Rex 1169) is gradually, line-by-line in the formal exchanges of stichomythia, forced to disclose the truth. But in this dialogue of confession the structure of action is almost everything, and the inward, psychological pattern is secondary. The inquisitorial exchange forces Oedipus to discover the *facts* of his origin and unconscious incest; his inward experiences are summed up in a four-line quasi-monologue; while the Herdsman's 'inner truth', the pain he finds in telling, is, as it were, a by-product of the exchange.

The central scenes of Shakespeare's major tragedies do embody the conscious self-expression of interacting characters, in full poetic complexity. Yet the great duologues of love (in *Romeo and Juliet* and in *Antony and Cleopatra*) and those of seduction and antagonism (in *Macbeth, Othello* and *Measure for Measure*) remain firmly action-centered and, despite their subtle psychology, are not primarily intended to enact a terrible process of mutual self-revelation through dialogue. The nearest approach to a 'confessional duologue' in Shakespeare can be seen in the paradoxically distant intimacy of Hamlet and Horatio. Hamlet does reveal himself to Horatio, the «just» man who is not «passion's slave» (*Hamlet* 3.2.60-72), bringing to the dialogue an integrity of self-expression and a naturalness of language otherwise only found in some of his soliloquies. But the duologue remains one-sided, Hamlet-dominated; Horatio remains relatively self-effacing and laconic, in keeping with the social convention between friends distanced by rank and the dramatic convention of the confidant.[2] In short, we are several stages from the sustained dual intimacy of the duologue in late Ibsen.

In Racine's purest tragedies, as in *Phèdre,* the action is centered on a series of confessions and revelations, reached tremblingly, through hints and indirections, which anticipate Ibsen and later drama. Nevertheless, even the most intimate confessional duologues of Phèdre retain a sublimity of expression which is at the opposite pole from «the genuine, plain language spoken in real life» (Ibsen's conversational model for the communication of deeply felt experience.) The degree of stylization, or incantation, found in Racine as it were shields the characters from full person-to-person encounter. A tragic character like Phèdre is isolated in the midst of felt eloquence that only *seems* shared, by her confidante and potential lover, in a confessional duologue. The formal exchange of speeches gives rise to a *dialogue solitaire.*[3]

[2] This material is drawn from chapter 3 of my *Dramatic Dialogue,* forthcoming, Cambridge University Press.

[3] Lucien Goldmann, *Racine,* L'arche, Paris, 1956, pp. 26—7, (using a pharse borrowed from Lukács).

This brief backward glance may help us to define Ibsen's duologues by underlining the elements of traditional drama that have been 'made new' and extended in *Rosmersholm* and the late plays. The Sophoclean quest for truth has been turned inward; and the confessional inwardness found in Hamlet speaking to Horatio, or Phèdre speaking to Oenone and Hyppolite, is converted into a full encounter of two interacting characters: a duologue fully expressing both duality and mutuality: Rosmer *and* Rebecca. These authentic duologues are then made central to the structure of action in an unprecedented way: they provide the most intense episodes while the 'plot' around them – the intrigue of politics, the world of Kroll and Mortensgaard – becomes a kind of carpentry for essences, or else a catalyst releasing self-revelation. The choice of a conversational model for deeper communication – something different from the 'imitation' of ordinary conversation, as we shall see – is a first, and precarious, attempt at expressing personal obsession, fantasy, dream, and other fragments of the haunted mind, within the linguistic limits of 'standard' speech: the audience *seems* to recognize a re-play of the way they talk, hardly aware of the degree of 'shaping' in the dialogue. In sum, the existential and structural heightening of the duologue coincides with a certain stylistic lowering (a seeming de-stylization) of the language of personal encounter. Such a conjunction, of psychological complexity and linguistic transparency, was hardly possible before Ibsen. And soon after Ibsen (and after Strindberg and Chekov) an increased self-consciousness, concerning both the inner mind and dramatic language itself, made the intimate duologue much more precarious. It is fortunate, in more than one sense, that *Rosmersholm* was a text for Freud and not the other way round; for the pre-Freudian and pre-Modernist mode of Ibsen's duologues goes with a certain robustly 'naive' language (in Schiller's approving sense). In the further complexities of self and style of later European drama, characters, to adapt Judge Brack, don't *say* such things any longer.

In keeping with Ibsen's privileged status as a robust innovator in the first phase of modern drama, we repeatedly find, in the central duologues, that even the tentative, indirect, language of self-revelation is placed in a robust structure, like an intimate picture in a conspicuously gilded frame. There is a tension between the firm structure of dialogue and its delicate texture, corresponding to a tension between explicit and implicit speech, between emphatic and groping self-expression. Take a paradigm-like example from a late play. In *Little Eyolf* (1894) Allmers returns from the mountains bearing within him the memory of some great, self-transforming experience. He hints at it early in the play and, under the pressure of questions from both Rita and Asta, his half-estranged wife and his supposed half-sister, he gradually unveils part of his experience, after these preliminaries:

RITA /*utbrytende*/. Du har opplevet noe på reisen! Nekt det ikke! for jeg ser det på deg!
ALLMERS /*ryster på hodet*/. Ingen verdens ting – i det ytre. Men –
RITA/*spent*/. Men – ?
ALLMERS. Innvendig i meg er der riktignok skjedd en liten omveltning.
RITA. Å gud – !
ALLMERS /*beroligende, klapper hennes hånd*/. Bare til det gode, kjære Rita. Det kan du trygt lite på.
RITA /*setter seg i sofaen*/. Dette her må du endelig straks fortelle oss. Alt sammen!
ALLMERS /*vender seg mot Asta*/. Ja, la oss sette oss, vi også. Så skal jeg prøve på å fortelle. Så godt jeg kan. /*Han setter seg i sofaen ved siden av Rita. Asta rykker en stol frem og setter seg nær ved ham. Kort opphold.*/
RITA /*ser på ham i forventning*/. Nå da – ? . . .

RITA /*exclaiming*/. You've been through something while you were away. Don't say you haven't. Because I can see by the look of you.
ALLMERS /*shaking his head*/. Nothing at all – outwardly. But –
RITA /*excitedly*/. But – ?
ALLMERS. But inwardly – there's certainly been a minor revolution.
RITA. Good heavens!
ALLMERS /*soothing her and patting her hand*/. Only to the good, Rita, my dear. You can rest assured of that.
RITA /*sitting on the sofa*/. Now you must tell us about this at once. All about it!
ALLMERS /*turning to Asta*/. Yes, let us sit down too. Then I'll try and tell you. As best I can. /*He sits on the sofa beside Rita. Asta pulls a chair across and sits near him. There is a moment's pause.*/
RITA /*looking at him unexpectedly*/. Well, now – ? . . .

(Akt I, Fakkel, p. 491, Penguin, pp. 227-8)

And so on, through further preliminaries, which Allmers himself calls a «sort of introduction», until the subject of Allmers' metamorphosis up in the mountains (which makes him put the crippled child Eyolf in the centre of his life instead of the great book on 'Human Responsibility') is broached. There is a further, more inward, almost numinous, experience hidden within the confessed metamorphosis; but the revelation of that inner core of experience is postponed until near the end of the play (where it is given such significance, by both the frame and the emphatic speech, that it seems to 'outshadow' the more direct action of Eyolf's death, and the painful discoveries of Asta and Allmers concerning their unfulfillable relationship). In a full confessional duologue with Rita this strange experience, outside the actional but within the thematic pattern of the play, is communicated by Allmers (in an image that recalls the meeting with the Strange Passenger in the fifth act of *Peer Gynt): «Jeg synes at der gikk jeg og døden som to gode reisekamerater.»* – *«It seemed as though death and I were going along like two good travelling companions.»* (Act III, Fakkel, p. 516, Penguin, p. 278). But before we reach this inner core of the confession, we witness once more the ritual of preliminaries, the attention-raising hints, which cease to be hints through repetition, and the solemn command to sit – on the bench by the summerhouse, as earlier on the sofa – twice repeated. The frame for the confessional is a pattern, a sustained ritual.

But is it not perverse, it may be objected, to point to the frame – functional and empty as it may seem – when it is the core of the duologue, the experience conveyed, that matters? My point is that this ritual of preliminaries in the confessional duologue is both typical (it keeps reappearing) and significant. Structurally, Ibsen needs the confessional prologue to carry trans'tion, 'suspense' and warning signals to the audience; existentially, it marks the first steps in a 'descent' towards deeper communion, the tremor before the taboo on speech is broken; linguistically, it marks the importance of 'naturalness' – people hesitate, repeat themselves, and go on hinting until their hints become explicit. (In later drama hints give way to subtler evasion or else to cruder attack.)

The explicitness of this groping towards an increasingly inward and authentic duologue can be traced back, briefly, to the well-made-play's ʿvisible' carpentry in the early plays. Bernick's confession of his guilt, in the final 'truth-telling' scene of *Pillars of Society* (1877) has about it an actor politician's address to a stage audience. Although ostensibly he is responding to the pressures of a duologue with Lona, the woman who embodies his conscience, the confessional speech itself is external, morally ambiguous, and cliché-ridden. The dialogue of the famous 'discussion' that brings to and end *A Doll's House* (1897) with Nora's declaration of new-found independence, is essentially the climax of the play's argument, not a fully personal encounter. This is repeatedly confirmed in performance. The final exchanges between Nora and Torvald (I agree with Raymond Williams here) «do not represent a 'living confrontation between actual people', but are rather straight, single declaration.» Torvald's questions are «rhetorical questions and could, essentially, be spoken by Nora herself.»[4] Nora's transformation springs from what she has just witnessed (her husband's totally disillusioning, self-centred response to their mutual crisis) and this transformation takes place in her mind, in the *silence* before she sits down, and bids Torvald to sit down, to communicate her resolution. The ensuing debate-duologue clarifies her new state of mind but does not itself transact the change, or change the speakers through what is being said.

The duologues in *Ghosts* (1881) are much more complex. Those between Mrs. Alving and Oswald certainly have a far greater emotional intensity than those between her and Pastor Manders (where the confessional urge is damped by the Pastor's willed conventional language, so that the repressed passion of one-time potential lovers is barely allowed to resonate – as it does in the key duologues of later plays). Moreover, the duologues of mother and son are spaced out and structured with great mastery: from Osvald's first and partial revelation of his illness in Act II (where the ritual frame, the verbal preliminaries and the sofa, become an essential antidote to the horror), to Mrs. Alving's counter-confession, prompted by Osvald's ghost-laden talk of joy, *livsglede,* and interrupted by Pastor Manders on the threshold of disclosure:

FRU ALVING /*som spent har lyttet, reiser seg med store tankefulle øyne og sier/*. Nu ser jeg sammenhengen.
OSVALD. Hva ser du?
FRU ALVING. Nu ser jeg den for første gang. Og nu kan jeg tale.

MRS. ALVING /*who has been listening eagerly, rises, her eyes big with thought and says/*. Now I see the connection.
OSVALD. What is it you see?
MRS. ALVING. I see it now for the first time. And now I can speak.
(Act II, Fakkel, p. 147; Archer, p. 154)

The careful preparation and underlining – listen, an important disclosure is about to be made – becomes an element in the play's 'suspense', further enhanced when Mrs. Alving's counter-confession is interrupted by Pastor Manders and postponed until Act III. At that point, the painful insight into the *sammenheng,* the connection (the recognition that Osvald's father was driven into dissipation by a conventional and repressive marriage) is mixed up with the revelation that Regina is the illegitimate offspring of that dissipation. Regina is present, the duologue between mother and son is thereby extended; but though this fits

[4] Raymond Williams, *Drama from Ibsen to Brecht,* Chatto and Windus, London, 1968, pp. 48—9.

in well with Ibsen's dramatic scheme, and further underlines the terrible irony of inheritance (Osvald's shattered hope to find in Regina a nurse-wife), it also smacks of well-made-play intrigue. The full authenticity of encounter is recaptured only in the final duologue, where Osvald reveals the imminent symptoms of syphilis (not named) and begs his mother to accept the task of administering a mercy-killing drug when the time is ripe. (This dialogue clearly breaks a long-held social and personal taboo; the son is allowed to demand from his mother a sacrifice for which there seems no precedent in drama before Ibsen. We need to recapture the terror of such taboo-breaking utterance, reflected in the otherwise so absurdly hostile reactions to the play a hundred years ago. At all events, that taboo is a good deal nearer to our own sensibility than, let us say, Antigone's horror at finding her brother lying unburied.)

The final duologue of *Ghosts* is so extreme and so compressed that it takes the speakers beyond the personal (in the sense of the individually personal as explored in later Ibsen duologues). What mother and son say to one another moves towards the elemental: Osvald tells of inexorable facts; Mrs Alving is faced with an unbearable dilemma, not worked out within the play; beyond that, the play points to á transpersonal situation, the emblematic Mother-son relationship, a profane *pietà,* as in a de-mythologized morality play. Within that frame there is no outlet, no 'leisure', for full and mutual self-recognition, leading to self-transformation, as in *Rosmersholm*. The language itself has something elemental and emblematic about it:

OSVALD. Ja, nu får altså du gi meg håndsrekningen, mor.
FRU ALVING *(skriker høyt).* Jeg!
OSVALD. Hvem er nærmere til det enn du?
FRU ALVING. Jeg! Din mor!
OSVALD. Just defor.
FRU ALVING. Jeg, som har gitt deg livet!
OSVALD. Jeg har ikke bedt deg om livet.

OSVALD. Well then, it's you that must come to the rescue, mother.
MRS ALVING *(screams aloud).* I!
OSVALD. Who is nearer to it than you?
MRS ALVING. I! your mother!
OSVALD. For that very reason.
MRS ALVING. I, who gave you life!
OSVALD. I never asked you for life.

(Act III, Fakkel, p. 155; Archer, p. 168).

Here the verbal exchange, with its semblance of argument and simple rhetoric (the 'I'-calls), becomes a primary dialogue – a notation for cries. It can be seen as one of the first attempts, within naturalism, to make characters in intimate encounter speak 'the unspeakable'; and it anticipates the inarticulacy of broken speech and screams in later modern drama.[5] And when Oswald collapses, the duologue, and with it the play, ends, appropriately, with fragmented speech, repetitions, whispers and cries.

III

The duologues of *Rosmersholm* (1886), as already suggested, extend and deepen the functions of the intimate duologue significantly. The final confessional duologue between Rosmer and Rebekka is unique: through it a sustained duel of opposed temperaments and values reaches a climax – in a unison of vision and voice. And this process of double self-transformation is enacted in such a way that the remnants of *plot* – testing and verifying the truth of Rebekka's final commitment to Rosmer and *his* values through the 'suicide pact' – are fused with the inward experience which the dialogue sounds with all its verbal echoes. To anticipate demonstration: Ibsen has succeeded in returning the theatre to the interaction of two inwardly linked minds, without that final immobility of near-solipsism which in the last plays, especially in *John Gabriel Borkman,* turns dialogue at times into double monologue. In keeping with this happy paradox of inward interaction through words, Ibsen avoids excessive reliance on the relatively static device of introspection, or on the relatively novelistic device (as Szondi argued[6]) of retrospection. The words are still exploratory, testing a new experiment in living (however burdened by the 'death-instinct'), and testing the validity of what is being said by issuing in action here and now. Finally, the language of this concluding dialectic of two minds is, correspondingly, at once compressed and fluid, carefully shaped and natural (by which I mean something distinct from raw naturalistic language in

[5] See: Inga-Stina Ewbank, «Shakespeare, Ibsen and the Unspeakable», Inaugural Lecture, Bedford College, London, 1975, and Andrew Kennedy, *Six Dramatists in Search of a Language,* Cambridge, 1975, pp. 23—5. Francis Fergusson found the end of *Ghosts* unsatisfactory – «brutally truncated» – despite its 'poetry of the theatre'. *The Idea of a Theater,* (1949), Doubleday, New York, 1954, pp. 158—74, 164.

[6] Peter Szondi, *Theorie des modernen dramas (1880—1950),* Suhrkamp, Frankfurt, 1956, esp. pp. 22—31.

drama[7]). The final duologue is made up of an inner series of circling confessions akin to the movement of the outer series of confessions in the play (which cannot be traced in detail here): circling towards the centre of 'truth' from the circumference of evasion and half-admission. The outer series of confessions passes from the tense intimate duologue of Rosmer and Rebekka at the end of Act II (including the ambivalent rejection of Rosmer's offer of marriage which aroused Freud's interest[8]) to the compulsive, but only half-true disclosure of her manipulative role in driving Beata to suicide, in the confession made to Rosmer in the presence of Kroll (as catalyst and domestic chorus) at the end of Act III. The threads of intrigue and hidden passion are inextreicably woven together in this pattern – in a dual style of declaratory statement and cryptic suggestion. The two threads and the two ways of speaking come together in the final duologue, in which the opening 'circle' presents estranged friends on the threshold of separation circling *away* from the intimate centre they had reached earlier (in the Act II duologue just mentioned). The intimate form, *du,* remains, but otherwise the opening is a verbal game bent on evading the confessional urge («Kjære, la oss ikke tale om *det* nu.» «My dear, don't let's talk about that now», p. 320; p. 105). Then, with a sudden reversal, in response to Rosmer's self-doubt and charge of lying, Rebekka chooses the present moment to grope her way towards a key confession:

ROSMER. Har du ennu mer å tilstå?
REBEKKA. Jeg har det store igjen.
ROSMER. Hvilket store?
REBEKKA. Det som du aldri har anet. Det som gir både lys og skygge til alt det øvrige.

ROSMER. Have you still more to confess?
REBEKKA. I still have the main thing.
ROSMER. What 'main' thing?
REBEKKA. The thing you've never guessed. The thing that gives light and shade to everything else.

(Act IV, Fakkel, p. 320; Penguin, p. 106)

[7] *Rosmersholm* forms part of my argument in distinguishing a 'natural language' in drama from naturalism in «Natural, Mannered, and Parodie Dialogue», *The Yearbook of English Studies,* Theatrical Literature Special Number, Vol. 9., 1979, p. 28—54.

[8] In «Some Character-Types Met with in Psychoanalytic Work», 1916, (published in James Stratchey (ed.), *Psychological Works,* Vol. 14, 1953), reprinted in James McFarlane (ed.), *Henrik Ibsen, Penguin Critical Anthologies,* Harmonsdworth, 1970, pp. 392—99.

until, with pauses, further circling, and broken speech, Rebekka reaches the next circle: «Da kom det over meg – dette ville, ubetvingelinge begjær – .» «There came over me . . . this wild, uncontrollable passion». The rhythm of utterance, at once urgent and hesitant, is to re-create for the audience, if only for a moment, the voice of the old, pre-Rosmer and pre-conversion, Rebekka: which might have been an ecstatic voice urging Rosmer on and on (as Hilde Wangel drives her Master Builder up and up the tower) in a duologue of spiritual temptation with erotic undertones. Yet, with a total irony of situation and language, Rebekka now renews the taboo on fulfilled love and adapts (in the bio-psychological sense) the grave and sublimated language of Rosmer and the Rosmer world: «Der fallt en sinnshvile over meg, – en stillhet som på et fugleberg. . .» «Peace of mind came down over me – like the stillness on the mountain-cliffs at home.» (p. 322; p. 108). The exchange of words amounts to full exchange of values and attitudes: Rebekka as convert to the puritanism of the Rosmer world, speaks in an 'ennobled' language.

Full communication – communion – is, even at this stage, inhibited, because Rebekka cannot bring herself to confess her fear of what happened in her past (the wholly un-named fear of unconscious incest with her father) while Rosmer cannot overcome his self-doubt, or his doubting of Rebekka. And so, the next circle of confession enacts, in an authentic language, their distrust of the words they *had* spoken to one another, and of the words being spoken *now*. For Rebekka's former confession of duplicity has cast doubt on her new confession of fidelity. How can words alone 'verify' untested feelings, be made the evidence of things not seen? (We have here a version of the Shakespearean tension between appearance and reality, which includes a tension between specious and trustworthy rhetoric.)

REBEKKA /*vrir hendene*/. Å, denne drepende tvil – ! Rosmer, – Rosmer – !
ROSMER. Ja, er det ikke forferdelig, du? Men jeg kan ikke gjøre ved det. Jeg vil aldri komme til å fri meg fra tvilen. Aldri vite visst at jeg har deg i hel og ren kjærlighet.
REBEKKA. Men er der da ikke noe innerst i deg selv, som vidner for at med meg er der skjedd en forvandling! Og at forvandlingen er skjedd ved deg, – ved deg alene!
ROSMER. Å du, – jeg tror ikke lenger på min evne til å forvandle mennesker. Jeg tror ikke på meg selv i noen sak mer. Jeg tror hverken på meg eller på deg.
REBEKKA /*ser mørkt hen på ham*/. Hvorledes vil du da kunne leve livet?
ROSMER. Ja, det forstår jeg ikke selv. Jeg begriper det ikke. Jeg tror ikke at jeg

kan leve det. – Og jeg vet jo heller ikke den ting som det kunne være verdt å leve for.
REBEKKA. Å livet – det har fornyelse i seg.

REBEKKA /*wringing her hands*/. Oh, this murdering doubt! John – John!
ROSMER. Yes, it's terrible, my dear, isn't it? But I can't help it. I shall never be able to free myself from the doubt. Never know for certain that I have your love, whole and unflawed.
REBEKKA. But isn't there anything in the depth of your mind that assures you that a change has come over me? And that the change has come through you – through you alone?
ROSMER. Ah, my dear, I don't believe any longer in my power to change people. I don't believe in myself in any way any more more. I don't believe in myself or in you.
REBEKKA /*looking gloomily at him*/. Then how are you to live your life?
ROSMER. That's what I don't know myself. I can't imagine. I don't see that I *can* live it out. And I don't know, what's more, of anything in the world it would be worth while to live for.
REBEKKA. Oh, life – it has a way of renewing itself.
$\qquad$ (Act IV, Fakkel, p. 323; Penguin, p. 111)

The more one attends to this exchange – in reading and in performance – the more authentic does the expression of Rebekka's assurance of change, *forvandling,* as well as the countering fear and doubt of Rosmer seem. The language of the dialogue itself authenticates the felt truth of what is being spoken: its spareness or 'purity of diction', its quiet rhythm carried structurally by the dovetailing of exclamation-question-declaration-question, by the repetition of key words *(leve/livet; live/life)* and by the crescendo of Rosmer's haunted negatives («Jeg tror ikke . . . Jeg tror ikke på meg self . . . Jeg tror hverken på meg eller deg. Jeg begriper ikke . . . Jeg tror ikke jeg *kan* leve det. – Og jeg vet jo heller ikke . . .» «I don't believe . . . I don't believe in myself . . . I don't believe in myself or in you. I can't imagine . . . I don't see that I *can* live it out. And I don't know, what's more . . .). These confessional utterances are, as it were, self-confirming – for the audience.

But for the speakers themselves, words alone are no longer certain good. So in the final circle, following the ironic counterpoint of Brendel's interruption, the duologue uses its own authenticity to show that the issue between Rosmer and Rebekka, given their state of transformation *and* arrest, cannot be settled by words, by confessional talk:

ROSMER. Jeg vil tro deg på ditt blotte ord denne gang også.
REBEKKA. Talemåter, Rosmer. . . Hvor kan du tro meg på mitt blotte og bare ord efter denne dag?

ROSMER. I will believe you on your bare word, this time too.
REBEKKA. Just words, John. . . How can you believe me on my bare word after today?

> (Act IV, Fakkel, p. 326; Penguin, p. 116—17)

The integrity of what has been spoken can only be tested by the double suicide into which Rosmer, with self-confessed fascination of the horrible, tempts Rebekka with his challenges («Så viker du. Vover ikke – hva *hun* vovet.» «You draw back. You dare not do – what *she* dared.» p. 326; p. 116). It is a brief dialogue of temptation, which may seem an ironic reversal of roles (since Rebekka was cast for the role of temptress in the play's retrospective action) and which complettes the reversal of values (from passion to self-transcending death, *eros* into *thanatos*). The tension of the dialogue, actional and verbal, still testing alternatives, still open, probing and groping, is sustained to the end – where the ritual marriage vow brings a quiet consummation. That final sharing of values – «For nu er vi ett» – is enseparable, as John Northam has shown[9], from a shared style. The dualism of opposed personalities and worlds leads to oneness; the duologue ends by confirming the unison of speakers in the silence of extinction.

IV

If in *Rosmersholm* the duologue remains throughout active and transformational – the words are the vehicles of subtle interaction between the speakers, here and now – in *John Gabriel Borkman* (1896) we have an early example in modern drama of a kind of post-actional dialogue. The three protagonists, (anticipating from the start the «one dead man and two shadows» of the end) are so to speak made to stand still on a platform or within a series of dramatic tableaux – to share a series of backward-looking confrontations, recognitions (of loss and betrayal) and a final epiphany (Borkman's vision). The whole play can be said to be constructed around the major duologues, some of them, like the act-long encounter between the two sisters, are so long and sustained that one of the first things the director of the Norwegian television film did was to reconstruct the duologues, interweaving those of Act I and II.[10] (For a duologue of that length and that degree of stylization may seem, to a contemporary television audience, as much a theatrical construct as the monologue.) Structurally, the duologue is, then more cen-

9 See note 1: *Ibsenårbok 1977*.
10 NRK, January 10, 1978, directed by Per Bronken.

tral than before; linguistically it is sparer – in the first three acts at times even stiff and static – until, in the final act, it modulates into the richly metaphoric language of Borkman's vision, stretching beyond personal dialogue, which may be said to lose the name of 'spoken action'. At first sight the Act I duologue of the two sisters, Mrs Borkman and Ella Rentheim, seems particularly stiff and colourless: carrying a load of expository material (concerning Borkman's bankruptcy and present death-in-life) and the slow first round of the battle over the possession of Erhart (thematically important, but, in my view, less charged with 'felt life' than are the past griefs of the protagonists).

But the dialogue gains tension through some built-in indirections which delay 'confessions' otherwise imminent. Such indirections, or seeming impediments to full utterance, represent the formal social code of the speakers: they must sound polite, must seem circumspect (to one another and the audience) in their emotional brutality. For example, the 'unspeakable' is skirted thus:

FRU BORKMAN /*tirrende*/. Jeg har nyttet disse åtte år – da jeg har hatt ham under øyne, ser du.
ELLA RENTHEIM /*behersket*/. Hva har du sagt Erhart om meg? Går det an at du forteller meg det?
FRU BORKMAN. Ja, det går så godt an.
ELLA RENTHEIM. Så gjør det da!
FRU BORKMAN. Jeg har bare sagt ham det som sant er.
ELLA RENTHEIM. Nå?

MRS BORKMAN /*provocatively*/. I used those eight years, you see – while I had him under my eye.
ELLA RENTHEIM /*controlling herself*/. What did you say to Erhart about me? Is it anything you can tell me?
MRS BORKMAN. Oh yes, certainly.
ELLA RENTHEIM. Then do so, please.
MRS BORKMAN. I only told him what's true.
ELLA RENTHEIM. Well?

(Act I, Fakkel, p. 528; Penguin. p. 302)

This use of words in a cat-and-mouse game (which depends on performance for full effect, and which seems to lose a good deal in this translation) foreshadows the future dialogue of fierce evasion within a subtext of banalities charged with emotion (as in Pinter). By contrast, the duologue between Ella and Borkman in Act II is turned, from what might seem predominantly retrospective and meditative, into a sense of new discoveries being made, in the course of recollection, about the

46

feelings concealed all those years by that pair of self-destructive potential lovers.[11]

ELLA RENTHEIM /*åndeløs/*. Sto det slik for deg den gang?
BORKMAN. Det forekommer meg så.
ELLA RENTHEIM. At *jeg* var det dyreste du visste?
BORKMAN. Ja, det svever meg for noe slikt.

ELLA RENTHEIM /*breathless/*. Was that how it was with you then?
BORKMAN. I rather think it was.
ELLA RENTHEIM. That *I* was the dearest thing you had?
BORKMAN. Yes; something like that comes back to me.

(Act II, Fakkel, p. 534; Penguin, p. 330)

The rise in emotion (here indicated by the stage direction − breathless)
is partly a matter of context and cumulative pressure, but partly carried by this natural-seeming exchange whereby Borkman's almost cas-
ual admission of past love is matched by Ella's incredulous and painful
discovery (soon to become rhetorically explicit).

But it is the transmuted duologue of Ella and Borkman in the final
act that calls for further comment. For here we have, first of all, a remarkable correspondence between the structural, the scenic, and the
verbal transcendence of naturalism at one and the same time: as the
backward-moving action suddenly turns to the future; and as those two
move from the claustrophobic bourgeois parlour into a scenography of
snow (which Edvard Munch called «the most powerful winter landscape in Scandinavian art»[12]), their dialogue itself is freed from their
constrained social and stylistic code − the spare and stiff language of
encounter. Moreover, this metaphoric language is not wholly dependent on visual effects. (I myself recall a radio performance where the *al-*
ternate symbolic landscapes of snow-and-ice and Borkman's invisible
Kingdom − of mines and factories, and of death − were clearly coun-
terpointed by words alone. And I am not quite sure how much is gained from seeing the new-fallen snow, etc., for the essential thing to be
communicated is Borkman bursting out into the chilling clearness of
winter air.)

The enrichment of the dialogue − expressing Rosmer's personal vi-

[11] See also Ella's key phrase of Recognition: «Jeg har aldri riktig visst hva der
egentlig var vederfaret meg for før nu kveld.» − «I've never really known till
this evening what it was exactly that happened to me.» (545; 331)

[12] Michael Meyer, *Ibsen,* London, 1967, 1974, p. 783.

sion through the imagery of that power-haunted *paysage intérieur* – is significant. But in the course of becoming rich and strange, the duologue, as interaction, also suffers a sea-change:

BORKMAN. . . Ella! Ser du fjellrekkene *der* – langt borte? Den ene bakenfor den annen. De høyner seg. De tårner seg. *Det* er mitt dype, endeløse, uuttømmelige rike!

ELLA RENTHEIM. Å, men der står et så isnende pust fra det rike, John.

BORKMAN. Det pust virker som livsluft på meg. Det pust kommer til meg som en hilsen fra underdanige ånder. Jeg fornemmer dem, de bundne millioner; . . . /*med fremrakte hender*/ Men jeg vil hviske det til jer her i nattestillheten. Jeg elsker eder, der I ligger skinndøde i dypet og i mørket. Jeg elsker eder, i livkrevende verdier – med alt eders lysende følge av makt og ære. Jeg elsker, elsker, elsker eder!

ELLA RENTHEIM /*i stille stigende opprør*/. Ja, der nede har du din kjærlighet ennu, John.

BORKMAN. . . Ella! Do you see the mountain-ranges *there,* far away? One behind another. They rise up. They tower. *That* is my deep, unending, inexhaustible kingdom!

ELLA RENTHEIM. . . Yes, John, but here's a freezing breath coming from that Kingdom!

BORKMAN. That breath is like the breath of life to me. That breath comes to me like a greeting from imprisoned spirits. I can see them, the millions in bondage; . . . /*With outstretched hands*/ But I will whisper it to you here in the stillness of the night. I love you, where you lie as though dead in the depth and in the dark! I love you, you treasures that crave for life – with all the shining gifts of power and glory that you bring. I love, love, love you!

ELLA RENTHEIM /*in silent, but rising emotion*/. Yes, your love is still down there, John.

(Act IV, Fakkel, p. 562; Penguin, p. 368)

This should be played and read, with the kind of pause that allows full realisation of the poignant irony: Borkman's vision is, from the point of view of relationship, a megalomaniac's final evasion of full encounter. As he turns from addressing Ella to addressing the spirits of the mine and of the bank-vaults, (strongly marked in the original by the untranslatable pronoun shift from *du* to the formal *jer* and *eder*), Borkman is allowing the intimate duologue to swell into his titanic monologue. The frame of the duologue is kept at this stage only by Ella (who still desires intimate encounter) – the whole transition masterfully controlled by Ibsen. It remains to be noted that the texture of Borkman's speech is also ambivalent: it is both a moving self-expression, and a piece of poetic property, an attack of bombast. It is one of the rare instances, in the prose plays, where Ibsen departs from what

Knudsen called «the idiomatic authenticity of the whole movement of speech» where «the syntax had to ring true».[13] It is, in short, an excursion into prose poetry, as distinct from the image-laden but spare poetry-of-the-theatre in *Rosmersholm*. It is a linguistic change appropriate to the change from dialogue as transformation to dialogue as epilogue: a final metamorphosis and recognition that is only partially embodied in an encounter of two minds in duologue. Ibsen is here creating a new mode of dialogue which, beyond its local interest, anticipates a future and problematic development: one speaker's 'excess' of speech, within dialogue, may become parodic (as in Gaev's address to the bookcase in the first act of *The Cherry Orchard)* or a symptom of dislocation, isolating speaker from speaker (ultimately the solipsistic voices in Beckett). Thus Ibsen opens up a new dimension of experience and expression – which is also a 'problem of style' – by breaking the mould of strictly naturalistic dialogue in Borkman's epiphanic yet egocentric duologue.

Editions used: Fakkel, *Nutidsdramaer 1877—99,* Gyldendal, Oslo, 1962.
Penguin, *The Master Builder and other Plays,* translated by Una Ellis-Fermor, Harmondsworth, 1958.
Archer, for *Ghosts* only, reprinted in *Seven Famous Plays,* London, 1950.

These were the only translations at hand at the time of writing; I resisted the urge to offer my own version here and there, as it seemed desirable to use a standard translation.

[13] See note 1: Knudsen, p. 162.

The end of *Ghosts*

EGIL TÖRNQVIST

«We have seen a good many plays of late which do not end, but simply leave off: at their head we might perhaps place Ibsen's *Ghosts.*»[1] William Archer, writing in 1912, is obviously not happy with the end of Ibsen's play. Referring to Aristotle's well-known requirement that a play should have a beginning, a middle and an end, he finds the latter lacking in *Ghosts.*

Much later, in 1949, Francis Fergusson comes to the same conclusion. Mrs Alving's quest, he writes, «is not so much completed as brutally truncated».[2] The end is unsatisfactory.

Sharply contrasting with these views is that of John Northam, expressed in 1953: «we see a process work towards its completion, and at its end we feel a sense of unity and roundness in the conception; it is not a play that simply leaves off.»[3]

«An end», Aristotle says (and what he means is a proper end), «is that which itself naturally follows some other thing, either by necessity or as a rule, but has nothing following it.»[4] As Butcher remarks, the purpose of this definition is to exclude endings which do not conclude the action.[5] A clear spelling-out of Aristotles' view on this point we find in the First Preface of Racine's *Britannicus:*

Pour moi, j'ai tojours compris que la tragédie étant l'imitation d'une action complète, où plusieurs personnes concourent, cette action n'est point finie que l'on ne sache en quelle situation elle laisse ces mêmes personnes. C'est ainsi que Sophocle en use presque partout.

---

[1] W. Archer, *Play-making,* New York (1912) 1960, p. 55.
[2] F. Fergusson, *The Idea of a Theater,* Princeton U. P. 1949, p. 164.
[3] J. Northam, *Ibsen's Dramatic Method,* London 1953, p. 74.
[4] S. H. Butcher, *Aristotle's Theory of Poetry and Fine Art,* New York, 1951, p. 31.
[5] Ibid., p. 282.

The plays of Sophocles, of course, served as Aristotle's chief source when he penned his ideas about tragedy in the *Poetics*.

How strong the Aristotelian tradition, also with regard to play endings, has been can be seen in the three statements on *Ghosts* I have just quoted. For although the three critics disagree on whether the play is rounded off or not, they agree about the premise, that a sense of completeness ought to be provided.

Actually, we are here faced with two questions which should be carefully kept apart. First, the question whether the Aristotelian idea of completeness is still valid. And second, the question whether the end of *Ghosts* is complete or incomplete. The word 'completeness', however, raises new questions: What does it mean? Complete, in what sense? How? To whom?

Before discussing these questions we must examine the end. Which brings us to another terminological problem: What do we mean when we talk about the end of a play? Where does the end begin? And where does it end? Oddly enough critics rarely seem to ponder such questions. As a result, the word 'end' can mean very different things to different commentators.

It is, of course, tempting to try a hard and fast rule. By the end of a play, we might suggest, is meant the last French scene or – as I prefer to call it – the last sequence. In *Ghosts* there are 41 sequences and the last one, leaving Osvald and Mrs. Alving alone on the stage would then, according to this definition, constitute the end. At closer inspection, however, this procedure proves highly unsatisfactory, since it means that in plays containing only one sequence – Strindberg's *The Stronger,* for example – the end becomes synonymous with the entire play. Thus defined the term is clearly meaningless.

More satisfying it is to let the end begin with a notable change of situation fairly close to the final curtain. Consider in this respect the following:

OSVALD. Ja, nu får altså du gi mig håndsrækningen, mor.
FRU ALVING. /*skriger højt*/. Jeg!

At this point it stands clear that Osvald has morphine at his disposal, that the crucial attack may occur at any time, and that Regine can no longer give him a helping hand since she has left. The only one who can take Osvald's life is now the one who has given it ho him: Mrs. Alving. Her violent reaction indicates that she realizes this.

There can be no doubt that this is a significant turning-point – as well as one of the major ironies of the play. But it is not the final change and so it is not valid in our context. For the end should properly begin with the last significant change of situation.

When Osvald asks his mother to give him the sun, we understand that the crucial moment has come, that he has, in his own words, become «hjælpeløs, som et lidet spædbarn, uhjælpelig, fortabt, håbløs». Note, incidentally, how Ibsen here insists on the hopelessness of his case. Up to this point Mrs. Alving could find release in the thought that what Osvald fears may not happen. Now she is faced with the brutal truth – not only Osvald's dementia but also her own promise to him that she make an end of his life, should it prove necessary. Now it is necessary.

Since Osvald's lines at the end refer to the sun which has just risen, it is logical to let the end begin with this striking change of light. What we get is the following (I quote the brief passage *in toto*):

Solopgang. Bræen og tinderne i baggrunden ligger i skinnende morgenlys.

OSVALD /*sidder i lænestolen med ryggen mod baggrunden, uden at røre sig; pludselig siger han*/. Mor, gi mig solen.
FRU ALVING /*ved bordet, ser studsende på ham*/. Hvad siger du?
OSVALD /*gentager dumpt og toneløst*/. Solen. Solen.
FRU ALVING /*hen til ham*/. Osvald, hvorledes er det med dig?
OSVALD /*synes at skrumpne sammen i stolen; alle musklerne slappes; hans ansigt er udtryksløst; øjnene stirrer sløvt frem*/.
FRU ALVING /*dirrende af rædsel*/. Hvad er dette! /*skriger højt*/. Osvald! Hvorledes har du det! /*kaster sig på knæ ned ved ham og rusker i ham*/ — Osvald! Osvald! Se på mig! Kender du mig ikke?
OSVALD /*toneløst som før*/. Solen. – Solen.
FRU ALVING /*springer fortvilet op, river med begge hænder i sit hår og skriger*/. Dette bæres ikke! /*hvisker ligesom stivnet*/. Dette bæres ikke! Aldrig! /*pludselig*/. Hvor har han dem henne? /*famler pilsnart over hans bryst*/. Her! /*viger et par skridt tilbage og skriger*/. Nej; nej; nej; – Jo! – Nej; nej! /*hun står et par skridt fra ham, med hænderne indfiltret i håret, og stirrer på ham i målløs rædsel*/.
OSVALD /*sidder ubevægelig som før og siger*/. Solen. – Solen.

It is easy to see that this end, though superficially realistic, is in fact carefully structured to meet the dramatic needs, that is: rather stylized. Osvald's motionlessness is strikingly contrasted with Mrs. Alving's mobility, just as his monotonous, obsessed repetition of that single word – the sun – markedly differs from her changing tone of voice, beginning on a normal pitch but soon turning into a scream, then into a whisper, and again a scream – an acoustic wave, dynamic, trembling with life. Until she becomes as immobile as her son, speechless, her

hands in her hair, a gesture indicating despair, bewilderment and iden-
tification with her victim: the suggestive phrase «med hænderne indfiltret i
håret» may be seen as a visual approximation both of Osvald's brain-
storm and of the entangled situation which has given rise to it. The
whole passage is rather like a film ending in a frozen picture.

Osvald's repeated reference to the sun can be interpreted in several
ways. On the most obvious level it informs us and Mrs. Alving that the
crucial moment has come. A single mention of the sun would not be
enough to bring home this idea; it is precisely his repetition of one and
the same word that makes it clear that Osvald has mentally regressed to
the state of a little child babbling his first word.

But why does Ibsen have him repeat this word in four different
speeches rather than in one? The reason is of course that the full truth
should not be brought home to Mrs. Alving all at once but step by step.
By distributing Osvald's appeal for the sun over four speeches, Ibsen is
able to demonstrate a gradual mental process within his protagonist
Mrs. Alving.

When he first asks for the sun, she starts but she has not yet any
reason to conclude – and she certainly represses all thoughts in this direction – that the fatal moment has arrived. His second reference to
the sun naturally increases her worry, and she now feels the need to
examine him at close distance. Precisely at this point, when mother
and son are physically close to one another, Ibsen suddenly alienates
them from each other: Osvald's last resistance breaks down; he now definitely turns into an imbecile, a helpless child, a living dead. Communication between the two is no longer possible. Mrs. Alving's questions
at this point illustrate above all her desire to cling to a last straw – as
does her desperate shaking of him. But everything is in vain. When she
realizes that there is no hope, she begins to tear at her hair, anguished
but still seeking a solution. Unable to accept the new situation which
she is now forced to recognize, she gets hold of the morphine. Killing
Osvald means not only making an end to his suffering (if he suffers) and
fulfilling her promise to him; it may also mean changing an unbearable situation.

However, both in action and words Mrs. Alving reveals that she is
not yet ready for this. Her shrinking back a step or two from Osvald is
clearly Ibsen's way of translating, in spatial terms, her shrinking back
from the idea of euthanasia. And her final speech, consisting of five
no's to a single yes similarly indicates that she does not, after all, dare
or wish to kill her son. Her last word in the play is no. Even when the
curtain falls she remains at a distance from him. To most interpreters

these four factors will suggest that Mrs. Alving does not kill her son.

Yet to others it may seem much more relevant that Mrs. Alving, momentarily, accepts the idea of euthanasia. Is this not an indication, so the argument may run, that she will eventually accept the idea wholeheartedly and proceed from word to deed? And is this not the logical continuation of the quest Mrs. Alving pursues throughout the play, her gradual breaking away from traditional moral values?

Noone would deny that Mrs. Alving undergoes a certain change in the course of the play, that she becomes more independent, more courageous. But the crucial question is: Does she liberate herself enough from traditional ethics to be able to perform the act of euthanasia? There is no clear indication of this in the play. Up to the very end she remains a split, vacillating person with regard to this issue.

Will Mrs. Alving kill Osvald? Different answers have been given. But in fact there is only one correct answer, Ibsen's own: «That I don't know.»[6] However carefully we examine her, there is no way of forespelling with any certainty how she will act.

So far I have paid attention only to the two characters proper appearing at the end. But there is, you might say, also a third 'character' appearing now for the first time: the sun. The entrance of the sun, I have already proposed, marks the beginning of the end. The end is literally set in another light than the rest of the play.

By general agreement the final sunrise carries symbolic connotations. But what kind of connotations? To Northam the sun is primarily a symbol of enlightenment, truth.[7] The light progression of the play – from gloomy rain through darkness to sunrise – corresponds to the gradual removing of one veil after another until the truth finally becomes visible. Preceded by such minor light sources as the lamp and the burning asylum, the sun brings enlightenment to Mrs. Alving and forces her «to face the facts as they really are».[8]

There is much to be said for this interpretation. Truth vs. appearances is a fundamental antithesis in *Ghosts* – as even the play title indicates. A true way of life – as well as freedom – is associated with the artists in Paris; hypocrisy and confinement, on the other hand, with Norwegian society or mentality. While Paris bathes in sunlight, Norway suffers from rain and darkness. Osvald's remark in Act II that he has

[6] *The Oxford Ibsen,* V, Oxford U. P. 1961, p. 475.

[7] J. Northam, *op. cit.,* p. 67ff., and *Ibsen. A Critical Study,* Cambridge U. P. 1973, p. 102ff.

[8] *Ibsen. A Critical Study,* p. 107.

never seen the sun shine at home is an exaggeration which brings out the symbolic truth of his statement. When Mrs. Alving states «Og så er vi så gudsjammerlig lysrædde allesammen», she is clearly equating light with truth. So is Osvald when he deliberately wants to synchronize his major revelation concerning his disease with the rising of the sun: «Nu vil vi snakke sammen, mor / – / og så rinder solen imens. Og så véd du det.»

Besides connoting truth and freedom, the sun also stands for the joy of life, «livsglæden»:

OSVALD. Ja det er bare det jeg mener, at her læres folk op til at tro, at arbejdet er en forbandelse og en syndestraf, og at livet er noget jammerligt noget, som vi er bedst tjent med at komme ud af jo før jo heller.
FRU ALVING. En jammerdal, ja. Og det gør vi det da også ærligt og redeligt til.
OSVALD. Men sligt noget vil menneskene ikke vide af derude. Der er ingen der, som rigtig tror på den slags lærdommer længer. Derude kan det kendes som noget så jublende lyksaligt, bare det at være til i verden. Mor, har du lagt mærke til, at alt det, jeg har malet, har drejet sig om livsglæden? Altid og bestandig om livsglæden. Det er lys og solskin og søndagsluft, – og strålende fornøjede menneskeansigter.

Just as the sunshine is here associated with the lust for life, so rain is the appropriate weather in a vale of tears; in the stage directions for Act I Ibsen significantly speaks of a *dystert fjordlandskab*. «Ja, livsglæden mor», Osvald points out, «den kender I ikke stort til herhjemme. Jeg fornemmer den aldrig.»

And yet it is not altogether lacking. Osvald himself admits that Regine might be able to save him: «for jeg så der var livsglæde i hende». And Mrs. Alving later reveals that what is true of Regine was once true also of her father, Chamberlain Alving:

I *ham* var livsglæden oppe, du! / – / Det var som et søndagsvejr bare at se på ham. / – / Og så måtte sligt et livsglædens barn, – for han *var* som et barn, dengang, – han måtte gå herhjemme i en halvstor by, som ingen glæde havde at byde på, men bare fornøjelser.

The Norwegian society is to blame. An so is Mrs. Alving for having adjusted to its norms:

Din stakkers far fandt aldrig noget afløb for den mægtige livsglæde, som var i ham. Jeg bragte heller ikke søndagsvejr ind i hans hjem.

Notice how Ibsen is here concerned with the original meaning of «søn-dag»: Sun-day, the day of the sun. At the same time Sunday of course connotes day of rest and, obliquely, of enjoyment, of happiness.

When the play ends it is at long last Sun-day, a day of the Sun. The Norwegian gloom has, so to speak, given way to the Parisian – or continental – joy of living.

Throughout *Ghosts,* then, two contrasting conceptions of life are depicted. As the action progresses it becomes increasingly clear that «derude» (in France) is primarily ethically opposed to «herhjemme» (in Norway). In the major part of the play only one of these outlooks is visualized: the Norwegian gloom; this is true both of the exterior and the interior, for Mrs. Alving's conception of life has always been highly determined by her surroundings. The other view of life – the French joi de vivre – is here merely described, reported, Osvald fulfilling the task of messenger. We see the rain and the darkness; we only hear of the sun.

At the end this situation is changed. The French conception of life, if I may call it so (the words 'French' and 'Norwegian' are here of course used figuratively), is now visualized in the exterior. «Derude» has become part of the stage picture and now contrasts with «herhjemme» in the sense: inside Mrs. Alving's home. Instead of the perpetual rain which makes us shortsighted, we now get a crisp air which enables us to see very far: *«Solopgang. Bræen og tinderne i baggrunden ligger i skinnende morgenlys.»* Our vision – and especially Mrs. Alving's – has been considerably improved. This is undoubtedly a beautiful and impressive view. Here is the sun of truth and of joi de vivre, the fresh air of freedom, the soaring white mountain tops of lofty idealism and purity. All the values that have gone into Osvald's paintings seem to be here. At last Osvald's Parisian sun sheds its light over a Norwegian landscape. A synthesis has been established.

How are we to understand this? Have the Norwegians suddenly converted from gloomy Christianity to 'pagan' joi de vivre? Naturally not. The sun at the end sheds its light only on two people. And one of the two cannot even see it. There is a stark irony in the fact that Osvald, who has spent a lifetime longing for the sun, is not able to see it when it finally rises. Sitting with his back to the window he can merely go on longing for it.

The only one who sees the sun – apart from the audience – is thus Mrs. Alving. It is her sun. The sunrise may therefore be taken to represent an inner experience on her part. And yet the fact that we, too, see it gives it a kind of objectivity.

All the values Osvald has longed for – and his father before him – are at long last fully recognized by her who has helped spoiling their lives because she has been but all too much a part of a gloom-promoting society. By having us share Mrs. Alving's vision – her experience – Ibsen brings us as close to her as he possibly can.

The sunrise comes to mean something very different from what Mrs. Alving had expected. Shortly before dawn she says:

Dagen begynder alt at gry oppe i højderne. Og så blir det klarvejr, Osvald! Om lidt skal du få se solen.

And just before the sun rises she speaks in the same terms:

Og ser du, Osvald, hvilken dejlig dag vi får? Skinnende solvejr. Nu kan du rigtig få se hjemmet.

For Mrs. Alving the sunlight here still has the illusory meaning of bright future. She wants the sun primarily because Osvald needs it, not because she herself is in need of it.

Once the sun has risen her hope is put to shame. There is no happy future in store for Osvald. And although the sunlight spreads to the interior, he is not able to see his home properly. Ibsen is clearly working in the tradition of Sophoclean irony.

But what *he* cannot do *she* can. For the first time she is able to see what kind of home Osvald has had. For the first time she is able to see the sun properly. Only if we regard the end in this way, only if we accept the idea that Mrs. Alving does indeed undergo an inner change at this point – only then can we regard the end of *Ghosts* as anything like the end of classical tragedy. Mrs. Alving has struggled bravely, and although she is defeated there is victory in her defeat; for at last she fully experiences the positive values her husband and son have stood for.

This view comes fairly close to that of Northam.[9] Mrs. Alving, Northam states, is finally «being forced to face the facts as they are». But if you are forced to do something you are anything but free and active. And I do not see how Mrs. Alving under such circumstances can gain any stature of significance. Only if we view the sunrise as an indication of her profound experience of the (true) values her men have been seeking can we accept the idea that there is victory in her defeat.

[9] Ibid., p. 105. Cf. also – with regard to the sun symbolism – B. Hemmer, *Ibsen og Bjørnson,* Oslo 1978, p. 184ff.

Let us now return to our initial question: Is the end of *Ghosts* complete or incomplete?

It is evident that Racine's Aristotelian demand that the audience should know «in what situation the characters are finally left» is not fulfilled. In that sense the play is incomplete and the end non-Aristotelian. But does this really bother us? Even Sophocles, if we may believe Racine, is not always perfect in this respect. And what about a play like O'Neill's *Long Day's Journey Into Night?* Surely, there is a tragedy of survival as well as a tragedy of death.

The tragic hero reaches his goal but the price he must pay is a heavy one. Oedipus finds the man who has committed parricide. Orestes and Hamlet revenge themselves on those who have murdered their fathers. Medea triumphs over Jason. Romeo and Juliet are united in death. Solness climbs his tower. What about Mrs. Alving?

It has been said that she differs from the classical tragic hero not in degree but in kind for she never reaches a goal: «just as she cannot give Osvald the sun, so the light of the sun has not been able to enlighten her». The final sunrise «sheds its rays as an ironic and bitter joke on a demented boy asking his equally helpless mother» for the sun. We are very far from the affirmation sensed at the end of classical tragedy.[10]

Contrary to Robert Corrigan, who is responsible for this view, I would claim that Mrs. Alving differs from the traditional tragic hero not in kind but in degree. Corrigan's analysis of *Ghosts* seems to me biased. He chooses to regard Mrs. Alving as a prototype of the modern, mediocre so-called tragic protagonist. She has to fit this pattern or she does not suit his purpose.

It is of course quite possible to regard the final sunrise as merely ironic and Mrs. Alving as utterly helpless. But is not this just scratching the surface? Helpless – yes. But who would not be in her situation? Can we really expect her to develop any superhuman faculties at this moment? If so, in what way? By killing Osvald? Or by abstaining from doing it? As for the sunrise, I think we may safely say that it is utterly ambiguous. The sun that rises is at once the sun of righteousness and the sun of grace, the sun of God, if you wish. (It is significant that it is the rain that is (falsely) attributed to God in the beginning of the play.) It is not necessarily an indifferent or ironic sun. Mrs. Alving's quest is not essentially different from that of Oedipus.

[10] R. W. Corrigan, «The Sun Always Rises: Ibsen's *Ghosts* as Tragedy?», *Educational Theatre Journal,* 1959. Here quoted from the reprint in R. W. Corrigan (ed.), *Tragedy. Vision and Form,* San Francisco 1965, pp. 401, 404.

Yet there is a difference in degree or should we say presentation which at least on one level should not be underrated. While the goal reached by the traditional hero at least on one level is explicitly formulated, the one reached by Mrs. Alving remains implicit and is consequently open to different interpretations.

More serious is Fergusson's criticism of the end:

Osvald's collapse, before our eyes, with his mother's screaming, makes the intrigue end with a bang, and hammers home the thesis. But from the point of view of Mrs. Alving's tragic quest as we have seen it develop through the rest of the play, this conclusion concludes nothing: it is merely sensational.

And again:

But the action is not completed: Mrs. Alving is left screaming with the raw impact of the calamity. The music is broken off, the dissonance unresolved – or, in more properly dramatic terms, the acceptance of the catastrophe, leading to the final vision or epiphany which should correspond to the insight which Mrs. Alving gains in Act II, is lacking. The action of the play is neither completed nor placed in the wider context of meanings which the disinterested or contemplative purposes of poetry demand.

Ibsen, in short, was unable to create a satisfactory tragic ending because he was writing in an essentially untragic period marked by realistic concern for petty parlours. This is Fergusson's thesis in a book significantly subtitled «The Art of Drama in Changing Perspective». The changing perspective, it appears, amounts to the gradual passing away of tragedy.

It is easy to agree with the idea that Ibsen, like any writer, was a child of his time. It is more difficult to agree altogether with Fergusson's description of the end of *Ghosts*. I fail to see in what sense Ibsen hammers home a thesis. He does not suggest any solution to Mrs. Alving's dilemma. All he does is formulate this dilemma with great precision and impact. That is something else.

It is also a gross overstatement to say that « the conclusion concludes nothing» and is «merely sensational». Fergusson would have come closer to the truth if he had said that the end is not as complete as that of classical tragedy, because the acceptance of the catastrophe is at most implied, not clearly demonstrated. We do not get anything like Maurya's «No man at all can be living for ever, and we must be satisfied», the closing line of Synge's *Riders to the Sea*. And I think we must admit that Ibsen has here sacrificed something essential. Why did he do it?

It is easy to see that he could have made the end more complete than it is. He could have let Osvald die a natural death or he could have had him commit suicide, leaving Mrs. Alving to mourn him much as Maurya mourns her dead sons. Or he could have let Mrs. Alving kill him. Death, as Archer notes, is much relished in tragedy because it makes the end so definite. [12]

However, a natural death or a suicide would have been rather pointless, since it would not have put Mrs. Alving, the protagonist, to the ultimate test. And to let her give Osvald a helping hand – well, that would indeed have meant turning *Ghosts* into the thesis play Fergusson thinks it is.

Ibsen rejected these possibilities in favour of the present question mark ending. In this way he could have the theatre audience play the part of judge. And the stage history of the play shows that audiences have avidly grasped the chance. Few plays have activated people the way *Ghosts* has.

Instead of regarding Ibsen as a child of his time we may, with regard to the end of *Ghosts,* see him as a forerunner of the epic theatre of our own time. Brecht wrote *Der Jasager und der Neinsager* to let the audience partake of the same situation from two opposite points of view. Mrs. Alving says yes and she says no. Both playwrights invite the audience to take a stand.

Once he had decided on an open ending Ibsen naturally had difficulties providing a complete one as well. He could not let Osvald die. Nor could he let Mrs. Alving act. All he could do was to hint at a completion of the protagonist's spiritual quest. The final sunrise is such a hint.

Viewed in this way, the end of *Ghosts* interestingly bears the stamp of the time in which it was penned, not in Fergusson's sense to be sure, but in the sense that it fuses Aristotelian with non-Aristotelian ideas.

It has often been said that *Ghosts* is dated, for Osvald's disease can nowadays easily be cured. This is of course taking a very superficial view of the matter and paying undue attention to the illness *per se* rather than to what it represents. More relevant, it seems to me, it is to ask whether the play will seem dated if euthanasia ever becomes generally accepted in cases of incurable dementia. If so, Mrs. Alving's dilemma must seem less acute than it did to the audience in Ibsen's time. However, although the attitude to euthanasia is more liberal today than it was in the 1880's, it is not likely that painless killing will ever be gene-

---

[11] Fergusson, *op. cit.,* pp. 164f., 169.
[12] Archer, *op. cit.,* p. 232.

rally sanctioned. Fundamentally, this is not a social but an ethical issue which everyone must solve for himself. There will always be those who will claim that genuine love prevents us from killing a child of our own. There will always be those who will claim that genuine love under certain circumstances forces us to kill – even a child of our own. And there will always be those who, like Ibsen himself, will vacillate between these standpoints.

Posing questions, not answering them, Ibsen considered his task as a playwright. At the end of *Ghosts* he poses a question which will continue to stir theatre audiences. If it ceases to stir them, there is every reason to worry – not about the play but about the receivers of it.

Ghosts as a Psychological, Social and Existential Work
– An Example of Ibsen's Tragicomic Vision

JOHN S. CHAMBERLAIN

Concluding, in *Fantasio,* a pessimistic commentary on the nineteenth century and its relationship to previous ages, Alfred de Musset's character, Spark, expresses his apprehensions and his sense of their ludicrousness in a memorably suggestive image:

L'éternité est une grande aire, d'où tous les siècles, comme de jeunes aiglons, se sont envolés tour à tour pour traverser le ciel et disparaître; le nôtre est arrivé à son tour au bord du nid; mais on lui a coupé les ailes, et il attend la mort en regardant l'espace dans lequel il ne peut s'élancer.[1]

Georg Brandes was so taken by this description that it is quoted to conclude one of his compelling accounts of the intellectual experiences of the group of writers whose work he discusses in *Emigrantlitteraturen.* Clearly, in Brandes' view, de Musset is delineating only the negative aspects of a complex process of transition. Where Spark sees only despair, impotence and absurdity, Brandes discovers also, and primarily, the germs – or, to pursue the metaphor, the robust fledgelings – of a confident emancipation of mind, body and spirit in nineteenth-century European life.

As is well known, Ibsen read Brandes' *Emigrantlitteraturen,* first published in 1872, with a kind of attention he devoted to few other books, with the exception of the Bible, and the excitement he felt is evident in the famous letter he wrote thanking Brandes in the warmest terms for the intellectual and poetic stimulation he had received:

Farligere bog kunde aldrig falde i en frugtsommelig digters hænder. Den er en af de bøger som sætter et svælgende dyb mellem igår og idag... Den *(Emigrant-litteraturen)* står for mig som Kaliforniens guldfeldter da de først forefandtes; man blev millionær på dem, eller man gik under i elendighed. Er nu vor ånde-

---

[1] *Théâtre Complet,* ed. Maurice Allem (Paris, 1968), p. 289.

62

lige konstitution robust nok hjemme? Jeg ved det ikke; men herpå kommer det heller ikke an; hvad der ikke kan bære tidens ideer, det ma falde.[2]

While this passage is often quoted by critics, as is Ibsen's remark that he found Brandes' letters more like poems than conventional correspondence, it is less often observed, and still less frequently demonstrated, that Ibsen meant every word he wrote when he implied that in his work from that time on *Emigrantlitteraturen* would serve as a goldfield. It did, in terms of ideas, attitudes, and even characters' names.[3] Psychologically, socially, even, broadly speaking, politically, and in literary terms (most specifically, perhaps, in relationship to Ibsen's secular existentialism), there is possibly no other book which has greater significance in Ibsen's intellectual growth, including other books by Brandes and works by Kierkegaard and Hegel which Ibsen is known to have admired.

An Englishman who has come from the Canadian West to make observations such as these to an audience consisting entirely of Ibsen scholars must inevitably run the risk of bringing coals (by a most circuitous route) to Newcastle (or timber products to Skien!), but with your indulgence, I would like to suggest the effects on Ibsen's dramatic imagination of *Emigrantlitteraturen* and only to a lesser extent to concentrate on verbal parallels between that work and *Gengangere*. And, to begin, I think it is useful to make a general observation about the nature of the influence of Brandes' explicitly proselytizing study on Ibsen's much more subtle and tragicomic play. Ibsen, being a poet and a major artist, did not take *Emigrantlitteraturen* as the tables of the law. He responded to it rather as an imaginative (and dramatic) history of the spirit of his age, which he could probe, assimilate and modify in any way which his genius suggested. He certainly did not use it as it has recently been claimed that he used Hegel's *Phänomenologie des Geistes*.[4] There is nothing schematic about the inspiration that *Gengangere* draws from *Emigrantlitteraturen*. In this play, as in so many others − from *Samfundets Stötter* on-

[2] *Samlede Verker,* Hundreårsutgave, ed. Francis Bull, Halvdan Koht and Didrik Arup Seip (Oslo 1928—'57), XVII, p. 31. This edition is subsequently referred to as *S.V.*

[3] Gunnar Ahlström, in his *Det moderna Genombrottet* (Stockholm, 1947) points out several thematic links between *Emigrantlitteraturen* and *Samfundets stötter, Et dukkehjem* and *Gengangere.* My own article «*Gengangere* and *Emigrantlitteraturen*» (*Scandinavica,* vol. 16 no. 1, pp. 1—10) attempts to demonstrate further connections.

[4] See Brian Johnston, *The Ibsen Cycle* (Boston, 1975).

wards – Ibsen was free to deride, if he chose, everything that he also seems to have in part admired in Brandes' book. *Emigrantlitteraturen* served as a medium transmitting an interpretation of great European cultural movements to Ibsen. It helped him to envisage, in an expansive framework, the dreams of the early nineteenth century and some of its archetypal dreamers. But even when he is most caught up with the hopes and the prophecy, Ibsen is clearly free to laugh at the postures of Brandes' heroes and to lament their possible ineffectuality.

During the past fifty years in particular a number of Ibsen critics have begun to refer to the «duality» or the «multiplicity» of Ibsen's dramatic vision. Shaw, in some early comments on *Vildanden,* effectively launched, for the English-speaking nations, the discovery that the Ibsen of the prose plays is a consummate ironic humourist,[5] while more recently, numerous distinguished critics and editors have contributed greatly to our appreciation of Ibsen's multidimensional and ironic vision. If we were asked to single out from among many interpreters one who has most clearly isolated a theory of tragicomedy in Ibsen, the choice would almost certainly be Karl Guthke; it is to Guthke's theories of «modern tragicomedy» in general that I am most consciously indebted. Guthke's isolation of the theory of the «synthetic phenomenon of the tragicomic»[6] is a major contribution to Ibsen criticism, even though, in terms of critical explication, he deals fully with only one Ibsen play, namely *Vildanden.* If, like Peer Gynt, one were looking for a signpost showing the «Master's intention» one could not, I believe, do better when considering *Gengangere* than to recall Guthke's statement about modern tragicomic writers in general:

... the tragicomedian... lacks ultimate reassurance. When he views the comic as tragic and the tragic as comic, he is face to face with the questionability of the smaller or greater scheme of things and denies himself the firm footing that more fortunate writers have. Or rather if there is one thing that he is sure of, it is that this firm footing can only be gained temporarily and precariously, for it is constantly threatened. Thus the tragicomedian, more often than not, is exposed to the challenge of ultimate and total meaninglessness, without, however, necessarily falling prey to it.[7]

[5] Shaw reviewed the second English production of *Vildanden,* in 1897, and commented on its ability to cause audiences «to look with horror and pity at a profound tragedy, shaking with laughter all the time at an irresistible comede.» Cited by James McFarlane, *The Oxford Ibsen* (London and New York, 1960), VI, p. 442.

[6] *Modern Tragicomedy* (New York, 1966), p. XIII.

[7] Guthke, p. 72.

In Ibsen, from *Catilina* onwards, heroism, especially tragic heroism, is constantly in doubt. He sees and questions the validity of the vision of the young artist in «På Vidderne» and he implies in a letter to Brandes that the shoemaker who stays at his last, avoiding the temptation to get on the stage and act, may be (but only may be) the real type of modern heroism.[8] Whereas, for Brandes, in *Emigrantlitteraturen,* such eagles as Mme. de Staël, Benjamin Constant, Charles Nodier and Prosper de Barante still fly, Ibsen's vision, in *Gengangere* as elsewhere, includes also the dark perceptions of de Musset's Spark. Unlike Carlyle, Nietzsche, Shaw and Lawrence, in their different, though related ways, Ibsen did not definitely hail an envisioned phoenix; neither, like European pessimistic dramatists from Jarry to Beckett, was he certain that he saw only maimed grotesques where eagles belong. *Gengangere,* like its companion pieces, *Samfundets Stötter, Et Dukkehjem* and *En Folkefiende* gives forceful expression to progressive views which Brandes and others popularized, but it does so within a structure of dramatic feelings as complex and ironic as that in *Peer Gynt,* or those in some of the best of Ibsen's poems. In boldly seeking to answer «Spørgsmaalet 'Hvorfor'» and such related questions as «hvorfor Mennesket fødes, hvorfor det lever, hvad det hele fører til. . .»[9] Brandes employs humanist and liberal formulations. These questions are, of course, the grand metaphysical ones and the fact that many questioners (unlike Brandes) found atheism a new nightmare rather than a simple incentive to liberalism and love free of legal restraint helps to increase the sense of existential isolation that is present in *Gengangere* and related Naturalistic works. When Helene Alving, accompanied by Osvald, comes to the edge of the eyrie, she has like Constant's character, Eleonore (Ibsen borrowed the name), or like Mme. de Staël's own Corinne and Brandes himself, a whole number of «answers» for the «angst» which grips the age: feminism, free love, the «joy of life», the «joy of work», artistic insight, charismatic leadership, mutual devotion of the sexes. And none of Ibsen's aspiring heroes is tested more sorely, more ludicrously, and with more apparently disastrous results.

In his comments on Benjamin Constant's *Adolphe* Brandes emphasizes the novel's seminal nature and, in particular, its skilful analysis of the psychology of love. The relationship of Adolphe and Eleonore is based upon Constant's own experience with Mme. de Staël. The element

[8] See the letter to Brandes from Dresden of September 24, 1871.
[9] These questions are posed in the second edition of *Emigrantlitteraturen* – which is substantially revised – (Copenhagen, 1877), p. 98.

of «psychical analysis» («psychologiske Studier»),[10] displacing interest in the supernatural, concentrates on the state of mind of Eleanore herself. Like Helene Alving, Eleanore is no young, soft-eyed Juliet but a woman of experience, a forerunner of an archetype which was to figure prominently in European drama and fiction as *la femme de trente ans.*

The positive aspects of the psychological conception of Helene Alving are clearly related to Constant's Eleanore as Brandes describes her. Eleanore is, according to Brandes, both mature and possessed of an iron will. But for all that, there is no touch of the virago about her. Love is her ideal and marriage, as conventionally understood, a mere legalistic formula against the pettiness of which she struggles to the end. Eleanore's understanding of both spiritual and erotic relationships between the sexes is strikingly similar to Saint-Simon's conviction, also mentioned by Brandes, that hope for real progress in sexual relations must be grounded in mutual respect and understanding. As Brandes also points out through a translation of a passage from Mme. de Staël's *Corinne,* such ideals are central to de Staël's own understanding of love:

Overfor Solen og Stjernehimlen føler man kun Trangen til at elske hinanden og føle sig hinanden værdig, men Samfundet, Samfundet, hvor gjør det hjertet haardt og Aanden letsindig, hvor bringer det En til at leve blot for hvad man vil sige om os! Hvis Menneskene en Dag mødte hverandre, hver for sig befriede fra det Tryk, som Alle udøve paa hver Enkelt, hvilken ren Luft vilde da trænge ind i Sjælen, hvormange nye Ideer, hvormange sande Følelser vilde da ikke forfriske![11]

The similarities of idea and imagery between this passage and the conversation of Osvald and Helene Alving about the sunlit freedom of love among the Parisian artists are significant.

No less crucial to an understanding of the heroic psychology of Helene Alving is a passage present in full only in the first edition of *Emigrantlitteraturen.* In it Brandes describes the battle of Mme. de Staël (Constant's Eleanore) and Napoleon in terms of tragic struggle:

Længe før Balzac, længe før George Sand, optræder da her Kvindens Kamp i Litteraturen, hendes Kamp med det Bestaaende og med Samfundet, og Eleonore kommer til at repræsentere denne Kamp, fordi hun er støbt over Aarhundredets mægtigste Kvindeskikkelse, over den Kvinde, der kjæmpede den største Kamp, som nogensinde i Verdenshistorien en Kvinde har kjæmpet

[10] Page 152 in the second edition.
[11] Pages 206—207 in the 1872 ed. Page 261 in the 1877 ed.

med rent aandelige Vaaben, med eet Ord over Mme. de Staël. Thi den Kjærlighedshistorie, som fortælles i «Adolphe», er den som virkelig fandt Sted imellem Benjamin Constant og Germaine de Staël. Ganske vist var dennes ydre Forhold andre end Eleonores; men det er denne store og sjeldne Kvinde, hvis personlige Livskamp var en Kamp med selve Datidens Verdensbehersker, og hvem Napoleon med smaaligt Had og uædel Frygt forfulgte, forviste, censorerede og underkastede alle de Plager, for hvilke et brutalt Despoti kan udsætte det geniale Individ, denne Kvinde er det, som giver Constant den nye Kvindetype.[12]

In *Gengangere* we encounter a similar great duel, though Helene Alving's heroic credentials are darkened by other and less desirable psychological motives than those just mentioned and Ibsen's Napoleon is ironically shrunken to the tyrant of committee and drawing rooms, Pastor Manders.

The positive aspects of social struggle in *Gengangere* are just as clearly foreshadowed in *Emigrantlitteraturen.* In translating a passage from *Adolphe,* Brandes could have been summarizing Helene Alving's plight when he wrote:

Den mest lidenskabelige Følelse kan ikke kjæmpe mod Tingenes Orden, Samfundet er altfor stærkt. Det gjør den Kjærlighed, som det ei har bekræftet og sanctioneret, altfor bitter. Ve da den Kvinde, som søger sin Støtte i en Følelse, som Alt forener sig om at forgifte og mod hvilken Samfundet, naar det ei er nødt til at respectere den som legitim, væbner sig med Alt, hvad der er slettest i Menneskets Hjerte for at nedslaae Alt det, som er godt.[13]

But in *Gengangere* there are negative psychological and sociological currents which are at least as powerful as Ibsen's interest in Brandes' own ultimate optimism. It is worth remembering, for instance, that when Brandes advised Ibsen to read George Sand, another of Brandes' favourite heroines, Ibsen expressed boredom,[14] and Brandes' request that Ibsen take an interest in John Stuart Mill was countered by the perhaps surprising reaction that an author so dependent on his wife was not worth reading.[15] In *Gengangere,* the psychology of atavistic sexual conflict erupts in dialogue which, perhaps deliberately, echoes the

[12] Pages 125—126 in the 1872 ed. A similar but less histrionic passage appears in the 1877 ed. (p. 166).
[13] Page 132 in the 1872 ed. Pages 175—176 in the 1877 ed.
[14] See the letter to Brandes from Christiania of October 11, 1896.
[15] See the letter to Brandes from Christiania of April 30, 1873.

murderous strife of Aeschylus' Clytemnestra and Agamemnon.[16] The relationship between Helene Alving and Regine at times suggests an archetypal hostility between a mistress and servant who is a sexual rival, and the Oedipal undertones of Osvald's behaviour to his mother are complemented by Helene's at least momentarily Jocasta-like attraction to her son.

In sociological terms, the negative aspects of *Gengangere* are based on intimations not, of course, that Napoleonic tyrants are right, but that Mme. de Staël and her supporters may be naive – mistaken, that is – to believe that men will ever be prepared, as an entire sex, to meet women on terms of equality, and no less in error to believe that women as a sex are aiming at a loving understanding with men and not at social dominance for themselves. Paul Lafargue's theories about the alternation of matriarchy and patriarchy as social and political institutions are known to have influenced Strindberg.[17] Apprehensions similar to Lafargue's are also present in *Gengangere*.

The more obvious psychological and social attitudes which find dramatic expression in *Gengangere* are those which have informed women's rights movements for two centuries and most educated men are now more likely to sympathize with the feminist ideology of *Gengangere* and *Et Dukkekjem* than with the paranoid chauvinism of Strindberg's *Fadren,* for example. But productions of *Gengangere* which are unilinear in their insistence on straightforward feminism (the perils of such interpretation are still more obvious in the case of *Et Dukkehjem*) miss much of Ibsen's ideological eclecticism and virtually all his tragicomedy. *Gengangere* is a disquieting work, not a simple call to arms: it is one in which the psychology of love, of feminism, and of social justice, is poetically examined «i hjertets og hjernens hvælv,» where, as always in Ibsen, trolls have not given up their powers of disguise, deception and predation.

The critical appreciation of «the synthetic phenomenon of the tragicomic» is an even more demanding task than its definition. Moreover, the appreciation of *Gengangere* as a representative example of Ibsen's tragicomic art cannot be achieved through general analysis of themes, characterization and structure. By definition, the moods of tragico-

[16] Francis Bull in his Introduction to *Gengangere* (*S.V.,* IX, pp. 19—20) refers to Schøtt's review in *Nyt Tidsskrift* which relates *Gengangere* to the Greek family tragedies.

[17] Martin Lamm, *August Strindberg,* trans. Harry G. Carlson (New York, 1971), p. 207.

medy change, interlock and replace each other in ways which are both subtle and varied in pace. Nor does such tragicomedy as Ibsen wrote preclude episodes which are primarily tragic or comic. The simultaneous presence of both tragic and comic effects ebbs and flows in the works themselves just as consciousness of it does in the minds of the receptive audience or reader. At times Helene Alving will remind us of a Phaedra, a Gertrude or even a Cleopatra: at other times she is more reminiscent of Nell in *Endgame* or Meg in *The Birthday Party* and often her dual – or multiple – dramatic identities are simultaneously observable: she can be high-minded idealist and doting mother, emancipated woman and victim of imprisoning conventions at the same time. For this reason the finest «criticism» of the play is necessarily a production of it which is open to all its intersecting crosscurrents and nuances. And in the absence of one (or complementary to it) the best critical method is probably close examination of the text.

Such detailed exegesis could, of course, go far beyond the necessary limitations of the present paper, so I would like to select some key passages from *Gengangere* for close comment, and to bridge these, if I can, with sufficient more general remarks at least to suggest how I think the play works as tragicomedy. Essentially, once some of the «fine tuning» is done, *Gengangere* is very well able to broadcast itself to receptive audiences. And, recalling how the learned men discussing the identity of tragedy and comedy in Plato's *Symposium* lapsed into sleep, (not, perhaps, induced solely by wine) there is probably much to be said for keeping critical theorizing within bounds. The passages on which I would like to concentrate are: the opening of Act I, the first appearance of Osvald, one of the confrontations of Helene Alving and Manders, and the closing sequence of the third and final act.

No better example of what Cocteau called «poésie de théâtre»[18] (John Northam has illustrated it very ably in Ibsen) could be found than the opening stage direction of *Gengangere*. I would like to emphasize its tragicomic implications. The references to «en rummelig havestue,» to the rain-soaked and gloomy fjord landscape outside and the association of Regine «med en tom blomstersprøjte i hånden» with both external nature beyond the windows and «civilized» nature indoors suggestively prepare us for the tragicomic treatment of Victorian contradictions with which the play as a whole is concerned. Indications are quickly offered that Jacob Engstrand, with his deformed left leg, is the presiding

[18] *Les Mariés de la Tour Eiffel* (Paris, 1924. rpt. in *Œuvres de Jean Cocteau, Theatre 1,* Paris, 1948), p. 45.

devil in this ironically secular hell. While Dionysian forces, soon to be named as «livsglæden» are present, they are clearly alien to the rituals of «hjem» and «plikt» which are implicit in this stage direction. But there is mention too of a round table covered with the progressive literature which Helene Alving has been reading, whilst near to a small sofa (presumably the one on which Captain Alving used to sprawl while readiis, ironically, a work-table. Far from being merely the «stuffy parlor» of which Francis Fergusson speaks,[19] the set is a visual embodiment of tragicomic tensions. A half-stifled Dionysus («livsglæden») is seen to be in conflict with a Pentheus who has informed, for instance, the improvements to the Rosenvold estate that Helene Alving has made: her declared commitment, like Regine's, has been to «plikt,» though her reading may already have given her a more positive conception of «arbejdsglæden.»

The action commences with a ludicrous *pas de deux* between Regine, a daughter who is not what she thinks she is and Engstrand, who is not the father he claims to be. Regine's snobbery and small-minded ambitions are played off against Engstrand's unscrupulous plans for a brothel. Like the episode which follows, in which Manders becomes the target of Regine's dubious aspirations to find employment in the home of «en rigtig reel herre», Manders' fear of scandal (he has taken lodgings near to the harbour to avoid any gossip about himself and Helene) and the preliminary conversations of Manders and Mrs. Alving, the duologue between Regine and Engstrand has both comic and tragic aspects. Tragically, life, vitality, potentialities are being wasted and perverted, and there is sardonic humour in the dramatic treatment of these themes. This humour is particularly effective when, for instance, Manders rises up, like the Troll King in *Peer Gynt,* to protect his Dovre with the odd, jingoistic insistence that progressive ideas have not got far in Norway: «Ja, men dog ikke her i landet vel? Ikke Her hos os?» It is apparent, again with Gyntian echoes, in Manders' ridiculous arguments about not offending the Almighty – or public opinion – by taking out insurance on the Orphanage.

Such tragic and comic elements are again brilliantly juxtaposed at Osvald's first appearance. He comes downstairs like an Apollo entering Helene's life: her face lights up with joy when she sees him and he brings a gospel of happiness such as Brandes approves, but we see immediately the foreignness of Osvald's position – he is wearing a light overcoat and cannot accustom himself to the Norwegian climate.

[19] *The Idea of a Theater* (1949, rpt. New Jersey, 1968), p. 152.

The sardonic humor associated with the pipe that Osvald is smoking is of crucial importance. It contains the Joycean idea (though Joyce's speculations about Osvald's biological paternity are incorrect) that there is a laugh against Manders as a father. Manders is as much Osvald's spiritual father as Alving, though he is, of course, quick to evade the suggestion. And, as well as recalling the guilt of adultery through thought (another Gyntian echo) the pipe is another hell image.

Osvald's description of having been forced to smoke by Alving has interesting dramatic likenesses to the suggested operation on Peer's eyes in the Dovre. Freudians may see here the experience from which a castration complex may grow, and this lends support to other such interesting diagnoses of Osvald's state of mind as those offered by Derek Russell Davis.[20] But the most important dramatic aspect of the pipe reminiscences is that Alving's laughter is shown to have been that of a human troll. And it is intriguingly ironic that it should be in this context that Manders (of all people!) speaks of «livsglæden:» to excuse Alving's sadism, Manders exclaims, «I sin ungdom var han en særdeles livsglad mand.» Manders is therefore in the same tragicomic relationship to Mrs. Alving as the fiddler is to the bear in the poem «Mindets Magt,» in which the tune to which the tortured creature dances is «Fryd dig ved livet.» – Manders speaks of life's joy to the very person to whom he has played tunes of anguish. Nor can her son be as free from that dance as he still might hope. With a genius for telling juxtaposition, Ibsen makes Osvald feel impelled to praise the joy of the Parisian artists' lives in the context of a conversation celebrating his own dreadful homecoming and the fictitious achievements of his father.

Once Osvald has departed, Manders and Helene Alving face each other like Norwegian versions of Brandes' Napoleon and Mme. de Staël. At the level of ideological thesis, the battle is deceptively straightforward, but beneath the thrust and parry of the arguments about duty and radicalism, about the supposed rights of the sexes and an idyllic view of their future relationships, and about opposed views on responsible parenthood and the value of art, other hideous troll scenes emerge. They are drawn out of Helene's past in her descriptions of home-life with Alving, of his drunkenness and disgusting talk, of her struggles to keep him and his life quiet. In the middle of what seemed to Brandes a cogent dramatic treatment of social evils which could be

[20] See «A Re-Appraisal of Ibsen's 'Ghosts',» *Family Process* vol. 2, no. 1, (1963), pp. 81—93 and «The Death of the Artist's Father: Henrik Ibsen,» *British Journal of Medical Psychology* vol. 46, (1973), pp 135—141.

removed, Helene utters the terrible confession of her Clytemnestra-like subjugation of Alving:

Og så tog jeg magten i huset – hele magten – både over ham og over alt det øvrige. For nu havde jeg våben imod ham, ser De; han turde ikke kny.

When the Orphanage is dedicated the «lange stygge komediespil» as Helene calls it will, she believes, be over. The guilt of marrying for money and status, her humiliation as a chattel-bride, the hypocrisy of her mother and aunts who advised the marriage, the hateful memories of sexual infidelities and of an endangered child will be as exorcised ghosts. The rest of the play reveals, of course, the power of those troll-like forces, and makes it clear that it is questionable whether any social changes and legislation can ever completely destroy them.

Between this first great battle between Manders and Mrs. Alving and the final passage I would like to discuss – the end of Act III – several complex tragicomic episodes occur. Act II begins with one of those mockeries of a joyous feast which are a feature of many of Ibsen's works and ends with a fire which is\tragic in its embodiment of wasted life and its inability to purge evil,\and comic in its implication that the devil Engstrand is in his element. Between these events, Helene Alving tries several times to take heroic flight, and it is left to the audience to decide whether she ever soars in more than imagination. On the one hand the evocation of deterministic forces is almost overwhelming: on the other the pathos and dignity of the isolated consciousness struggling to make sense of a world that is ludicroisolation of Helene Alving is the principal source of our sympathy for her as the action moves on.

The existential nature of this isolation is emphasized by the satirical treatment of other characters: the hypocritical bargain struck between Manders and Engstrand and Regine's abrupt departure from Rosenvold are good examples of this. The ending of the play is overwhelming, abrupt, and lacking in all the harmonies that are sometimes associated with tragedy. It is, in fact, the tragicomic duality of identity in both Helene and Osvald Alving that are most striking at the very end. Osvald has something of the noble Roman about him as he seeks for a friend strong enough to help him to end his life: he is a champion of euthanasia as he demands that his mother take back the life he did not ask for and does not want. He is also surely – with grotesque comedy – the worst of trolls, selfishly and cruelly demanding that a mother destroy the only person who gives her life meaning. Like the overgrown brat of the Woman in Green in *Peer Gynt,* he comes home to demand an obnoxions «right» from a parent in an hour of sorest trial.

Helene's last coherent speech is made as she bends over Osvald, and it is as full of sunlight and hope as *Corinne* or Soria Moria Castle, and as she makes it, the sun actually rises upon Osvald's inanity. Heroically, Helene Alving has become an advocate of uninhibited love, and spiritual spontaneity. She has comforted Osvald to the last iota of her strength and understanding. It would be folly to deny that she may and actually seems to rise in herioc flight. But birds, even eagles, sometimes take to the wing in evasion, and the implication is in the play that much of Mrs. Alving's soaring may be avoidance even when she is at her most truthful. The dreadful crisis of the ending reduces her, as it reduces Åse in comparable circumstances, to incoherence and tearing her hair. In tragicomic terms (especially when she runs to escape from Osvald, and is brought back) her situation is remarkably similar to that of the trapped and stunned bird in «Fugl og Fuglefænger.» At the very end, Helene's situation is the embodiment of the cruellest aspects of tragicomedy: she is a woman full of love with only an imbecile to cherish, and one who has defined high purposes unachievable in her or perhaps any other genuinely human situation.

The comic element of *Gengangere* is more assertive than that in some other Ibsen plays: some critics have found it an excrescence. I hope I have shown that it is more subtle than is often thought: while some of the humour is farcical (one thinks of Engstrand's pursuit of Manders, for example, or some of the recollections of Regine's mother's relationship with Alving), it is farce which works together with many levels of sardonic humour to penetrate deeply the tragic movements of the play, and, ultimately, to call all unilinear interpretations of life into question. In psychological, social and existential terms, Helene Alving pursues an inspiring quest for truths. But the truths she discovers, good and evil, are left ultimately unclear or, at least, unendorsed by Ibsen.

Group Interaction in Ibsen's play *Ghosts*

A Literary Sociological Reading

ALEX BOLCKMANS

In this paper I shall try to approach Ibsen's play *Ghosts* with the sociological concept of «grouping». I am fully aware of the problems this may cause in the sociological field of study but I am not concerned with these points. I intend to discuss the three categories, a division largely agreed upon by sociologists: the group, the collectivity and the social category.[1]

The distinction between said categories can be summarized as follows. The group is a small entity whose members interact frequently and inevitably f.e., the family; its members are in direct social contact and all relevant questions concern their lives. The collectivity is the grouping of people with indirect relationship; they may be included in a body in which interaction between the members is infrequent, determined by structures of authority or external organization. The special category is the grouping of people without interaction, or where interaction is negligible or almost nonexistant; its members belong to the same large community but their relationship is vaguely determined by matters as social position, class, etc.[2]

These three terms are difficult to determine because the difference between them is vague. Besides, other classifications intersect and it would be difficult to combine them with other grouping classifications starting from quite different views such as primary and secundary groups (Ch. S. Cooley), socio- and psyche-group (Maucorps). This would be the case in purely sociological discussion, but in the field of literary sociology the said division will prove a working instrument of value, as I hope to show in my analysis.

Ibsens play *Ghosts* puts five characters on the stage. To get an accurate impression of their interaction, it is imperative also to consider the

[1] See R. K. Merton, *Social Theory and Social Structure,* 1949 and other works.
[2] The distinction mainly follows the description of the phenomenon given by J. A. A. van Doorn and C. J. Lammers, *Moderne sociologie.* (1964), p. 150—152.

characters that are simply mentioned or referred to by name. Here I recall the two characters whom the author named and who died before the action of the play takes place: Mr Alving and Johanne, the chambermaid seduced by him; also the characters the author does not name: the man in the street, the men of quality pastor Manders talks of, Mrs Alving's mother and aunts, the tipplers and artists who play their part in the lives of Mr Alving and Osvald respectively and the seamen mentioned by Engstrand; in brief each and every person referred to who plays either an active or passive part in the society of the play.

The structure of this society in *Ghosts* might be described as consisting of two groups: the family Alving, the Captain, his wife Helene, their son Osvald. In fact there was another group, viz. the Engstrand family, which consists of the carpenter himself, his wife Johanne, former house-maid of the Alvings and Regine. In the play however this second group no longer really exists: Johanne is dead, Engstrand lives by himself, Regine is at Mrs Alving's, after having been received into the bourgeois «Intimsphäre» of the Alvings. As a matter of fact Manders, Helene Alving, Engstrand, Osvald and Regine may be considered as a collectivity where as the social category is made up by those «men of quality», Helene Alving's relatives on one hand and Osvald's artist friends, Alving's drinking companions, and the seamen Engstrand talks of, on the other.

When speaking of social distinction, only the higher middle class and the lower classes are represented. In fact the play *Ghosts* is only concerned with the higher middle class – although the important part taken by Engstrand and Regine – covering both classes – in the play, makes necessary the contrast between higher and lower classes.

In the group interaction, pastor Manders is the catalytic agent; in fact he is the destructive force of society, although he represents the existing society and tries to guide the interaction. His activities failing dismally ended in complete disaster. Everyone has acquired their own resistance against the kind of world he represented and propagated. These various sorts of resistance had one thing in common: they turned aside in order to avoid clashing with the existing social order. Only one person showed enough courage to resist actively and to challenge social order: Helene Alving. Thus her efforts led to a tragic ending, at the same time revealing both the hollowness and destructiveness of the entire social system.

Schematically the grouping of the characters in the play can be represented as follows.

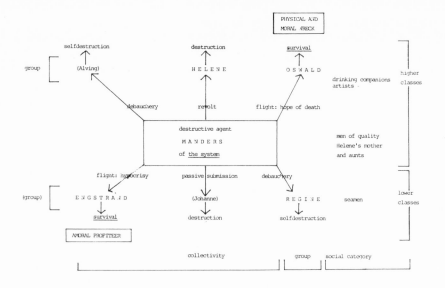

The action of the play starts with Manders' arrival at Rosenlund. He is about to add the finishing touch to the festivities by which Helene Alving will attempt both to bury the past once and for all and to atone for her mistakes. These efforts mean an active interfering with the social order, Manders (its representative!) being her executive agent. In spite of the fact that these efforts entirely correspond with the social system and order, they will turn out to be Helene Alving's complete destruction. This process proves clearly that any meddling with the existing social system in order to put things right can only lead to ruin, as it did (and will continue to do so) for those who did not resist but were looking for an alternative solution.

This has been or will be the case with all Ibsen's other characters. The meddling in the other one's affairs by Manders as a representative agent of the existing bourgeoissystem resulted in passive resistance to that system and led to self-destruction. Captain Alving in whom the joy of living has been killed took to drink and debauchery and this brought about his physical and mental downfall. Osvald at first ignorant of the true situation and its consequences takes to flight when he discovers the truth: his trying to marry Regine and his preparations for euthanasia. His physical as well as his mental destruction is brought about. Engstrand has been crippled by the system − just as Alving was a physical wreck so Osvald becomes a mental one. Being both a victim and a destructor Engstrand has taken to the alternative solution of hypocrisy in order to survive. Johanne submitted passively to her sufferings, where as Regine takes the right into her own hands. Following her father's example she resists fate by seeking pleasure and gain for her own benefit, although in a very short time this will lead to self-destruction.

In all these cases Manders has been the destructive element causing ruin for all involved – except for Engstrand his executive. Manders lends the breakdown of the system a helping hand: social conformism must lead to destruction. Active resistance cannot ward off destruction as long as one has been integrated into the system, as is shown by Helene's fate: she becomes aware of the connections but her efforts to stave off consequences are ineffective because she has submitted before to the laws of the system. The only way of survival is hypocritical acceptance of these laws, combined with self-interested motives.

In fact all the people involved develop a mechanism of resistance to Manders' destructive activity which instinctively they feel to be ruinous but find impossible to escape because in any case it will lead to destruction.

There is a remarkable likeness in the mechanism: Alving and Regine who seek refuge in debauchery end in self-destruction; Johanne and Helene try opposite reactions, passive submission for the former and revolt for the latter, but either's end is destruction, Johanne is bullied to death while Helene's entire world collapses; Engstrand and Osvald who both take to flight, hypocrisy and hope of death, both survive, somehow: Osvald a completely impotent human wreck and Engstrand an amoral profiteer of the system.

People acting like Manders leave behind them nothing but human wrecks and profiteers of the system.

The interaction of the play is on two levels, that of the group (Helene Alving, Osvald and Regine) and that of the collectivity (Helene, Manders and Engstrand). The fact that Helene Alving in both cases is the leading character, makes her into the primordial part of the play.

The interaction in the group originates in Helene Alving's awareness of what is going on between Osvald and Regine (end of the first act): the couple in the garden house. In the end it brings about Helene's confession while Osvald's solution is his marriage to Regine (end of the second act), a marriage approved by Helene and refused by Regine (third act). This refusal leaves but one issue: Osvald must beg his mother for help and by doing so subject Helene to her dramatic inner conflict, euthanasia or not.

In the group-interaction Manders naturally takes no part. He is a looker on, an appalled looker on who does not understand a thing. But he did bring about the situation which in the end led to interaction: at one time he had forced Helene to return to her debauchee-husband in spite of the love bonds between himself and Helene, which were pushed back and ignored, as we are told at the outset of act II.

The other level of interaction – the one in the collectivity – is interwoven with the first. The characters involved are Helene Alving, Manders and Engstrand, where as Osvald and Regine remain in the background. The main topics are: the practical affairs of the new home, and Helene's and Manders' disagreement on social and moral ideas in act I; Engstrand flattering the minister, the truth about Alving, and the fire in act II; Engstrand's final master stroke to win Mander' confidence in act III.

The interaction begins in the collectivity and ends in the group: *Ghosts* is a «familjedrama» as is made clear by the subtitle. All along the interaction shifts from one level to the next in subtle composition.

The entire first act is devoted to interaction in the collectivity which is understandable as it is the exposition of the drama, revealed by three minor scenes that foretell the future: Regine and Engstrand (partner-to-be in the Seamen's brothel), Manders and Regine (the girl is confronted with the prospective moneylender), Helene Alving and Manders (the hoped for ceremony of the next day). The central scene (between Osvald, Manders and Helene) deals with the present: artists' life in Paris. The last two scenes deal with the past: Helene and Manders talking about Alving's true life; Regine and Osvald repeating the scene between Alving and Johanne.

The second act too opens with interaction in the collectivity: two scenes, the first between Helene and Manders on their joint past, the second between Manders and Engstrand on Engstrand's past. And so the interaction in the group can properly start; the conversation on past and future of Helene and Osvald, Osvald's illness in Paris, his plans concerning Regine, and finally Helene's preparations for the new solution – interrupted by the news of the fire.

The third act once again opens in the collectivity with a scene of the fire and its consequences, the present and future situation. The remainder of the play is devoted to the final interaction in the group: Helene's understanding of the situation and her interpretation of the past, which results in Regine leaving the house; and the final conversation Osvald Helene which leads to the open ending.

The first act deals with collectivity, the beginning of both acts II and III culminates in group interaction, where as the interaction shifts from past and present to the future. Schematically: three minor scenes on the future, one on the present, one on the past (act I); two scenes on the past, one on the past and the future (act II); a scene on the present and the future, one on the past and the future.

It is to be noticed that in the interactions of both group and collectivity, triangles occur in all themes in which two people confront a third one, while the themes themselves show well defined contrasts. In the love theme we have the triangle Alving – Helene – Manders, with Manders as outsider, although the alternative (Alving being the outsider) should also be taken into consideration. Then we have the triangle Alving – Johanne – Engstrand, and Engstrand is the outsider, or the alternative (Alving as outsider). There is a definite contrast between the fashionable bourgeois-marriage (with the unfashionable – but shunned love relationship) and the unfashionable arranged marriage (with its natural but morally condemned love relationship). In the social theme we have the triangle Manders – Helene – Engstrand for the Children's Home (Manders – Helene against Engstrand) in contrast to the triangle Engstrand – Regine – Manders for the Seamen's Brothel, where Manders acts as outsider. In the moral theme both Osvald and Helene approve of the artists' free lives while Manders, the third man involved disapproves. As to the incestuous relationship Helene and Osvald both approve of the situation where as Regine bluntly refuses to do so. Here the contrast in the themes is negligible.

On the other hand the social category is kept in the background. It is nothing more than a background setting, chiefly invoked by Manders, both positively (to stress the importance of the «men of quality») and negatively (to belittle the artists, Captain Alving's drinking companions), while Osvald and Engstrand only occasionally invoke the social background: Osvald to exalt the free and independant artists' lives, and Engstrand who mentions the seamen he is going to allure into entering the home he is intending for them.

Although in this play class distinctions as a whole are not to be overlooked, the fact that Manders is the destructive factor of his own class must be stressed where as Engstrand could be called his bad spirit. Blind and naive Manders guided by a wicked Engstrand unwittingly heaps calamity on calamity for his own class: the childishly confident minister allows himself to be led blindly from one calamity to the next by a self centered, hypocritical and devilish carpenter. Thus the higher classes are wrecked by individuals who act slyly for their personal benefit. Perhaps personal benefit and self interest are a means for the lower classes to realize something in the system as they cannot act as a class.

Considering Habermas' outlines of the bourgeois society one could say of *Ghosts* that in the collectivity – and perhaps the old subdivision into primary and secundary groups would be more helpful here – all four provinces of society (intimacy, social life, and cultural and political life) are repeatedly mixed. This will contribute to our understanding of Manders' helplessness. He fails to grasp the social mechanism, which Helene Alving has read. This explains her radical attitude while on the other hand Osvald is only vaguely aware of what is wrong and Engstrand and Regine know by natural instinct what is wrong. They do not hesitate to profit by the situation: their grip on the situation is immediate and correct while the higher class characters find self understanding so much more difficult.

The symbolism of the play may possibly be explained from the social interaction. Manders represents the bourgeois system.[3] Superficially the system is both harmless and innocent, naive and full of good intentions as Manders is, in spite of its carefully hidden drawbacks which are also Manders'. It is guided however by hypocrisy, the bad spirit Engstrand whose single aim is to profit by the system. It is his sole chance of survival in this self same system where everything leads to destruction, even though Engstrand's solution will kill the system from inside. This hypocrisy is the proletarian class' defence mechanism – never having been given the chance in the bourgeois world to develop a social system of their own (see Oskar Negt and Alexander Kluge's *Öffentlichkeit und Erfarung*) since the proletarians in fact are crippled and hypocritical bourgeois, full of well concealed malignity and devilish slyness. So the title symbolism of «ghosts» is represented by the couple Osvald-Regine: a bourgeois boy physically wrecked and mentally demoralized is courting helplessly and in vain a proletarian girl who although healthy in body is morally depraved. Here we have the ghosts of the couple that is made up of the sprightly, self indulgent man (Captain Alving) who makes love to Johanne, the proletarian woman. The bourgeois system only survives in the ghostlike world of bodily ruin and mental demoralization exploited by proletarian cupidity. In the system the merging of bourgeoisie and proletarianism can only lead to a dead end (the character of Regine).

---

[3] Using the word «bourgeois» here I am well aware of the fact that Ibsen is describing a pre-capitalist situation: a world of civil servants. But this world clearly prefigures the coming capitalist situation (as «the men of quality», the artists' situation etc. indicate). Therefor the social system Ibsen writes about may be identified with it. So the words «bourgeois» (meaning «the propertied classes») and «proletarian» (the lower classes) may be used too.

The Children's Home intended to perpetuate and exalt the system is not insured as the social system is unaware of any danger. But the Home burns down, the fire having been caused by «subversive» malignity which is smoothed over as carelessness of the system's warden. So the fire symbolizes the impending destruction of the social system from within – the alternative for the moment being a caricature – The Seamen's Home, viz. brothel, Engstrand has in mind – because no true alternative has been built up or even briefly outlined as yet. In connection with this alternative it is worth remembering that all three women in the play are prostitutes of sorts: firstly Regine, the true prostitute, intended as such; secondly Johanne, the bourgeois victim who is looked upon as a fallen woman; finally Helene who by marrying sold herself body and mind for hard cash. It is noteworthy that the male characters in the play, without exception, are alcoholics of sorts: Engstrand, the vulgar drunkard, Alving, the debauchee, and Osvald, the heavy social drinker. In this bourgeois system alcoholism and prostitution are omnipresent although officially nonexistent and ignored. Manders is free of all sins: he never heard of prostitution, and alcohol does not tempt him.

The bourgeois institution of holy wedlock the trustworthiness of which is symbolized in part by the Children's Home – but in fact replaced by the Seamen's brothel – shows nothing but disaster: Alving's marriage is a whited sepulchre – Helene selling herself for a fortune, Alving becoming a debauchee and Osvald being a human wreck. Engstrand's marriage to Johanne is based upon fraud and perjury, Johanne is bullied to death, Regine is an «amoral» being. Any marriage of Osvald and Regine would be an incestuous alliance. The man and woman relationship, based upon love and spiritual human attraction – the bond between Helene and Manders – is never realized.

Manders, the representative of the system, who has performed both marriages and carefully broken off any bond with Helene, is indignant and appalled when he hears the truth – and flabbergasted on hearing Osvald's intention to marry Regine, which is to be Osvald's last protection against his illness.

The symbolism of the scenery which John Northam explains – the evolution from the misty rainy afternoon light over the artificially bright light of the fire to the cold light of the morning sun across the glacier, may be brought into connection to the interaction of the collectivity as well as that of the group. The first act takes place in the light of the rainy afternoon, as does the beginning of the second act. But the group interaction of the last scenes of the second act is interrupted by the bright and artificial light of fire, indication of a provisional solution – which is replaced at the end of the third act by the sunny morning light – the sun being the symbol of warmth and joy of living, but in this instance the example of a situation finally cleared up, situation which had been hidden all along in the twilight of deceit and hypocrisy – as at the beginning of the play. The interaction in both collectivity and group against a background of social categories has eventually cleared up the situation by doing away with immanent contradictions of the system which inevitably lead to catastrophe that must destroy the fundaments of the system.

I am quite aware of the fact that some of my interpretations do not open new perspectives but I hope nonetheless to have proved that a sociological reading may well be suited to shed a new light on certain points, even if a narrow starting point is taken.

Rosmersholm: Existentialist Tragedy or Escapist Fantasy? A Dialogue

DEREK RUSSELL DAVIS AND DAVID THOMAS

DRD – The tragic climax of *Rosmersholm* comes when bride and bridegroom fall from the bridge into the millstream. Before their marriage each had lost sense of purpose and identity: Rebekka, crushed by the Rosmer traditions, her courage lost, her love hopeless, her will infected, her past confronting her like a barrier, and with a crippled existence in prospect; and Rosmer, no longer believing in his own cause, and facing desolation and emptiness after abandoning his task of ennobling the minds of men. The marriage restores their relationship with one another on new terms, and gives them the courage to go with gladness – mutually – the two, man and wife, as one – the way Beate went – on to the bridge and into the millstream.

These actions, combine in a composite set of condensed images, meaning and energy derived from several themes: the spiritual marriage; the loss of hope; flight from desolation and emptiness; yet, in Brendel's words, homesickness for the great void; the carrying out of justice over themselves, with retribution, expiation and atonement; the acknowledgement of the past, and reunion with Rosmer's dead wife; and the power of the dead.

We offer an interpretation of the Fourth Act, and try to say what it means, what it expresses. According to our interpretation, which is, of course, only one of many interpretations, the essence of the play lies in the efforts made by Rebekka and Rosmer each to work out terms on which to relate to the other after their fine, clear friendship has been disrupted by the intervention of Rektor Kroll. They need to relate, and are driven by the existentialist anxiety lest they should lose each other and be alone. But there are obstacles: the differences in their social position, Bebekka, without position or property, and Rosmer, the scion of the district's leading family; the differences in their religious and political views, Rebekka, radical and free-thinking, Rosmer, conservative and Christian; Rebekka, experienced and passionate and affected by urgent physical desire, Rosmer, repelled by sexuality; and, of special importance, Beate's death.

DT – There are a number of puzzling things in Act 4 that particularly interest us. In this final act of the play, a new and destructive pattern of interaction is established between Rebekka and Rosmer. Why? And why was the initial basis of the relationship, as we saw it in Act 1, so fragile that it collapsed at Kroll's very first intervention?

When Brendel appears in Act 4, why does he articulate thoughts that seem to link moral imperatives from the Gospels with implicitly sexual imagery?

When Rosmer and Rebekka leave the stage at the end of the play to commit suicide together, what is it that is actually happening? Are we witnessing the final scene of an existentialist tragedy in which the protagonists recognise their inability to overcome the limitations of social process and assert their essential freedom in the only way left to them by committing suicide? Or are we watching a lethal fantasy game played out by emotionally immature protagonists hiding their real motives from each other and hence acting existentially in bad faith?

DRD – We depend on the interactional approach of modern psychotherapy, which has evolved from the interpersonal theory current in the nineteen thirties or in Britain the object-relations theory of the nineteen forties. The emphasis shifted then from the biological processes to which Freud attached importance – the libido and the need to reduce instinctual tension, for instance – to psycho-social processes, especially to the need people show to relate to one another – to create relationships; these are based on the assumptions and expectations they make about each other.

This shift reflected a development of ideas in many disciplines: Martin Buber, for instance, referred to the meaninglessness of the category «I» without the category «You». Yerkes, the primate psychologist, remarked that «one chimpanzee is no chimpanzee at all»; Brecht: «The smallest social unit is not one human being, but two human beings»; and Laing: «The sense of identity requires the existence of another by whom one is known».

We shall focus on the relationship of Rosmer and Rebekka, who form a couple in that, at the crucial time, the relationship they had with each other was stronger than, and more or less independent of, that either had with others. They make up a system – an organisation composed of objects or persons, showing the tendency to react to external events in such a way as to preserve the relationship between the components. Systems show a «dynamic conservatism», but adapt through learning to changing circumstances. If they do not, they become precarious, and are then brought to a crisis by any event of sufficient force or significance.[1]

The concept of «systems» was introduced into psychotherapy by Gregory Bateson and his colleagues[2][3] at Palo Alto, California. It is derived from cybernetics, a theory based on analogies between the behaviour of man and machine, and is concerned with the regulation by two or more persons of each other's behaviour and communication. The theory recognises that when two or more persons are connected with one another in a system, the behaviour of one person changes only when there are corresponding changes in the behaviour of the others. One condition in which changes come about is when the relationships between the persons are disrupted by an intervention from outside.

What happens usually fits readily into a three-Act scenario. Act 1. *External challenge*. The intervention challenges the assumptions two or more persons have been making about one another, and brings their relationships to a crisis, i.e. turning point. The system is disrupted. Act II. *Exploration*. During the period of instability following the crisis, the implications and consequences of the challenge are explored, and attempts are made to find a basis on which to restore the system. Act III. *Reorganisation*. The relationships stabilise on new terms. The scheme used by Lifton[4] in his studies of «thought-reform» is similar; he refers to «confrontation», «reordering» and «renewal».

A lover's quarrel starts, for instance, when something happens which obliges them to review the basis of their relationship. Intense feelings may be expressed during the exploration, so intense that the instability may amount to illness. In Act III, the lovers become reconciled, sometimes on terms more satisfactory than before, with a clearer recognition of each others' needs. The outcome is not always a happy one. Sometimes they split up. Sometimes the new terms are more restrictive or more disabling. Sometimes events move inexorably towards tragedy.

Let us illustrate the application of the interactional approach by dis-

---

[1] Schon, D. A. *Beyond the Stable State*. Harmondsworth, 1971.

[2] Bateson, G. *Steps to an Ecology of Mind*. London, 1973.

[3] Watzlawick, P., Beavin, J. H. and Jackson, D. D. *Pragmatics of Human Communication*. London, 1968.

[4] Lifton, R. J. *Thought Reform and the Psychology of Totalism*. Harmondsworth, 1961, p. 526.

cussing David Thomas's paper in the 1974 *Ibsen Årbok* «Patterns of Interaction in Ibsen's *Ghosts*»[5].

DT – I suggested in this paper that *Ghosts* should be seen as a far
more dynamic play than is normally the case, with characters not simply responding to a situation beyond their control, but saying and doing things to each other that have discernible and far-reaching human
consequences. I tried to show in my analysis that one can find the roots
of Osvald's lapse into what appears to be a catatonic state in the things
Mrs. Alving and Osvald actually say and do to each other. Traditionally
in Act 3 Mrs. Alving is considered to be a helpless spectator confronted
by a situation she can do nothing to remedy, as her son succumbs to an
inherited disease. This is illustrated by Edvard Munch's well-known design for Max Reinhardt's 1906 production, with the mother behind the
chair in which Osvald is slumped. But Act 3 actually consists of a violent and ugly quarrel between mother and son in which destructive
and hateful things are said and done by both parties.

As I wrote in my paper,

The way Mrs Alving and Osvald respond to each other here indicates clearly
enough that they are caught in a vicious spiral of confusion, misunderstanding
and mystification which thwarts all their real feelings and emotions. The
problem facing them is the nature of their relationship together, but that is
the one issue they never discuss. . . They talk at each other and past each other,
but never to each other. It is this that makes their pattern of interaction so lethal. When it comes to the final catastrophe, there may be no absolute certainty as to who is provoking whom into doing what, so complex is the nature of
their interacton. One thing is, however, certain. The spiral in which Osvald
and Mrs. Alving are caught is deadly and it ends with Osvald's madness. That
actually happens.

DRD – They deny each other status. They fail to recognize each
other's needs. Osvald tries in various ways to deal with the problems
besetting him; one way is to demand that his mother give him morphine. Lapsing into catatonia represents the frustration of all the
solutions available and defeat. The catatonic patient is aware of what is
going on around him, but feels incapable of doing anything active
about it.

DT – There is, as it were, a pattern of mutual disconfirmation: the
point is of course that Osvald ontologically is less secure than his mother, which is why it is he who collapses at the end of the play.

5 Thomas, D. «Patterns of Interaction in Ibsen's *Ghosts*.» In: *Ibsenårbok*, Oslo,
1974.

Re-interpreted in this light, *Ghosts* can be seen, not only as a more dynamic play than is normally the case, but also as a more complex document in human terms. And this opens up important new perspectives for the theatre. Interpreted as the tragedy of the helpless mother or even the hapless son, *Ghosts* is an admirable vehicle for star acting, with a star actress presenting the mother's tragedy (as with Agnes Sorma in Max Reinhardt's production) or a star actor (as in the case of August Lindberg or Josef Kainz) showing the son going mad. Re-interpreted as an existentialist tragedy in which the two protagonists fail to escape the web of process in which they are entangled, *Ghosts* becomes a play that demands ensemble acting of great subtlety and sensitivity.

DRD – This is a theatre concerned with relationships, and communication between people, verbal and non-verbal, and meta-communication, i.e., communicating about communicating. These concerns are shared by playwrights and psychotherapists.

Biological and social processes

Osvald's collapse is not to be explained, your paper argues, by reference to what Helene and Osvald say and do to one another. You go further than I did in my paper[6] on *Ghosts* in «demedicalising» (to use Illich's term)[7] Osvald's illness.

Ibsen does suggest a medical explanation when he refers to the Paris physician and somatic symptoms like headaches, and uses the word «vermoulu», but nowhere did he confirm that he intended to describe a case of cerebral syphilis. Osvald's regression and deterioration have causes lying in processes in his family. Syphilis may stand as a symbol of these processes, but you show, as the dramatists of ancient Greece, Shakespeare, and others have done, that psycho-social processes in families can be as destructive as biological processes, and that it is unnecessary to resort to biological processes for an understanding of what was happening to Osvald. Surely it is time for the public to face up to the real nature of Osvald's illness, and to give up the comfortable belief, which Ibsen allowed them, that it was caused, in any literal sense, by syphilis. The essential issues, which the medical explanation confuses and disguises, lie in the relationships of Osvald and his mother, with his father

---

[6] Davis, D. R. «A Re-appraisal of Ibsen's *Ghosts*.» In: *Henrik Ibsen: Penguin Critical Anthology*. Harmondsworth, 1970.

[7] Illich, I. *Limits to Medicine*. London, 1976.

intruding although absent, in the setting of Rosenvold. So to regard the illness adds to the excitement of the last Act.

DT – At the conscious level Ibsen writes about an inherited disease and structures much of the play's symbolism around the notion of inheritance. But at an intuitive level, in the dialogue, he shows a mother and a son doing and saying dreadful things to each other. My own suspicion is that Osvald's lapse into a catatonic state at the end of the play explains very clearly why Ibsen never went back to his own mother's house.

DRD – In *Rosmersholm,* the significance Ibsen gives to Beate's illness illustrates one of the points we have been making. Adherence to the belief that Beate was «a sick unhappy woman of unsound mind» defended Rosmer against acknowledging that he had played a crucial part in her death. He refers to her «wild fits of sensual passion . . . she expected me to respond to», her self-reproach and «dreadful agony of mind about something (her childlessness) that wasn't her fault», and her «disordered mind that drove her to those wild aberrations». Very soon, the defence being annulled as a result of Kroll's revelations, he has to recognize «her despair and quite alone . . . And, then, in the end, her triumph . . . that agonizing indictment . . . in the millstream». Rebekka and others collude with him in his belief that Beate was mentally ill. Ibsen made it plain in *Rosmersholm,* as he did also in *The Lady from the Sea,* that to regard someone as of unsound mind serves to deny one's own part in causing disturbed behaviour and in this way evades and subverts the truth.

Macro- and micro-politics

DT – Part of the problem with *Ghosts* lies in the fact that so much of the action seems to follow from an unbroken chain of determinism. The way the characters think, feel and respond to each other is socially determined; their attitudes and their patterns of interaction are shown to be the products of social process. Even Mrs. Alving's conscious attempt to rid herself of the ghosts of social process fails. Not surprisingly, the various characters in the play, including Osvald himself, are inclined to view his illness in a deterministic light.

If I might express the matter in slightly different and slightly more precise terminology: in *Ghosts,* as in *Pillars of Society* and *A Doll's House,* Ibsen seems primarily concerned with the way macro-politics shapes micro-politics,[8] i.e. with the way society and accepted social values shape and fetter individual patterns of response, or, in rather more Marxist terms, with the way 'social existence determines consciousness'.

By the time he wrote *Rosmersholm* Ibsen saw a far more complex and dynamic relationship between macro- and micro-politics. To begin with in *Rosmersholm* a great deal of attention is paid to the contemporary macro-political situation. The various characters in the play are carefully located within the macro-political structure of the day and we are shown how this structure determines their life-styles and attitudes. Rosmer, for instance, as the only son of a wealthy family can afford the luxury of giving up his living as a priest in order to retire to the family property and live the life of a dilettante academic. His innately conservative views can also be attributed to his family background.

Rebekka, by way of contrast, as the daughter of a socially inferior midwife, can only work her way into polite society as companion to Rosmer's wife. Even her emancipation, stemming from her affair with Dr. West, can, with some justification, be attributed to her lowly origins, as Kroll points out.

During the course of the play, however, micro-conflicts assume ever greater importance for the major characters so that, by the end of the play, macro-politics are simply used as fantasy images to be manipulated by the various characters, and above all Rosmer and Rebekka, in their pattern of interaction. In the last act of the play it is no longer social existence that determines consciousness, in the traditional Marxist sense, but rather the intensely personal fantasy stratagems of two almost hermetically isolated human beings.

DRD – The processes are two-way. The macro-political situation and the micro-politics of the family interact. Kroll's macro-political campaign represented his efforts to retrieve on the national scene the defeats he had suffered in his own home, with his son, an avid reader of *The Beacon,* and his daughter, embroidering covers for it.

Three crises

There were three crises at Rosmersholm which we want now to discuss. The first was caused by Rebekka's challenge. Before the play begins, Rosmer and Beate maintained steady relationships with Kroll and his

[8] For a more detailed definition of these terms see – Collier, A. *R. D. Laing: The Philosophy and Politics of Psychotherapy.* Hassocks, Sussex, 1977, p. 163 ff.

wife as a foursome living in a small-town community. Rebekka intrudes into this system, with some persuasion by Beate and some support from Kroll. She cannot be incorporated, and the system becomes unstable. It is in these circumstances that Beate becomes ill, her illness reflecting in some degree her efforts to create the conditions in which a reorganised system might stabilise.

DT – I want to suggest that the system was less stable initially than you indicate, and that Rebekka's arrival exacerbates an already untenable situation. Rosmer's relationship with Beate was fraught with problems long before Rebekka's arrival. Rosmer had a horror of life's physicality: his whole up-bringing had taught him that any manifestation of spontaneous life was wrong, evil, wicked. Beate, on the other hand, appears to have been a warm out-going personality who expected Rosmer to reciprocate the emotional and physical attraction she felt for him. (Interestingly, a critic like Herman J. Weigand,[9] writing in the mid-1920s, commented that Beate was highly sexed. Today in a society that is just beginning to accept female sexuality, it is perhaps easier to see Beate as an out-going personality with perfectly normal sexual needs.) Inevitably, Rosmer found himself rejecting Beate's advances. In some distress he even turned to Kroll for advice, but with no success. His next stratagem was to begin a disconfirmation of Beate's personality: she must be both bad and mad to feel the way she did. And as so often happens, his wife, in her confusion, accepted his definition of her personality, even though it denied the validity of her feelings. Even before Rebekka's arrival therefore, Beate was showing obvious signs of disconfirmation in the shape of neurosis and depression.

After Rebekka's arrival, Beate's condition deteriorated rapidly. At one and the same time she was infatuated with Rebekka (Kroll hints at the lesbian nature of her feelings for Rebekka) and yet jealous of her – Rebekka was after all succeeding with her husband in a way she could not. She also found herself subjected to a more insidious disconfirmation of her personality on the part of Rebekka. Viewing Beate as a hindrance to the fulfilling of her aims with Rosmer, Rebekka began quite deliberately to undermine Beate's already fragile ontological security. It is therefore hardly surprising that Rebekka had a de-stabilising effect on the relationship system at Rosmersholm. She fully intended this and went out of her way to achieve it.

DRD – The second crisis grew out of the first and was produced by Beate's death, in circumstances calculated to bring disruption. The

9 Weigand, H. J. *The Modern Ibsen.* London, 1925, p. 170.

90

place and manner of a suicide accuse. After twice visiting her brother, Kroll, and writing to Mortensgaard, Beate falls into the millstream outside the windows of Rosmersholm. It was indeed a triumph and an indictment. Kroll and his wife break off their relationship with Rosmer and Rebekka, who settle into a quiet, orderly routine. There are several remarkable features of their new life together.

They show no 'bereavement' reaction, no grief and no mourning. They do not explore – work through – the implications and consequences of Beate's death. They share thoughts and feelings, and help each other to plan their lives anew, but do nothing to put into effect their plans to ennoble and liberate their countrymen. These are strange plans when one remembers the ignoble parts they had played in Beate's death. What does ennobling mean? Does it mean to desexualise, to purify? Or to restore the Rosmer family's tradition of tight control over feelings? Rosmer's concept of ennobling seems to have been fantasy not defined in terms of realities or practicalities.

Their friendship during this period is described as pure – as Kroll pointed out, an apostate and an emancipated woman, living under one roof . . . without a morality rooted in the faith of the Church . . . saying a cool good-night and going to their separate rooms. What has happened to their sexual feelings?

Another feature is the self-enclosure. Sometimes two persons with a precarious relationship with one another protect the relationship by shutting themselves off from others; the relationship can only survive if it is protected from the rough-and-tumble of everyday life. Rebekka and Rosmer sought the self-enclosure, but this was also in part a quarantine imposed by Kroll. Their restricted life together lasts for about eighteen months until the third crisis, which is brought about by Kroll's intervention.

DT – In his book *Self and Others* R. D. Laing[10] defines collusion as «the game of mutual self-deception. . . an essential feature of this game is not admitting that it is a game». Mutual self-deception is the game Rebekka and Rosmer are playing at this stage. Now that Beate is dead they have established a collusive fantasy about the life they shared with her and the ideals that motivate them. Both fail to admit the nature of their game, that is, until Kroll intervenes.

Initially Kroll's intervention in their relationship is entirely motivated by macro-political considerations. He wants Rosmer's help in his crusade against the Liberals. This event brings to a head the collusive

[10] Laing, R. D. *Self and Others.* Harmondsworth, 1971, p. 108.

fantasy Rosmer and Rebekka have shared. Faced by Kroll, Rosmer must now act and declare himself to be an emancipated liberal. And as he does so, Kroll immediately leaves the macro-political sphere and looks for a micro-political explanation for this conversion. In view of his own former feelings towards Rebekka he does not have to look very far. It seems obvious to him that Rebekka must have put Rosmer up to this; Rosmer is so impressionable and Rebekka is a hard-headed young lady. Remembering Beate's strange comments to him about Rosmer's relationship with Rebekka, Kroll assumes, not unreasonably, that he has a duty to protect his former brother-in-law from a cunning adventuress. He therefore consciously inervenes on two further occasions. In Act 2 his intervention is intended to open Rosmer's eyes to what is happening, and in Act 3 his intervention is intended to break Rebekka's spirit. These two interventions are decisive. Effectively, they destroy the various fantasy stratagems on which Rosmer's and Rebekka's relationship is based. After this, there are only two alternatives left them. Either they have to break with each other completely, which almost happens, or else they have to re-establish their relationship on a completely new basis. In fact the latter happens, but the new basis is a destructive one and it culminates in suicide.

Existentialist and psychological viewpoints

At this point we once again face the issue of what it is that brings Rosmer and Rebekka to the mill race. Are they the victims of tragic process, or are they caught in a web of fantasy, self-deception and bad faith? Are Rebekka and Rosmer by the end of the play able to act as responsible agents facing up to a conscious burden of choice with complete honesty and self-awareness? Are they aware of the true conflict facing them or are they a prey to false conflict and therefore, as Laing states in *Self and Others,* «in danger of psychosis»?

Laing and existentialist philosophers have emphasised the importance of choice and action. As Sartre puts it in *Existentialism and Humanism:* «Man is nothing else but what he purposes, he exists only insofar as he realises himself. he is therefore nothing else but the sum of his actions, nothing else but what his life is». For the existentialist, existence precedes essence. Man's essence is the sum of his actions. That this was a view Ibsen shared is clearly demonstrated in *The Lady from the*

[11] Sartre, J. P. *Existentialism and Humanism.* London, 1975, p. 41.

Sea, which is a play about choice in the existentialist sense. In that play Ibsen stressed the importance of choice, action, responsibility. Although man may live out his life in the shadow of determinism, both in macro and micro terms, in the end he can only break through the imprisoning web of process (crystallized praxes, unwritten assumptions, material determinism) and become himself by acting and taking responsibility for his actions. Ellida faces up to the various threats from her past and the unresolved tensions from her present and chooses to act with freedom and responsibility.[12] Her choice may not be particularly idealistic and it certainly involves both renunciation and resignation. But it is made freely and responsibly. That way lies sanity! In many of his other plays Ibsen shows figures who long to break through the various chains of process in which they are imprisoned, but fail. *Ghosts* is one example; *Hedda Gabler* is another. Where the attempt is dignified and the failure painful, as in *Ghosts,* one is confronted by existentialist tragedy; where the various stratagems used to break through process are brittle or even frivolous, as in *The Wild Duck* or *Hedda Gabler,* one is left with a peculiarly dark kind of existentialist comedy. In *Rosmersholm* one is confronted by neither but rather by shimmering ambiguity.

DRD – There is a conflict between the psychological and existentialist view. Psychologists make the methodological resolution to regard behaviour, normal or disordered, as causally determined. Their job is to define the conditions under which behaviours of a certain kind occur. They test hypotheses by discovering whether predictions from them are borne out. But they have to live with a paradox. Essential to mental health is to feel free to choose. To feel that one's will is not free, that one is under the control of others, or imprisoned by the past or the passive victim of circumstances, is a symptom of illness, perhaps psychosis. To choose responsibly is required of the well; the sick tend to be excused from doing so.

On the existentialist view, Rebekka and Rosmer exercised choice when they went on to the bridge. On the psychological view such choices are causally determined and potentially capable of being predicted, given full knowledge of the circumstances and the antecedents. Rebekka and Rosmer search in a trial-and-error way for a solution that is the best fit. They consider and reject one solution after another. Rosmer offers marriage in terms which propose that Rebekka takes the

---

[12] Davis, D. R. «Intervention into family affairs.» *British Journal of Medical Psychology, 41,* 1968, pp. 73—79.

place vacated by Beate. Rosmer seeks reconciliation with Kroll. Rebekka prepares to leave Rosmersholm. In Act 4, the lines of the final solution gradually emerge. This has to take account of the hang-ups of their pasts and the current circumstances. Spiritual marriage, death, and reunion with Beate are the elements of the package that fits best.

The final solution

A point of interest in this, the final solution, is the triangulation. One way in which two insecure people can stabilise their relationship is to bring in a third party.[13] This is a part a psychotherapist sometimes has to play. The relationship of a husband and wife tends to be stable when they are components of a larger system, which may include their children, for instance, or their extended families. Rebekka and Rosmer were on their own. Kroll might have given them some stability, on his terms, but did not. Reunion with Beate might promise to give them the stability they were otherwise denied. Beate while alive seems to have explored the possibility of some sort of ménage à trois. To paraphrase Mrs. Alving's comment on another kind of irregular arrangement – Unheard of, you say? Do you think there aren't plenty of couples all over the country who find this solution?

In each of the plays *Ghosts, Rosmersholm* and *The Lady from the Sea,* there is a third party, an absent intruder – the ghost who returns. For Osvald and Helene, the third party is Chamberlain Alving. Their relationship comes to a crisis when the orphanage is burnt down, and Osvald's illusions about his father are destroyed. In *The Lady from the Sea,* the third party is the stranger. He is dismissed when Ellida and Dr. Wangel are able to make a responsible choice. Rebekka and Rosmer have not worked out, through the processes of mourning, their relationship with Beate, and they have not broken free from her.

At the inquest on the double suicide, one might have asked: What else went wrong between Rebekka and Rosmer? We have referred already to their collusion in deceiving themselves about the causes of Beate's death and the grave responsibility each had had for it. Rosmer, especially, failed to recognize Rebekka's true needs and to respond authentically, i.e. genuinely, to them, just as he had failed to respond authentically to Beate's. The purity of their friendship after Beate's

[13] Bowen, M. «Family therapy after twenty years.» In: *American Handbook of Psychiatry,* Vol. V. New York, 1975, pp. 367—392.

death was merely an illusion. The friendship was «pseudo-mutual»[14], in that it lacked true reciprocity and mutuality. The contrast, to which Mrs. Helseth refers, is with Mortensgaard's response to the needs of the woman deserted by her husband. The reasons for Rosmer's failure are to be found, as Mrs. Helseth keeps telling us, in the traditions of Rosmersholm.

Several similar failures are described in Ibsen's plays. Pastor Manders and Mrs. Alving are at cross purposes in this passage:

MANDERS . . .the hardest struggle of my life.
MRS ALVING. Call it rather your most pitiful defeat.
MANDERS. It was my life's greatest victory, Helene; victory over myself.
MRS ALVING. It was a crime against us both.
MANDERS. Was it a crime to say to you: Woman, go back to your lawful husband. . .

At the end of the exchange, Manders says: «We two don't understand each other».

Another example is Mrs. Alving's denial of Osvald's needs as he perceives them, when she says: «What terrible ideas they were to get into your head, Osvald. But all just imagination. All these upsets have been too much for you. But now you'll be able to have a good long rest. At home, with your mother beside you, my darling Anything you like you shall have, just like when you were a little boy . . .» The choices she offers Osvald are all disagreeable.

In what degree, in what respects, did Rebekka and Rosmer achieve before they died a genuine recognition of each other's needs and a true mutuality?

DT – The problem confronting Rebekka and Rosmer at the beginning of Act 4 is to determine on what basis they will in future relate to each other. By this stage in their interaction they have faced up to a number of uncomfortable truths. Rosmer has accepted that his political idealism was pure fantasy. He has also accepted that what he felt for Rebekka was love and not merely platonic friendship. He is deeply shocked at Rebekka's confession of complicity in Beate's death and yet aware that his own feelings towards Rebekka, which Beate obviously noticed, must have contributed to her suicide. Confronted by this burden of guilt, his instinct is to opt out, to go the way Beate went. Re-

[14] Wynne, L. C., Ryckoff, I., Day, J. and Hirsch, S. «Pseudo-mutuality in the family relations of schizophrenics.» *Psychiatry 21,* 1958, pp. 205—220.

bekka for her part has openly admitted her complicity in Beate's death; she has faced up to the prospect that she lived for many years in an incestuous relationship with her real father Dr. West; she has admitted her overwhelming sexual passion for Rosmer, which helped drive Beate into the millrace. She believes that her former wild passion has subsided and she confesses to loving Rosmer now in a pure, ennobled (i.e. essentially sexless) manner. However, such is her disappointment at the lack of genuine reciprocity in her relationship with Rosmer that her instinct is to fly from Rosmersholm and return 'home' to the North. In phenomenological terms, this is the actual situation by the beginning of Act 4.

Where does this leave them? Too many lies, too many subterfuges have clogged their interaction for them to trust each other. Their relationship is built on shifting sand. And here Ulrik Brendel appears out of the dark night, almost like a figure out of an absurdist comedy by Samuel Beckett, to articulate thoughts at the back of their minds and flesh them out in the dialogue. At the heart of their problem lies sexuality, something Rosmer seems incapable of accepting and something that has driven Rebekka to a course of action tantamount to murder. Ulrik Brendel suggests a way out. Trust can be renewed. Rosmer's:

success is assured. But – mark well – upon one unavoidable condition. . . That the woman who loves him goes gladly out into the kitchen and chops of her dainty, pink little finger. . . here, just here near the middle joint. Furthermore, that the aforesaid loving woman – likewise gladly – cuts off her incomparably moulded left ear.

Finger and ear are well-known Freudian symbols for male and female sexual organs. Rebekka, who has taken on herself the thrusting role of the male in her relationship with Rosmer while yet, paradoxically, still longing to be penetrated as a woman, must kill both desires in herself. She must divest herself of her sexuality. And of course the only way she can fully be divorced from her own sexuality is in death.

Brendel's imagery also has strong biblical overtones. Apart from the obvious reference to shifting sands (Matthew 7:26—27) there is a clear reference, as Inga-Stina Ewbank[15] has pointed out, to an earlier passage in the Sermon on the Mount:

And if your right hand is your undoing, cut it off and fling it away; it is better

[15] Ewbank, I. S. «Ibsen and 'The Far More Difficult Art' of Prose» In. *Contemporary Approaches to Ibsen.* Oslo, 1971, pp. 77—78.

for you to lose one part of your body than for the whole of it to go to hell. (Matthew 5:29—30)

In linking these moral imperatives from the Gospels with overtly sexual imagery, Brendel foreshadows the stratagem to be adopted by Rosmer and Rebekka.

After Brendel's exit there is a sense of almost adolescent excitement and expectancy as Rosmer spells out to Rebekka the kind of proof he wants of her new-found love for him. Like a tongue-tied youth asking his girl friend to yield herself to him, Rosmer sits on the edge of his seat stumbling over every word:

Have you the courage to − are you willing to − gladly as Ulrik Brendel said − for my sake, now tonight, gladly − to go the same way − as Beate went?

Even though he wants Rebekka to kill herself for him rather than yield herself to him, the note of erotic arousal is unmistakable. He admits that there is «a horrible fascination» in his thoughts, and the feeling of folly or madness, which might be expected in the early stages of any sexual adventure, is heightened for Rosmer by the knowledge that what he has in mind is not making love to a beautiful young woman but using her corpse, or rather the thought of her corpse, as a vehicle for erotic satisfaction.

Rebekka not only catches Rosmer's mood, sharing his excitement, she seems to know what is in his mind almost before he shapes his thoughts and words. She even eggs him on. Now that Rosmer actually offers her his trust and love on the only terms he can, Rebekka finds it impossible to refuse. No longer is she the arrogantly calculating woman who once exploited Kroll and abused Beate. Gradually, during the course of the play, she has relinquished her dominant position and now willingly accepts a one-down role in relation to Rosmer, allowing him to suggest the nature and shape of their relationship, even if this means death for both of them.

Viewed in this light the suicide of Rosmer and Rebekka represents surrender to a world of destructive fantasy. And yet both of them claim that their death may be seen as an expiation for sin and guilt. Rosmer claims, like an existentialist, that he is judging himself (presumably on the basis of his past actions); Rebekka expresses the more traditional ethical notion of «where I have sinned . . . it is right that I should atone». But are they not disguising thwarted sexual longings under this pious imagery, in exactly the same way as Ulrik Brendel did?

Of course their suicide does promise some kind of expiation. For Rosmer it offers expiation for his complicity in driving Beate to the millrace. In proposing a similar course of action to Rebekka, he can only hope to absolve himself from complicity in her death by joining her. Faced by the anguish of his confused and tortured thoughts, the dark night, the peace of death seem to him infinitely more attractive than the guilt of life. For Rebekka suicide offers expiation for a number of equally tangible sins: she has committed incest, albeit unwittingly, with her father; she has ruthlessly manipulated people; she has used her sexuality to encourage a woman, infatuated with her, to commit suicide. And yet one is left with the nagging doubt that what they both want is not so much expiation as escape.

The ending of the play is strangely ambiguous. Rebekka and Rosmer, like a bridal couple, are almost light-hearted as they leave the stage. We have just witnessed a moving wedding ceremony, made all the more poignant by the realisation that this is a wedding that can only be consummated in death. Now of course any wedding ceremony represents a channelling of man's deepest sexual longings and urges into a socially acceptable pattern. As the Anglican Prayer Book puts it:

Holy matrimony is «an honourable estate . . . ordained for a remedy against sin, and to avoid fornication»

And this wedding is no exception. Potentially explosive emotions and urges lie hidden under the restraint and decorum of Rosmer's and Rebekka's behaviour. At the back of their minds are racing thoughts. Memories of incest, falsehood and even murder in Rebekka's case; guilt-ridden fantasies, frustrated sexual longings and possibly even thoughts of necrophilia in Rosmer's case. But all that is expressed in words and movement is: «Now I lay my hand on your head and take you in marriage for my true wife». It would be difficult to envisage neo-classic understatement taken any further.

DRD – Another purpose for which holy matrimony was ordained, according to the Prayer Book, was «for the mutual society, help and comfort, that the one ought to have of the other». Rebekka and Rosmer acknowledged through their marriage their need to relate to one another.

DT – The ending of the play, in its neo-classic tightly structuredness, seemingly represents the triumph of Apollonian order, restraint, civilisation. And it is perhaps above all in terms of its shape, its structural decorum, that the play gives credence to the notion that the final suicide of Rebekka and Rosmer reflects a desire for justice, expiation, atonement on their part; in other words that they are acting maturely, responsibly, authentically, albeit tragically.

However, an interactional analysis suggests that what is acted out is far more questionable, namely, that the suicide of Rebekka and Rosmer in fact represents their surrender to a world of barely articulated and essentially destructive fantasy. In committing suicide together, they are acting neither maturely nor responsibly but rather evading their responsibilities to each other. They can and do offer each other companionship but it is only the companionshop of yet another collusively shared fantasy, one of those «white horses» of the heart and mind. The difference this time is that they *choose* to deceive themselves. When Rebekka asks the leading question:

Suppose you were only deceiving yourself . . . Suppose it were all a delusion . . . one of those White Horses of Rosmersholm

the game of collusion is given a new set of rules. Rebekka and Rosmer now know and admit that they are playing a game. Hence the light-hearted, almost bantering tone of the dialogue. The end result, however, is still a shared fantasy, only this time they collude about colluding in a game played for lethal stakes, a game that ends in the millrace.

Ibsen, ironically, perhaps even mischievously, builds into this ending, with its clash of form and feeling, an element of deliberate mystification. (Certainly the jarring clash between the romantic, vibrantly erotic quality of the action and the decorum and restraint of the structure seems quite deliberate.) As a result, in the closing lines of the play, not even Rebekka and Rosmer seem sure who is doing what to whom:

REBEKKA: Yes, but tell me. Is it you who follow me? Or I who follow you?
ROSMER: We shall never really know.
REBEKKA: I'd dearly like to know.

Is this the final scene of an existentialist tragedy in which the protagonists choose to die as a conscious act of atonement and expiation? Or is this the final move in a complex escapist fantasy? I suspect it is the latter. But as Rosmer says «we shall never *really* know».

Yet again the Master Builder covered his tracks and gave the critics something to think about, as indeed we all still are. One thing we are certain of. Although our interactional approach may seem to us one of the more interesting and fruitful avenues of enquiry open to Ibsen

scholars today, particularly Ibsen scholars interested in the living theatre, we are quite certain that we have not said the last word on the
complexity and ambiguity of *Rosmersholm*.

DRD – Plays like *Ghosts* and *Rosmersholm* deserve to be reinterpreted
over and over again in order to put what they express into the context
of contemporary themes. Relating; obstacles to relating; and the
quality and authenticity of relationships; these are some of the themes
that are important in our contemporary world. The illumination plays
like *Ghosts* and *Rosmersholm* give a hundred years after they were written
to the themes of our to-day testify to their greatness.

Rosenvold and Rosmersholm:
Protagonist implies interpretation

SANDRA E. SAARI

The sound similarity of «Rosenvold» and «Rosmersholm» does not ex-
haust their resemblance. Both function as symbols of the antagonistic
force against which the protagonist fights. In both *Ghosts* and *Rosmersholm*, moreover, there has been or still is some question about which
character is the protagonist. The historical first choice in each case was
the dominant male character. In both cases, the interpretation then
viewed the male protagonist as weak or helpless, and consequently defeated by those forces greater than himself, symbolized by Rosenvold or
Rosmersholm. If the dominant female character is considered to be the
protagonist, however, the interpretation of the play shifts dramatically.
Because of its production history, this is easy to demonstrate in the case
of *Ghosts*.

The subject matter of Osvald's syphilis in *Ghosts* caused such outrage
that none of the traditional theatres would venture at first to produce
it. A Swedish director refused it saying, «The play is one of the filthiest
things ever written in Scandinavia.»[1] Consequently, *Ghosts* was first interpreted by the naturalistically oriented avant-garde theatres whose
actor-directors were males who cast themselves in the presumed leading role, Osvald. The Swedish actor-director August Lindberg prepared himself for the role of Osvald by visiting a hospital to study children
who were insane from inherited syphilis.[2] Though he suffered repeated
nightmares during rehearsals, Lindberg so profoundly portrayed Osvald's increasing debility and final, lifelessly mechanical repetition that
he succeeded in converting a previously scandalized Scandinavia. Zola
urged Antoine to present *Ghosts* at the Théâtre-Libre.[3] Recognizing «the
most beautiful role that an actor could play,»[4] Antoine himself played

[1] Michael Meyer, *Ibsen: A Biography* (Garden City: Doubleday, 1971), p. 484.
[2] Ibid., p. 518.
[3] André Antoine, *Le Théatre* (Paris: Les Editions de France, 1932), p. 248.
[4] André Antoine, *«Mes Souvenirs» sur le Théâtre-Libre* (Paris: Arthème Fayard,
1921), p. 184. The translation is mine.

Osvald. George Moore saw Antoine's production and was overwhelmed by its impact: «we learn though there be no gods to govern us, that nature, vast and unknown, for ever dumb to our appeal, holds us in thrall.»[5]

Moore's characterization of the play reflects the dominant interpretation of *Ghosts* for several decades:[6] Osvald is the play's protagonist, naturalism its stance. Assuming the former, the latter absolutely follows. With Osvald as protagonist, the organization, that is to say, the plot, can be summarized: Osvald is so controlled by forces of heredity and environment that he is ultimately reduced to existence at a non-human level.

Osvald initially enters smoking his father's pipe, looking, according to Pastor Manders, exactly like his father. So much do external forces control his actions, that, given his similarity to his father, the same environment produces identical behavior. Act I closes with an exact repetition in place, action, and word of Captain Alving's dalliance with the maid: his son Osvald dallies with the maid's daughter. Since the audience already knows the actions of the father by the end of Act I, it has only to compare Osvald's actions to discover the identity. Mrs. Alving's horrified statement, «Ghosts! The pair from the conservatory . . . walk again,»[7] serves not as information for the audience but merely as a *quod erat demonstrandum* of the results that the audience has already seen reproduced.

Osvald's entrance in the middle of Act II is preceded by his off-stage drinking; in quick succession the audience hears Osvald take three glasses of strong liqueur. The knowledge of Captain Alving's heavy drinking, together with Osvald's reason for drinking, «It is good against the dampness,» and his complaints about the weather and the lack of sun, reinforce the perception that once again heredity and environment are determining Osvald's actions. His confession to his mother that he is ill, that the doctor said, «there has been from birth something wormeaten about you . . . the sins of the fathers are visited upon the children,» suddenly clarifies the full import of Mrs. Alving's statement in Act I that a doctor said her husband was debauched. Osvald throws himself on the

[5] Michael Egan, ed., *Ibsen: The Critical Heritage* (Boston: Routledge and Kegan Paul, 1972), p. 185.

[6] Halvdan Koht, *Life of Ibsen* (New York: Benjamin Blom, 1971), p. 328.

[7] Henrik Ibsen, *Nutidsdramaer 1877—99* (Oslo: Gyldendal, 1962), p. 133. The translation is mine. Further quotations of *Ghosts* are likewise my translations from this volume.

sofa, and from a position that duplicates visually the verbal picture in Act I of his father «laying there all day long on the sofa,» says, «Had it only been something inherited. . . something that one could not have helped.» Thinking himself to blame for his debility, Osvald is full of shame and remorse about his own responsibility for his degeneration. The audience and Mrs. Alving know that guilt to be groundless, for Osvald is no more responsible for the physical condition that he inherited than he is for the darkness and incessant rain outside. Act II nears the end with Mrs. Alving imbibing with her son as she had in the past with her husband. With similar persons the environment again has produced duplicative actions. Osvald says of this force of environment, «Live the same life here at home as abroad, and yet it would not be the same life.»

The conflagration closes Act II and not only symbolizes the destruction of the ideal Captain Alving, but also precipitates in Osvald the consuming effect of the inherited syphilis. In Act III Mrs. Alving tells Osvald that his father was «a broken man,» believing that this truth will take away Osvald's remorse and self-reproach. But Osvald's horror of the progressing disease has so advanced by this point that guilt or lack of guilt is meaningless; human responsibility has no significance in face of the knowledge that he will be reduced to an existence with no human capacity. To counteract the horror of this, he extracts from his mother the promise that, at such a time, she will give him a lethal dose of morphine. The final act ends with Osvald's humanity, that is, his rational powers, totally destroyed by the ravages of heredity syphilis. The play concludes, leaving unanswered the question whether his final wish, one even more modest that that of Gervaise, will be granted. Osvald has been revealed as the unwilling but passive victim of what Haskell Block calls «the enchainment of material circumstances,»[8] the Zola-esque deterministic pattern of physical, physiological, and social environment.

The difficulty with this interpretation of the play is evident from criticisms of productions in which Oswald was cast as protagonist. Archer politely says of the Lindberg production that Manders was «decidedly the weak point of the cast.[9] Moore's remonstration is much more outspoken:

[8] *Naturalistic Triptych: The Fictive and the Real in Zola, Mann, and Dreiser* (New York: Random House, 1970), p. 13.

[9] *The Oxford Ibsen, Vol. V*, trans. and ed. James Walter McFarlane (London: Oxford University Press, 1961), p. 480.

But what shall be said of the parson? Who is there, I ask, who could utter one word of praise or even mild defence of this dreary old bore who spoils so far as it is possible the first and second acts with such intolerable sermonizing. . .? I make no exception either in favor of Mr. Ibsen or Mr. Archer; neither could find a reasonable word to say in defence of his parson.[10]

The fact is that with Osvald as protagonist, there is no dramatic justification for the length and weight of Manders' role, since his relation to Osvald is merely that of a foil for Osvald's free-thinking position. However, with Mrs. Alving as protagonist, the length of his role is fully justified since he is a mummified embodiment of the hypocritical social morality and absolutistic religious posture that have enchained her and that return to haunt and test her.

The plot of the play is dramatically different with Mrs. Alving as protagonist. Stated simply it is: to confront the ghosts of the past. These take two forms, mental and physical. Manders' visit in Act I is the occasion of what Mrs. Alving believes to be her final act of ridding herself of the physical past. She has built the Orphanage with a sum equal to Alving's fortune when she married him. By giving the Orphanage to the town she will dispose of the Alving money, so Osvald will inherit only from her. But the Alving inheritance is biological as well as monetary. This aspect of the plot unfolds, as outlined earlier, to reveal Osvald's final inheritance from his father, which she is powerless to prevent.

The mental ghosts are more elusive. Her free-thinking books, to which Manders so objects, represent what she asserts to be her present beliefs. Superstitions of the past, however, are not easily discarded. Manders' insistance in Act I on not insuring the Orphanage because of public opinion, echoes his insistance 29 years earlier that Mrs. Alving return to her husband because of duty and public opinion. That her mental habits have not totally altered in the intervening years, is demonstrated by her acquiescence to Manders' arguments, again against her better judgment. Though she fails this preliminary test of insuring the Orphanage, no moral issue is at stake. Her three subsequent choices are increasingly difficult tests of her freedom from the social and religious dicta of the past. Shall Osvald honor his father or shall he know the truth about his debauched progenitor? Mrs. Alving finally chooses to tell the truth rather than to conform to the Commandment by which she had lived for the past 28 years. Shall Osvald be allowed to marry his half-sister or shall the incest taboo be upheld? Mrs. Alving chooses to tell the whole truth about Captain Alving in order to fore-

[10] Egan, p. 185.

stall an incestuous marriage, though she had admitted earlier, «If only I were not such a miserable coward, I would say to him: marry her, or arrange things as you both will.» Her final test is the most crucial, whether to grant Osvald the death he wishes. Not only is the Commandment, thou shalt not kill, at issue, but also the more deeply rooted response of the mother for her child. She has made one ethical choice out of freedom from, and one choice out of obedience to, the ghosts of the past. Though she is not always able to choose freely, Mrs. Alving's capacity to exercise choice is so important to the plot that Ibsen concludes the play precisely at the moment of her greatest ethical decision. Many have argued that she will, or that she will not, administer a fatal dose; none has been able to demonstrate the logical inevitability of either choice, which is to say that Ibsen has constructed the terms of the play so that Mrs. Alving has a *real* choice.

With Mrs. Alving as protagonist, her psychological and metaphysical positions take precedence over Osvald's physical, physiological and social victimization. Her free will becomes a major consideration in the play. From this perspective, the plot concludes precisely at the moment of Mrs. Alving's greatest existential choice.

The title, *Ghosts,* names the abstracted and generalized antagonist of that play. The preliminary title of Rosmersholm was «White Horses,» a title which was to have functioned precisely as «Ghosts» does, the «White Horse» motif in the play indicating that aspect of the reputedly dead past that still walks abroad. The Second Draft has this exchange: «*Rosmer:* My earlier self is dead. I look upon it as a corpse. *Mrs. Rosmer* (the Rebecca character): Yes, but that's exactly when those white horses come.»[11] The conversation goes on to elaborate white horses as a symbol of those forces of traditional beliefs that block the way to complete emancipation. For the Third Draft, Ibsen has changed the title to *Rosmersholm,* and in the final form Kroll defines the significance of Rosmersholm:

Rosmersholm has since time immemorial been a cornerstone of propriety and orderliness – of respectfull honor in front of all that which has been upheld and sanctioned by the best in the society. The whole region has taken its impress from Rosmersholm.[12]

11 *The Oxford Ibsen, Vol. VI,* trans. and ed. James Walter McFarlane (London: Oxford University Press, 1960), p. 399. Subsequent citations of the Second Draft and the Third Draft are taken from this volume.

12 Henrik Ibsen, *Nutidsdramaer 1877—99* (Oslo: Gyldendal, 1962), p. 300. The translation is mine. Further quotations of the final copy of *Rosmersholm* are likewise my translations from this volume.

This function of Rosmersholm – providing the mold for the regional character – is confirmed in less laudative terms by Mrs. Helseth, when she identifies the source of the absence of laughter in the region:

It began at Rosmersholm, they say. And then it spread out, like a kind of infection, I suppose.

Rosmersholm is the matrix in which the germ of the past culture was preserved and cultivated. Whereas «Ghosts» concentrates on the nature of the infection, the title «Rosmersholm» identifies the source and specific matrix of the debilitating disease.

Those characters who fight on behalf of this force are Kroll and Mortensgaard. Though on opposite political sides and themselves bitterly antagonistic toward each other, in the combat that constitutes the action of the play Kroll and Mortensgaard perform identical functions. They both come to Rosmersholm for the same reason: to obtain the weight of the name of Rosmer for their political causes. Upon hearing of Rosmer's apostacy, they both attempt to prevent him from making a public break with the Church.

The conservative Kroll: I say that if this madness shall be, then think and mean and believe in God's name what you will – both with respect to the one thing and to the other. But only keep your ideas to yourself. This is a purely private matter. There is no necessity for such things to be shouted out over the whole land.
The liberal, less loquacious Mortensgaard: So it is most advisable that you keep silent about all suthe public.

Both see a public stand by Rosmer to render him politically detrimental, so they both urge public conformity and no external change of status. As Ibsen stated in his speech to the workingmen of Trondheim in 1885, those that have been irreparably harmed by party pressure cannot deliver the nation into a new freedom and nobility of character. Kroll and Mortensgaard receive their stamp from party pressure. They share, therefore, the role of antagonist in the play.

The critical question again is – who is the protagonist? The clear majority of Ibsen critics responds, «Rosmer is the protagonist.» Most then hasten to add, «but a very weak one.» However, if one compares the Rosmer of the Second Draft with the Rosmer of the final copy, one can see evidences of a deliberate weakening of Rosmer's character. In Act I of the Second Draft, for example, the Rebekka character wants to tell the Kroll character about Rosmer's newfound position. «Yes, for now I'm going to tell you straight. . . Rosmer responds, «No, let me say it myself . . .» Here Rosmer is cast in a self-assertive position. In the final form, Rebekka's speech remains the same. Rosmer's response, however, alters. He quickly says, «No, no, let it be! Not now!» His reaction has shifted from assertion to evasion.

Similary in Act II, Rosmer is given a stronger stance in the Second Draft than in the final copy. In the Second Draft, he argues with the Kroll character on an equal and vigorous footing:

KROLL. I consider that faith and morality cannot be separated. And I recognize no other morality than our Christian one.
ROSMER. And I recognize no Christian morality; I recognize no other morality than the one I have in my blood.
KROLL. Private, human morality is a feeble defense.
ROSMER. Oh, this unbounded fanaticism that has taken hold of you!

Here, Rosmer's stance is a counter-assertion to the position of Kroll. Kroll fights on one side; he fights on the other. In the final copy, this exchange is expanded and greatly altered in form.

ROSMER. Ah. . .! So you don't think there is any sense of virtue to be found among free-thinkers? Doesn't it strike you they might have a natural instinct for morality?
KROLL. I don't place much reliance on any kind of morality that is not rooted in the faith of the Church.
ROSMER. And you include Rebekka and me in that too? My relations with Rebekka?
KROLL. . . I cannot bring myself, merely on your account, to abandon my view that there is no tremendous gulf between freethinking and . . . hmm!
ROSMER. And what?
KROLL. . . and free-love, if you must have it.
ROSMER. (gently). And you have no shame in saying that to me? You who have known me since I was a boy.

The obvious rhetorical shift is from Rosmer's declarative statements in the draft to his series of questions in the final copy. This shift from assertion to query is paralleled by an alteration in the content of Rosmer's responses from that of defining his own position to that of inquiring about the limits of Kroll's position. The effect of this change is that Rosmer no longer directly confronts Kroll. On the basis of these and other evidences of shifts from the early drafts, such as the disappearance of Rosmer's book ennunciating the goal of human happiness, one is justified in concluding that by the final copy, Rosmer has been extricated from his originally conceived position as protagonist.

Who, then, is the protagonist combatting the forces of Rosmersholm? Rebecca West, née Gamvik. Gamvik stands opposed to Rosmersholm: a place name above the 71st parallel in Finmark that evokes the turf huts of the Samer against a Western Norway estate name and manor house of the old ruling class.[13]

In inverse proportion as Rosmer becomes weaker from the Second Draft to the final copy, Rebekka becomes stronger. A major factor involved in Rebekka's increase in stature is, of course, the fact that Ibsen abandoned the Second Draft shortly after the beginning of Act III. The acts said to be «Rebekka's acts,» III and IV, are missing in the Second Draft.

Agreeing with Halvdan Koht that Ibsen «realized that the ending had to receive an entirely different emphasis than he had first intended,»[14] one can argue that Ibsen ceased in his attempt to develop Rosmer as the play's protagonist after the beginning of the third act and began again.

In addition to Rebekka's assumption of the major role in Acts III and IV, there are clear evidences in Acts I and II of her position being deliberately strengthened. Her conversation with Kroll at the beginning of Act I, for example, shifts from Kroll dominating and defining the conversation in the Second Draft, to Rebekka and Kroll as equal participants with her character being defined and elaborated by the conversation as much as Kroll's. The most significant addition in the first half of the play however, occurs in Act II. Whereas in the Second Draft Rebekka is largely absent from the stage, in the final copy she is present during virtually all of Act II.

I am going to argue that the strengthening of Rebekka's role does not result, as several including Professor McFarlane have persuasively argued, in dual protagonists, that Rebekka's and Rosmer's roles do not become equally strong. I am going to argue that the strengthening of Rebekka's role results in Rebekka becoming the protagonist.

Knowing Ibsen's concern in this and other of his modern plays for

[13] Professor Emeritus Einar Haugen, having consulted *Norsk stadnamnleksikon,* Jørn Sandnes and Ola Stemshaug, eds. (Oslo: Samlaget, 1976), stated in a telephone conversation with me on 17 May 1978 that the most likely etymological association with «Gamvik» for Ibsen would have been the Old Norse «gamme,» meaning «a turf hut.»

[14] Koht, p. 375.

what can be termed «family inheritance,» one would be justified in assuming that Ibsen's choice of career for Rebekka's mother was not accidental. Every bit as much as Rosmer's career as pastor was determined by his being a son of the Rosmers of Rosmersholm, so Rebekka's career is delineated by her being the daughter of a midwife. The function of Rebekka's role as protagonist is to perform the actions of a midwife in a play whose plot can be stated in these terms: to birth the free soul. In his Trondheim speech the year before *Rosmersholm* was published, Ibsen singled out workingmen and women as the two groups capable of delivering a noble spirit from the nation. Rebekka is the midwife of this delivery.

If the plot is seen to be that of birthing the free soul, then the dominant imagery of the play can be seen to reinforce this plot and the actions of all the characters in the play can be seen to forward or to block this action. Forwarding the action are the protagonist Rebekka and the secondary protagonist Rosmer. Blocking the action are the antagonist Kroll and the secondary antagonist Mortensgaard. Brendel, Beata and Mrs. Helseth reflect in specific ways the action of the main characters.

Rebekka, in her confession in Act IV, describes her motive for coming to Rosmersholm. Having heard from Kroll that Ulrik Brendel with his revolutionary ideas was a major influence on the youthful Rosmer, she thought it possible that she could continue that effort. She expresses her perception in terms that reinforce the birthing and midwife action. Arriving at Rosmersholm, she saw that there was «an insurmountable wall between [Rosmer] and whole, complete freedom.» She realized wherein deliverance lay, «the only deliverance.» So she acted. When Rosmer asks how she could have acted in a way that brought about Beata's death, she responds, «I thought that it was a question of choosing between two lives, Rosmer,» a statement reflective of the traditional choice of the midwife in critical circumstances between mother and child.

In Act I Rebekka tries to push Rosmer to emerge into the public world. But, although it has been 18 months since Beata's death, the double gestation period appears to be insufficient: Rosmer protests that it is not the proper time. Only after Brendel's first appearance, where he is repeatedly invoked as a boy, does he emerge, declaring, «There has come a new summer in my heart. A new youthful view.» In Act II Rebekka hovers, an unseen presence, to oversee the welfare and progress of her newly birthed soul in the public world. Kroll and Mortensgaard prove too fierce an environment for Rosmer. After their departure Rosmer confesses, «Oh, never before have I felt that I needed you like this.» He goes on to develop his guilt for Beata's death. Rebekka reminds him of his new beginning. «Now you were about to begin to live, Rosmer. You had already begun.» She encourages him to form new relations with the outside world. Rosmer rallies: «But now opens itself before me a life with strife and with unrest and with strong moods. For I *will* live my life, Rebekka! I will not let myself be beaten into the ground by dismal possibilities.» Rebekka encourages him, «Be entirely a free man, Rosmer!»

In Act III Rebecca attempts to infuse new life in Rosmer by her confession, giving him what he says is absolutely necessary for life, innocence. But that does not succeed in severing him from the matrix of Rosmersholm: he still cannot cross over the bridge separating the two worlds – the dark, inner, private womb-world of Rosmersholm from the light, external public world. Despairing, Rebekka plans to leave, until she realizes that Rosmer's «killing doubt» about her now blocks Rosmer's freedom. He says, «I don't think I can live. And neither do I know of a thing in the world which could be worth living for.» And so she acts to remove the insurmountable barrier of doubt in the only way possible; again it is a question of choosing between two lives. Again she chooses on behalf of birthing the free soul. This time it is not the wife, but the midwife that must die in order to give birth to the new life.

Rosmer has been convinced by Rebekka that midwifery is to be his vocation also. As a pastor he had been dedicated to containing people within the folds of the Church; as midwife he will emancipate them from that confinement. At the end of Act I he ennunciates to Kroll his mission to try to arouse people to free themselves. He develops this theme further in Act II: «I think that is is a compelling duty for me to kindle a little light and happiness where the Rosmer family has caused darkness and oppression all this long, long time.» In the case of Rosmer, however, the annunciation is followed by no subsequent live birth. He is instead pushed back into the matrix of Rosmersholm by the very forces of oppression that he had sought to overcome. Not sufficiently strong himself in his newly entered world, he is incapable of assisting others in their re-birth. By the beginning of Act IV he has retreated, under the pressure of Kroll and «all our old circle of friends,» back into the Rosmersholm womb.

The trajectory of his career as secondary protagonist is similar to that of Mortensgaard, the secondary antagonist. Both espoused liberal positions, but because of potentially vulnerable private lives, retreat back into the safety of the publicly acceptable Christian posture. Ibsen intertwines Mortensgaard's past private vulnerability with Rosmer's former public denunciation of it, and Rosmer's present vulnerability in his private life with Mortensgaard's present capacity to recognize its defaming potential. Both are marked men for similar reasons. Each has revealed that mark to the other. Both cease supporting anything opposed to the Church, though each had seen that as a crucial opposition at one point in his career.

The three remaining characters, Mrs. Helseth, Beata and Brendel, function as an obverse reflection of the action of the main characters and, particularly in the case of Brendel, provide an alternate perspective from which to view that action.

Mrs. Helseth's function is easiest to define. She is the living embodiment of Rosmersholm in the same way as Berte is the living embodiment of the Tesman household in *Hedda Gabler*. Mrs. Helseth demonstrates by her commentary on the action, the transmutation effect that the Rosmersholm way of life has upon any events that come within its purview. The clearest examples of this are in Act IV. As soon as Rebecca announces her intention to leave, that is, as soon as she is prepared to take a public action, Mrs. Helseth casts the motive into the stereotype of the fallen woman unredeemed by the man, revealing her long-standing, unspoken judgment about the affairs at Rosmersholm despite the fact that she has been there constantly to see first-hand what had and what had not occurred. At the conclusion of the play, it is she who provides the context for the interpretation of the white thing as the White Horses of Rosmersholm. It is she who delivers the judgment on behalf of Rosmersholm, that Rebekka and Rosmer are sinful creatures and that the dead woman has taken them. In this respect, Mrs. Helseth is intimately connected with her opposite, Beata.

The dead Beata is as much of a character in the play as Mrs. Helseth. In a very crucial sense, Beata is the prime example of the effect of the force embodied in the concept of Rosmersholm. Like Rebekka, Beata had a passionate nature that was unrequited at Rosmersholm. Like Rosmer, she accepted Rebekka's midwifery guidance about birth. Unable physically to give birth to a child, she commits suicide to free Rosmer for a new life, from her death seeking to engender rebirth. That purpose had been successful for 18 months. Rosmer had approached closer and closer to the verge of freedom. When, however, at the end of Act I he steps over the boundary, the forces of Rosmersholm move swiftly and unerringly to pull him back, to reassert their jurisdiction. Kroll and Mortensgaard convert Beata's liberating act into a Rosmersholm act: that is to say, into an act creating guilt and oppression.

Beata's action of liberation has been transmuted by the forces of Rosmersholm into an action of condemnation.

This transmutation process is clearly developed. As the influence of Rosmersholm had made Beata sicker and sicker until ultimately she was unable to bear the sight or smell of life even in the form of live flowers, so do the forces of Rosmersholm coerce and shape the effect of her action after her death. Kroll begins by saying that «Beata made an end to her own life so that you [Rosmer] could live happy – could live free and – according to your desire.» Several speeches later he is concluding with the accusation that Rosmer's philandering with Rebekka was the direct cause of Beata's commiting suicide. As is typical of many of Ibsen's modern plays, one never knows the precise nature of crucial actions, of Solness' kiss or Hedvig's father. The reason for Ibsen's deliberate vagueness and imprecision is nowhere so explicitly stated as in *Rosmersholm*. Rosmer, after Kroll's accusation, says:

«Listen to me. For more than a year now – ever since Beata died – Rebekka West and I lived alone here at Rosmersholm. In all that time you have known of Beata's accusation against us. But never a moment have I noticed that you took offense at Rebekka and me living together here.
KROLL: I didn't know before yesterday that it was an apostate man and an – emancipated woman who led that life together.

Granted the fact of Beata's suicide and the fact of Rosmer and Rebekka living alone at Rosmersholm subsequent to that, the significance, the meaning of those facts depends on time, context and interpreter. As long as Kroll believed that Rosmer was within the context of Rosmersholm, he was content to assign no significant meaning to reflect adversely on Rosmer. Rosmersholm, that is, the traditional context, defined Rosmer and the significance of his actions and Beata's suicide. When, however, Rosmer is no longer perceived against that background, Kroll's interpretation of the facts alters greatly. The facts have not changed, as Rosmer points out. What has changed, to use the terminology of perception theory in psychology, is the perceived relationship between the figure and the ground. As long as Kroll looks at the ground, i.e., Rosmersholm, as the definer of figure, he perceives one thing. As soon as Kroll looks at the figure, i.e., Rosmer, he perceives a totally different thing. The shift is similar to the perceptual shift operant on a typical figure-ground illusion: if one looks at the white as the ground, one sees two faces facing each other in silhouette; if one looks at the black as the ground one sees a white goblet. The facts have not changed, only the perception, the interpretation has altered. Kroll's shift of perception alters the interpretation of Beata's suicide, causing the act of liberation to become, 18 months later, the act of bondage.

Brendel's career confirms this transmutation process, the major emphasis in his case being on time rather than on the context and the perceiver. When Brendel appears in Act I, his first comment is «Had you expected that you should ever see me again? Especially within these hated walls?» Not only has he returned to the confines of Rosmersholm, he also dons the garb of Rosmer before he goes forth «to strike a blow for life.» His brief appearances in the play, thereby, provide a comic exaggeration of Rosmer's own rebirth. His appearance in Act I acts as a catalyst for Rosmer's emergence into the public light. Immediately after Brendel leaves, Rosmer tells Kroll about his new stance in life. Brendel's reappearance as a failure in Act IV outlines Rosmer's own defeat. «So you observe the transformation,» Brendel says. He elaborates the cause. «For 25 years have I sat as a miser sits on his locked moneybox. And then yesterday – when I opened it and would take the treasure out – then there was nothing. Time's teeth had crushed it to dust. There was absolutely nothing in the whole mess.» If one relishes one's ideas of freedom in private, like Brendel, time transforms them into dust. Rosmer cannot do nothing, for that will create nothing. If on the other hand, like Beata, one does a public act, then the forces of tradition, as symbolized by Rosmersholm, can transmute that into its opposite.

Brendel not only provides another example of the transmutation process, perhaps more importantly he provides an alternate interpretation from that of Mrs. Helseth of Rebekka and Rosmer's last actions.

In his departing scene, Brendel the tutor gives his final, mantic instruction to Rosmer and Rebekka. He first calls Rebekka «min tiltrekkende havfrue.» Eight years ago at the meeting of this seminar, Professor Gravier pointed out Ibsen's awareness of the Danish ballad «Rosmer the merman and Agnes» and others containing a seductive merman.[15] Certainly Ibsen was working with the content of these ballads as late as the Third Draft, where Rebekka is not designated as a mermaid, but rather is apprised of Rosmer, the seductive merman: «Stay my fair

[15] Maurice Gravier, «Le drame d'Ibsen et la Ballade Magique,» in *Contemporary Approaches to Ibsen: Proceedings of the Second International Ibsen Seminary, Cambridge, August 1970,* ed. Daniel Haakonsen (Oslo: Universitetsforlaget, 1971), pp. 153—55.

lady. For you there is no danger lurking. He's not likely to lure you into deep water.» However, this depiction of Rosmer is replaced in the final copy by Brendel's designating Rebekka as the «alluring mermaid.» Furthermore, in the final copy Brendel goes on to instruct Rosmer in the formula for his successful life mission:

That the woman who loves him gladly go out into the kitchen and chop off her fine, rosywhite little finger − here − exactly here near the middle joint. Likewise that the aforesaid loving woman − equally gladly − slice from herself that so incomparably formed left ear.

The elaborate precision of detail combined with the violence of the actions creates an incantatory, compulsively magical effect. This magical sacrifice motif, while not present in the Danish ballad material, is an essential motif of Hans Christian Andersen's reworking of the *havfrue* material in his tale, *The Mermaid.* There, from the sea-witch, the mermaid obtains a magic draught conferring human shape at the price of her voice, the most beautiful in all the sea. The witch cuts off the mermaid's tongue. This sacrifice of the incomparably beautiful by severing an appendage is strongly echoed in Ibsen's phrases, «chop off her fine, rosywhite, little finger,» «slice from herself that so incomparably formed left ear.» The motif is essentially identical.[16] Brendel thus evokes in his mysteriously charged departing scene a mythic motif of the magical sacrifice linked with the mermaid. As opposed to the interpretation of sin and death, white horses and the dead woman, pronounced by Mrs. Helseth, Brendel's perspective brings to the final scene the interpretation of love, sacrifice and transformation, with the emphasis on Rebekka as conscious agent.

Further parallels between *Rosmersholm* and «The Mermaid» elaborate this aspect of Rebekka's role in the play. Upon her exposure to the world of the prince, the mermaid, unlike her sisters who became indifferent to the world above the sea, desires to become part of the human world: «she became fonder and fonder of mankind, and longed more and more to be able to live among them; their world seemed so infinitely bigger than hers.[17] Rebekka, upon coming south from Fin-

[16] Ibsen, of course, knew H. C. Andersen, had been with him on several occasions, and had received from him in 1872 the final volume of his *New Tales and Stories.* Meyer, p. 359.

[17] Hans Christian Andersen, *Fairy Tales* (1907; rpt. London: J. M. Dent, 1956), p. 11. Further quotations from the tale are taken from this volume.

mark to the world of Rosmer, felt «like there opened up a new, big, wide world for me. . . I wanted to be a part of the new day that was breaking forth. To be a part of all the new thoughts.» Both desire to participate in a world of greater potential than their old world.

For both, the means to that participation is by engendering a man's love. The mermaid desires to gain an immortal soul, thereby to partake in human felicity. The mermaid's grandmother formulates the sole method by which this could occur.

Only if a human being so loved you, that you were more to him than father or mother, if all his thoughts and all his love were so centered in you that he would let the priest join your hands and would vow to be faithful to you here, and to all eternity; then your body would become infused with his soul. Thus and only thus, could you gain a share in the felicity of mankind. He would give you a soul while yet keeping his own.

Determined to win the prince's love and thus to gain an immortal soul, the mermaid transforms herself into human shape. She becomes the daily companion of the prince, who grows very fond of her. However, «it never entered his head to make her his queen,» because the memory of another woman, the princess, obtrudes. The mermaid sorrows that it is she who saved his life, yet it is to the memory of another woman that the prince clings. The prince believes that that woman «will never return to the world.» Therefore, the mermaid and he will be inseparable companions, because, as the prince explains, «you almost drive her image out of my heart.» The mermaid continues in the belief that she will become the center of the prince's love and his wife, until the moment she sees the prince clasp the princess to his heart.

Rebekka likewise saw the means of participating in that new world to be through engendering a man's love. Coming to Rosmersholm, she determined to free Rosmer, so they could «go together forward in freedom. Ever further. Ever further forward.» Beata was the obtruding woman. Despite Beata's departure from the world, her memory remained in Rosmer's heart as that of the princess remained in the heart of the prince. Like the prince, Rosmer therefore never conceived of the idea of marrying Rebekka though they became sole and inseparable companions. Rebekka continued in her daily companionship, hoping that one day Rosmer would recognize and reciprocate her love, which by the time the play opens has shifted from the passionate to the selfless.

Near the end of Act II, Rebekka tries to bring Rosmer to the point of relinquishing his memory of Beata and recognizing the love that stands waiting. She asks, «Listen, Johannes, if it lay in your power to call Beata back to you, to Rosmersholm, would you then do it?» Rosmer does not know. Rebekka then, with her arms on the back of his chair, evokes their past companionship: «How fine it was when we sat down there in the living-room in the twilight. And we then helped each other to lay out the new life-plans. . .» As she calls forth those memories to fill Rosmer's thoughts, she shifts from the past tense into the modal form, «du ville gripe, du ville gå,» and then elliptically, into the infinitive, «vinne, skape,» as she attempts to bring him closer to a present union. Rosmer demurs at the absence of happiness: «I shall never more be able to luxuriate in that which makes life so miraculously lovely to live. » Rebekka, believing that Rosmer is going to aver that love is the precondition of happiness which ennobles the spirit, is prepared to reciprocate with a declaration of her own love for him. «Leaning over the back of the chair, softly,» she says, «what is it that you have in mind, Johannes?» Rosmer responds, «Den stille, glade [Rebekka can anticipate «kjærlighet» as the final word] skyldfrihet.» Rebekka is visibly taken aback by this response, as the stage directions indicate, «et skritt tilbake,» and, dumbfounded, can only repeat the word, «Ja. Skyldfrihet.» Her shock is emphasized further by the momentary freeze indicated in the stage directions, «kort opphold.»[18]

As Rosmer continues to elaborate the theme of lack of freedom from sin and guilt, Rebekka becomes increasingly afraid that he is going to break with her. The source of this fear is what she did and did not hear during her earlier eavesdropping. She heard Kroll's adjuration to Rosmer that Rebekka was a questionable character and that Rosmer «must move to escape in time.» What she did not hear, because she had to go downstairs to meet Mrs. Helseth, was Kroll's conclusion that if Rosmer and Rebekka were both going to continue living at Rosmersholm, then at least Rosmer should conceal his religious defection in order to preserve the Rosmer name. Since Rebekka extrapolates Kroll's effect on Rosmer from what she had heard, when she sees Rosmer walk to the door in the final of Act II and then come back to say, «A question occurs to me. Haven't you also asked yourself that question, Rebekka?» she thinks that Rosmer is going to break with her. Hardly able to force out the words, Rebekka responds «(with labored breathing) Let me . . .

---

[18] The nature of Rebekka's expectation and its being thwarted here has been variously undervalued. Arvid Paulsen, for example, entirely eliminates Rebekka's visual and verbal response in his translation, *The Late Plays of Henrik Ibsen* (New York: Harper and Row, 1962), p. 66.

have quickly . . . what it is.» Rosmer continues with a question that seems to be leading precisely in the direction of the separation she fears: «How do you think *our* relationship will turn out after this day?» The conversation continues, all of Rosmer's statements seemingly circling around the issue that Rebekka fears, until Rosmer asks the presumed final question, «But do you know then what I am thinking about? Don't you know? Don't you know how I best can win freedom from all the nagging memories – from all the miserable past?» Rebekka, fearing severance in the next statement says, «Well?!» Rosmer's answer justifies her fears: «By opposing them with a new, a living reality.» Though she had anticipated this conclusion, its impact is still crushing. Rebekka «gropes for the chairback» for support but nevertheless is grimly determined to hear it out to the fatal finish: «A living . . .? What is . . . that?»

For the second time in as many minutes, Rebekka is completely stunned by Rosmer's response. He proposes marriage. She, «(for a moment dumbfounded, then cries out in joy), Your wife! Your. . .! I!» This total reversal of her expectations has caught her off guard. For a moment Rebekka believes she has reached her goal; proffered is the long-awaited union. Then she recognizes the full implications of such a union. Rosmer, like the prince, wants Rebekka to erase the memory of Beata. However, Rebekka realizes that if she became one with Rosmer, far from taking Beata's corpse from Rosmer's back, she would be permanently wedding Rosmer to guilt for Beata's death. She answers: «It is more impossible that I could become your wife. Never in this world can I become that.» Acts III and IV, «Rebekka's Acts,» explicate the reason for Rebecca's response. They elaborate the transformation that has occurred in Rebekka by the end of Act II: her selfless love has so created in her a new soul that the very goals she had formerly sought become, by that very love, impossible. When the sisters of the mermaid loved a human man, they sought to be united with him in their own world, thereby causing his death. The mermaid, to the contrary, recognized that her world was fatal to the prince and so sought to become part of his world. Rebekka, like the mermaid, recognizes that freedom from guilt is essential to the life of Rosmer's free spirit and thus foregoes the union to save him. This renunciation is the first deed of her new soul.

At the end of Act IV, having confessed her love for Rosmer, she is faced with the choice that faces the mermaid: her own death or that of the beloved. She, like the mermaid, chooses out of selfless love her own death. Like the mermaid who throws herself into the water and can only be seen as a bit of white foam by the prince, Rebekka's end is characterized to the external world by the residual glimpse of white. In Andersen's tale, this act of selfless love has won for the mermaid the opportunity as a daughter of the air to create by her own good deeds an undying soul. In Ibsen's tale, this act of selfless love creates the union of souls. The wedding absent in Andersen, takes place in Ibsen. Rosmer fulfills the response necessary to unite the souls: he forsakes his familial heritage and focuses solely on Rebekka. They become wedded and go to their united death, though they recognize that their action may be the result of delusion – a result of the White Horses of Rosmersholm. The repeated emphasis on the absolute and equal union, on their becoming one, in the concluding dialogue can be interpreted from this perspective as the affirmation of the birth of the new soul through an act of selfless love, as the mermaid's grandmother had stipulated.

But that is not the final perspective on the action. Ibsen in not a Romantic. He concludes not with absolutes but with ambivalence. The possibility of delusion that prevents Rosmer from acting with the assurance of absolute truth is presented to the audience as well. Mrs. Helseth's interpretation of White Horses and the dead woman taking them ends the play. But this cannot be taken as the conclusion of the play any more than Brack's response, «But, good God, people don't do such things!» can be taken as the conclusive perspective of *Hedda Gabler*. If the audience operates from within a Rosmersholm context, then it will see the «ground» as the final determinant: Beata will be seen, as Mrs. Helseth sees her, as one of the forces of Rosmersholm ultimately preventing any escape of the struggling soul, ultimately recreating the very act of escape into an action reaffirming the power and predominance of the force of Rosmersholm. If, on the other hand, the audience operates from without a Rosmersholm context, than it will see the «figure» as the final determinant of value: Rebekka will be seen as having successfully birthed the free soul from out the matrix of Rosmersholm – in fact, two free souls, that of Rosmer and by virtue of that, her own. From this perspective *Rosmersholm* can be seen to be concluded at the moment of Rebekka's greatest existential action.

In *Ghosts* and *Rosmersholm* the figure of the protagonist emerges out of the ground of Rosenvold or Rosmersholm. As with the figure-ground illusion used in the psychological study of perception, so in these plays Ibsen creates for his audience a conclusion which, rather than resolving into a single interpretative focus, maintains the double perspective of the reversible ground and figure with conterminous lines. If Osvald and Rosmer are seen as protagonists, the conclusion resolves into a single interpretive focus that views their defeat against the forces of Rosenvold and Rosmersholm. If Mrs. Alving and Rebekka are seen to be the rightful protagonists, then the conclusions of the two plays remain ambivalent, that is capable of a double focus. In one focus, one can see the picture of the traditional forces as a final definition of the action of the protagonist *and* in the other focus one can see the picture of the protagonist at the point of emerging from a traditional context in an act of free choice, in an act that births the free soul.

La conversion de Rebekka

MAURICE GRAVIER

Nombreux sont dans le répertoire universel, et plus particulièrement dans le théâtre espagnol au Siècle d'Or, les drames ou les comédies portant un sous-titre tel que «le voleur volé» ou «le trompeur trompé». Les auteurs dramatiques aiment à présenter un personnage excessif á la longue puni parce qu'il voulait faire sentir à son prochain les effets de sa propre supériorité et qui se voit appliquer le traitement qu'il entendait faire subir à autrui. Henrik Ibsen aurait sans doute pu intituler son drame *Rosmersholm* d'une tout autre façon, par exemple *Rebecca ou le convertisseur converti*. En effet Rebekka, libre-penseuse, femme émancipée, prétend convertir le pasteur Rosmer à sa propre doctrine et planter le drapeau du libéralisme sur Rosmersholm, forteresse des conservateurs. Au moment même où elle semble être parvenue à ses fins, elle doit avouer qu'elle à elle-même subi l'influence de Rosmer. L'atmosphère de Rosmersholm l'a si bien pénétrée, si complètement brisée, qu'elle n'est plus tout-à-fait la même personne, sa volonté est comme malade, son insolente hardiesse est comme domptée, elle renonce à ses audacieux projets, elle renonce même à sa conquête du bonheur. *Forvandling,*[1] «métamorphose», «conversion», «det store omslag,» ces termes sont employés par Rebekka au 4eacte, ce sont peut-être les mots-clés qui nous aident à comprendre et même à admetre un dénouement qui pourrait par ailleurs nous dérouter.

En nous plaçant sous le signe des idées et des doctrines, rappelons comment se déroulent les évènements. Essayons en particulier de définir le rôle que joue la conversion dans l'enchaînement des faits et l'évolution des personnages. Qui dit conversion considère qu'un croyant abandonne sa foi et se tourne vers une autre doctrine pour donner à ses nouvelles idées non seulement une adhésion intellectuelle mais encore pour s'engager corps et âme à leur service. Qu'en est-il d'abord de Rosmer? Descendant d'une illustre famille qui a donné à la Norvége

[1] «det store omslag», p. 428, «forvandling» p. 430.

nombre de dignitaires ecclésiastiques et de solides officiers, Johan Rosmer s'est laissé persuader de devenir pasteur dans l'Eglise luthérienne de Norvège. Il professe très officiellement sa foi et s'acquitte consciencieusement de sa tâche au sein de l'Eglise. En politique, il appartient tout naturellement au parti conservateur. Sans être tout-à fait fanatique, il applique avec rigueur les principes de la morale traditionelle. Puis survient Rebekka, «femme émancipée, tempérament de feu.»[2] Elle s'introduit à Rosmersholm. Elle y assume les fonctions de dame de compagnie et garde-malade auprès de la pauvre Beate, l'épouse stérile et hypocondre de Rosmer. Mais elle s'occupe aussi du pasteur. Elle le prend souvent à part. Insinuante et discrète, la petite libre-penseuse n'hésite pas à mettre en question les croyances mêmes de Rosmer, sa foi religieuse et ses convictions politiques. Des évènements graves s'inscrivent dans l'histoire de Rosmersholm. Beate l'égrotante, un beau jour, se jette d'un ponceau dans le bief de la rivière, à deux pas du manoir. Et puis Rosmer, sans trop fournir d'explication, se démet de sa charge ecclésiastique. Il se retire du monde pour se consacrer à des recherches personnelles, ne quittant guère Rosmersholm que pour faire tout seul sa promenade quotidienne. Personne ne semble sérieusement s'interroger sur ces deux évènements apparemment sans relation immédiate l'un avec l'autre. Beate s'est donné la mort. Qui peut s'en étonner? N'avait-elle pas l'esprit quelque peu dérangé. Le pasteur ne veut plus prêcher ni administrer sa paroisse. Ce digne homme n'est-il pas un peu «fin-de-race»? La mort de sa femme a pu ébranler sa santé. On le savait taciturne, peut-être un peu aboulique. En tout cas, nul ne mettait en cause Rebekka. Cette belle fille avait apparemment développé à Rosmersholm des verus qui s'étaient déjà manifestées: n'avait-elle pas jadis prouvé ses capacités de dévouement avec son père adoptif, le Docteur West? De même elle avait soigné avec beaucoup de zèle Beate, elle semblait aussi très attachée au Pasteur Rosmer, elle lui servait sans doute d'intendante. Nul ne s'inquiétait de voir l'éclatante créature vivre dans le manoir avec le pasteur veuf qui n'etait son aîné que de douze ou treize ans. Après tout, Rebekka, par les services rendus, avait acquis le droit de rester au manoir aussi longtemps qu'il lui plairait. Tel était l'avis du proviseur Kroll, beau-frère de Rosmer, et même de Madame Helseth, la bonne servante, qui voyait Rosmer et Rebekka évoluer chaque jour devant elle. Elle ne suspectait en aucune manière leur moralité. Un pasteur! Et une garde-malade, si réservée dans ses manières et si attachée à la famille!

[2] 444.

Mais bientôt Kroll découvre que Rosmer n'est pas le calme érudit qu'on imaginait et qui aurait quitté l'Eglise, parce qu'il n'etait pas bien sûr de la servir comme il fallait. C'est un apostat, il a perdu la foi, il est passé de l'autre côté de la barrière; en politique, il se désolidarise d'avec les conservateurs. C'est un libéral, qui sait? peut-être même un radical, prêt a pactiser avec Mortensgård, ce libertin, ce mécréant, cet adultère. Et, au fait, puisque Rosmer a perdu la foi, quelle confiance peut-on avoir en lui? Sans doute est-il aussi perdu de moeurs? Et Kroll, le proviseur, sent grandir en lui une âme d'argousin. Il commence une enquête sur Rebekka. Il cherche à comprendre le pourquoi de cette conversion si inattendue chez Rosmer. Et il nous aide à découvrir une étrange aventure, il essaie de déterminer le rôle qu'y a joué l'idéologie et la place que tiennent sans doute certains sentiments assez troubles. A notre tour reprenons l'enquête de Kroll. Demandons-nous d'abord quelles sont ces idées si agissantes qui auraient pu désorganiser la conscience et l'existence même du pasteur et en quoi consiste cette prétendue conversion, puis la conversion en sens contraire de Rebekka. Ensuite nous essaierons de voir quelle place prend dans cette double évolution l'amour, ou le vertige des sens, ou encore, comme on dirait aujourd'hui, le sexe. Enfin nous tenterons de comprendre comment Ibsen a pu conférer une grandeur tragique aux destins unis de Rosmer et de Rebekka, ces convertis qui n'arrivent pas à s'arracher à leur condition, aux lois brutales de l'hérédité et de la contrainte sociale.

Rosmer et Rebekka ont donc eu − en aparte − de nombreuses conversations pendant la maladie de Beate. La malade a dû souffrir, rien qu'à constater le plaisir avec lequel ces deux personnes chaque jour se retrouvaient. On apprendra assez vite que Rosmer a évolué moralement, sous l'effet de ces fréquentes rencontres. Rebekka aurait gagné Rosmer à sa vision du monde, à sa conception de la vie. C'est sans doute sous l'influence de Rebekka que Rosmer abandonne sa foi religieuse et ses convictions politiques. Quelle sont donc les idées que propage Rebekka? Dans la version définitive, Ibsen ne se donne pas grand'peine pour nous les faire connaître avec précision. Nous apprenons toutefois que Rebekka n'a pas inventé grand'chose en tout ceci, elle transmet simplement les idées de son père adoptif (et probablement aussi naturel) le docteur West. D'ailleurs elle parle rarement pour son propre compte, elle se contente de présenter et de commenter les ouvrages contenus dans la fameuse «caisse de livres», le seul héritage qu'elle tienne du Docteur. Cet homme est le défenseur des thèses matérialistes caractérisant cette seconde moitié du 19e siècle: darwinisme et autres apports des sciences naturelles, en ce temps dominantes. De toute évidence aussi Rebekka entre en guerre contre la morale traditionelle, celle qui s'appuie sur les commandements de Dieu et les impératifs de l'existence familiale, morale de l'autorité et de l'ascèse. L'aspect positif de cette morale nouvelle, la référence au bonheur individuel est beaucoup plus explicite dans l'ébauche de la pièce, les *Chevaux blancs (Hvide heste),* plus préciséments dans la seconde version de ce texte. «Je veux une bonne fois commencer à vivre. Je veux connaître le bonheur une fois dans ce monde» proclame Rosmer, dûment chapitré par Rebekka. Gylling (c'est-à-dire Kroll) se récrie devant cette impudente chasse un bonheur. Et Mademioselle Dankert (c'est le nom que porte ici Rebekka) vole au secours de Rosmer: «c'est le propre de notre temps. Une des conquêtes capitales dont notre jeune génération peut s'enorgueillir, c'est que nous osons proclamer que le bonheur est le but de notre vie.»[3] Les raisonnements de la jeune novatrice ont aussi pour but de soulager autant que possible la conscience de Rosmer. Il a le droit de prendre des positions hardies, de présenter à tous l'aspect d'un homme libéré. Qu'il ait le courage de s'affranchir une bonne fois. Qu'il ne s'embarrasse pas d'inutiles scrupules. Elle réussit fort bien, puisque Rosmer répond à Gylling qui se scandalise: «Je me sens libre et pur.»[4]

Rebekka s'entend fort bien a utiliser ces idées, ce qui ne signifie pas forcément qu'elle y attache une si grande importance, en ce qui la concerne elle-même. Pour les deux personnes qui lui tiennent à coeur, elle choisit les arguments qui porteront et les livres qui ont le plus de chance de les impressionner, dans la situation ou chacune ces deux se trouve. Pour ce qui est de Beate, il s'agit de l'amener à s'effacer, au besoin par le suicide. Il faut donc lui donner le sens de la culpabilité, non pas de tuer en elle le scrupule. Epouse stérile, elle n'a pas sa place dans la société, elle fait obstacle au bonheur de son mari. Pour elle, Rebekka trouve un ouvrage de physiologie qui expose les vues de la science moderne sur la finalité du mariage. Sur Rosmer, Rebekka effectue le travail inverse. Les scrupules du pasteur, de ce puritain, dernier représentant d'une longue lignée austère, gênent considerablement les projets de l'intrigante. Il s'agit donc de lui prouver sans cesse, au nom de la Science et selon les critères de la conscience moderne, que sa manière d'agir est juste, simple, naturelle. Ce n'est seulement le faisant marcher sur cette voie-là qu'on réussira à le «libérer». Rebekka n'est en aucune manière une apôtre qui serait accidentellement tombée amoureuse de l'homme qu'elle cherchait à convertir. La «cause» ne compte quère

[3] 477.
[4] 478.

pour elle. Rebekka a un but devant les yeux et les idées l'aident à progresser vers ce but. Non pas en galvanisant son courage à elle, mais en anéantissant ceux qui la gênent, ou en les obnubilant. Elle agit par la suggestion plus que par le raisonnement. Elle fascine plus qu'elle ne persuade. Rosmer est pour elle un «sujet» de qualité exceptionelle, plutôt qu'un disciple authentique et passionné. Pourquoi travaille-t-elle à «convertir» Rosmer? Non pas parce qu'elle croit au scientisme du Docteur West comme on croit à la vérité, mais parce que cette attitude philosophique laisse les mains plus libres et permet de mieux profiter de l'existence. Si elle s'attaque aux convictions de Rosmer, c'est qu'elle veut tout d'abord conquérir Rosmersholm et la conquête de Rosmersholm est impossible si on ne subjugue pas tout d'abord Rosmer. Or – elle en fera elle-même l'aveu au pasteur beaucoup plus tard – Rosmer est prisonnier de sa croyance religieuse et de son attitude conservatrice. Pour triompher de Rosmer, il faut faire de lui un autre homme.

Mais cette femme si habile à *combiner,* à calculer sait aussi *charmer.* Et réciproquement, elle subit le charme de son interlocuteur:

«Nous étions si contents de rester dans la grande salle, le soir au crépuscule. Nous nous aidions mutuellement en dressant ensemble des plans pour l'avenir. Tu voulais intervenir dans la vie des hommes; dans la vie des hommes au fil des jours, comme tu disais.»[6]

Cet enseignement ne se faisait pas, bien sûr, à sens unique. Rebekka donnait et recevait. Entre eux s'établissait sinon un échange d'idées, du moins une complicité intellectuelle et sentimentale. Ces heures d'entretien les rapprochaient de plus en plus. Aucun effort, aucune contrainte n'était nécessaire, car Rosmer était un élève qui n'offrait guère de résistance aux suggestions de Rebekka. Kroll lui fait remarquer qu'il a toujours été réceptif aux impressions venues du dehors. Mais, en ce qui concerne l'affranchissement religieux, Rebekka prêchait presque un converti. Pasteur, il ne l'était devenu que pour faire plaisir à son père le commandant et pour se conformer à la tradition tracée par les Rosmer de Rosmersholm: alternativement un militaire et un ecclésiastique. Le père avait été militaire, il fallait donc qu'il devînt homme d'Eglise. Mais l'enthousiasme lui avait de tout temps fait défaut. Rosmer avait étudié la théologie et il avait fallu le bousculer pour l'amener à prendre une charge dans l'Eglise. D'ailleurs le terrain

[5] 417.
[6] 394.

124

n'avait-il pas été préparé pour Rebekka par un précepteur libéral, le pittoresque et génial Ulrik Brendel que le Commandant Rosmer avait ignomignieusement chassé? Dans ce monde de revenants qu'est le théatre d'Ibsen, il est aisé d'imaginer ce qu'avait èté alors le dialogue entre le commandant Rosmer et Ulrik Brendel: l'officier devait tenir à l'audacieux partisan des réformes le langage arrogant que nous retrouvons sur les lèvres de Kroll, quand celui-ci s'adresse à Johan Rosmer, à Rebekka ou à Ulrik Brendel lui-même. Brendel, Rebekka et Johan Rosmer appartiennent à la même famille spirituelle qui doit faire face au clan des conservateurs, aux défenseurs de *l'establishment* aussi bien politique que philosophique et religieux. Ils se constituent les défenseurs du bonheur individuel, tandis que les autres s'attachent à maintenir en place les institutions traditionnelles. Mais si Rosmer et Brendel sont purs, seul Brendel possède en plus le don de prendre ses distances, d'observer le monde avec un détachement véritable, de manier avec naturel la poèsie et l'humour.

Rebekka remporte donc une victoire facile. Même si sociologiquement Rosmer est encore rivé aux formes du passé, psychologiquement il est mûr pour renouer avec un mode de pensée qui lui était familier, au temps où il suivait l'enseignement de Brendel. Habile, Rebekka tire profit du plaisir Rosmer prend à dialoguer avec elle, ce sont les idées qui l'aident à se placer à Rosmersholm, à gagner la confiance de Rosmer. Leurs rapports deviennent ambigus, on peut parler d'amitié amoureuse.

Le zèle de Rebekka, apôtre de la foi nouvelle, ne se manifeste que d'une manière: elle enrage à l'idée que Rosmer, timide ou indifférent, ne rende pas manifeste son changement d'attitude. Il a quitté son poste de chef de paroisse. Mais il a laissé courir le bruit (au moins dans les *Chevaux blancs)* qu'il s'est heurté aux cohortes fanatiques et obscurantistes du piétisme, d'où sa décision. Il ne fait savoir à personne qu'il a perdu la foi et qu'il ne quitte pas seulement sa paroisse, il abandonne l'Eglise. Il faut que Rebekka bouscule à plusieurs reprises Rosmer pour que celui-ci fasse une déclaration semi-publique. Encore la visite d'Ulrik Brendel joue-t-elle ici le rôle d'un déclic. Rosmer reconnaît enfin devant Kroll qu'il n'est plus pasteur, qu'il n'appartient plus à l'Eglise et il se refuse catégoriquement à combattre dans les rangs des conservateurs et des traditionalistes. Certes, Rebekka veut compromettre définitivement Rosmer, le contraindre à rompre les amarres, l'arracher à son clan et à sa caste. Ceci fait partie de son plan, mais nul n'oserait affirmer qu'elle attache une importance capitale au contenu de sa «doctrine». S'agit-il d'ailleurs d'une doctrine cohérente? Rétrospectivement elle découvrira et reconnaîtra que ce comportement était criminel. Il n'est pas possible cependant que cette pseudo-idéaliste n'en ait pas pris sur le moment complètement conscience, puisque'elle mêle sans cesse le mensonge à la prédication orientée d'une philosophie moderniste et «scientiste». Elle ment, par exemple, quand elle anticipe, annonçant à Beate des victoires qu'elle n'a pas encore remporteés: Beate croit à l'apostasie de Rosmer qui n'est pas alors un fait accompli. La pauvre femme est encore la victime d'une odieuse comédie que lui joue Rebekka: celle-ci déclare qu'elle va quitter Rosmersholm, pour éviter le déshonneur. Elle veut donner à penser qu'elle est enceinte, ce qui signifierait qu'elle est déjà la maîtresse de Rosmer. Et Beate, si prompte à douter d'elle-même ne met jamais en doute ce que lui dit Rebekka.

De fait Rebekka, tout en «agissant», ne ferme pas toujours les yeux sur sa faute, c'est elle-même qui nous le dit. Nous pouvons la croire. Rosmer lui en veut d'avoir tout si bien «combiné». Elle prétend cependant qu'elle a été prise dans un tourbillon, comme dans un engrenage. Elle n'a pas réussi à conserver constamment la tête froide. Chaque fois qu'elle aurait voulu s'arrêter, elle se voyait entraîner plus loin par la logique même de la situation qu'elle avait crée et qu'elle ne parvenait plus à dominer. Elle conserve nettement la notion du bien et du mal. Mais le mouvement l'entraîne.

REBEKKA /*vivement*/. Mais croyez-vous que j'aie alors agi constamment la tête froide, en mesurant et calculant chacun de mes actes? Je ne ressemblais alors à ce que je suis au moment ou je vous parle. Il y a bien deux sortes de volonté en nous, il me semble. Je voulais que Rebekka disparaisse. D'une manière ou de l'autre. Mais malgré tout, je ne croyais pas que j'aboutirais à mes fins. A chaque pas que je faisais, je me disais: Jusque lá, pas plus loin. Nous ne ferons pas un seul pas de plus! – Et puis je ne pouvais quand même pas abondonner la partie. Il fallait à tout prix que je fasse encore un tout petit effort, que j'avance encore un petit peu. – Et puis c'est arrivé – et c'est comme cela qu'on aboutit à des résultats de cette sorte. . .[7]

Les évènements inattendus qui suivent la visite de Kroll, puis celle d'Ulrik Brendel et enfin celle de Mortensgård mettent en vue, pour Rebekka, le but du voyage. Rebekka entend avec stupéfaction, avec ravissement Rosmer lui offrir ce qu'elle n'osait lui demander. Face à Kroll (qui incarne l'opinion publique inquiète et irritée), par soumission ou par bravade, on ne sait, Rosmer se déclare prêt à épouser Rebekka. Mais Rebekka refuse. Pourquoi? Elle a brusquement pris conscience de

[7] 418.

la situation qui se présentait à elle, à eux deux, a partir du moment où Rosmer avait rompu son mutisme.

La «conversion» de Rebekka est tout d'abord prise de conscience et renonciation, avant de devenir une marche vers la mort. Cette *forvandling* ne saurait donc en aucune manière être assimilée à la démarche d'un fétichiste qui demande à devenir chrétien ou du protestant qui passe au catholicisme. Rebekka ne brûle pas ce qu'elle a adoré. Elle ne renonce pas solennellement au fétichisme de la science. Elle ne revient pas à Dieu, comme l'Inconnu du *Chemin de Damas*. Il s'agit plutôt de la conversion du pécheur. Rebekka mesure l'étendue de ses fautes. Elle les reconnaît ouvertement. Elle se proclamait affranchie *(frigjort)* pas seulement affranchie des croyances commune, mais libérée de plus des scrupules que chacun éprouve. Elle se plaçait plus ou moins consciemment par-delà le bien et le mal. Désormais elle renoue avec la morale commune, c'est-à dire qu'elle refait connaissance avec le scrupule et même avec le remords, dès qu'elle tourne ses regard vers le passé. Mais dans ce domaine, comme dans l'examen prospectif de la situation, elle se montre toujours ferme et lucide.

Qui a ramené Rebekka sur le chemin de la morale? Elle nous le dit elle-même: c'est le commerce avec Rosmer, c'est aussi le climat moral de Rosmersholm. Comme nous l'avons vu, dans les conversations avec Rosmer, Rebekka a sans doute autant reçu qu'elle a donné. Or Rosmer, même dégagé de tout lien formel avec l'Eglise, reste encore une sorte d'apôtre, de pasteur désacralisé, un homme d'oevre qui veut continuer à visiter les foyers, à porter ses conseils et ses consolations à tous ceux qui cherchent et qui souffrent. Même si Rosmer croit désormais que l'homme doit consacrer tous ses soins à la quête de son bonheur individuel, il restera malgré tout attaché à une éthique solide, toute proche de la morale des commandements. Toute tendance frivole, toute pente vers la recherche égoïste lui demeurent étrangères. Le bonheur n'est sûrement pas pour lui une somme de jouissances matérielles. Il reste noble, réfléchi, pondéré. Nous le devinons voué à une sorte d'ascétisme atavique. Non seulement il est sérieux, mais, comme tous les hommes de sa race, il ne sait même pas rire. Mais il est toute finesse, toute délicatesse et il fait passer en Rebekka chacune de ses impressions, chacun de ses sentiments.[8] A aucun signe extérieur les observateurs qui l'entourent n'ont pu déceler en ces derniers temps la moindre déviation dans son mode de vie.

Rosmersholm, forteresse austère de la tradition, de la religion et du

[8] 428.

conservatisme, a exercé sur Rebekka une étrange fascination. Elle a été élevée par sa mère dans le monde de la pauvreté et de l'inconfort. De là elle est passée, avec le Docteur West, dans la sphère de la bohême et du dérèglement moral. Ce père adoptif à qui le confie Madame Gamvik, sage-femme fort peu sage, est un homme instruit mais dépravé, capricieux, mal portant. Rebekka l'admire certes et elle éprouve sans doute aussi, quand elle repense à lui, comme un sentiment de répugnance. Par contraste avec le modeste garni où vivait sa mère et avec l'appartement désordonné où West a supporté les épreuves de sa dernière maladie, le monde riche, harmonieux et austère tout-à la fois, que constitue Rosmersholm a par à Rebekka comme un havre de grâce. Rosmersholm est vite devenu pour Rebekka un objet de convoitise, elle a voulu régner sur Rosmer et, à travers Rosmer, sur Rosmersholm. Réaction fréquente chez les dames de compagnie, les éducatrices d'enfants et autres membres du personnel domestique du stade intermédiaire, nous dit Siegmund Freud – Mais Rosmersholm fournissait aussi, avec ses portraits d'ancêtres, une image de la société bien établie, de la soumission à l'Eglise et au pays, d'une certaine solidité morale, la matérialisation d'une conscience collective et traditionelle, de la famille, avec sa solidité et la somme même de dévouements que la survie de la grande tribu laisse supposer. Rosmersholm apparaissait à Rebekka comme un autre partenaire – moins facile que Rosmer – avec qui elle devait, même à son corps défandant, dialoguer et qui remettait constamment en cause les principes mêmes de sa morale individualiste. C'est sans doute Rosmersholm qui finalement tue en elle cette volonté insolente de braver la morale et la loi divines et lui dictait les décisions les plus audacieuses et les plus paradoxales. Elle ajoute aussi que Rosmersholm a tué de plus en elle la joie de vivre et la soif du bonheur.

Reste une dernier interlocuteur que Rebekka ne nomme pas mais qui a puissamment contribué à sa conversion, c'est le proviseur Kroll. C'est lui qui pose à Rebekka les questions décisives. Il est venu a Rosmersholm avec de bonnes intentions. Rebekka par elle-même l'intéresse peu. Il ne la suspecte pas. Et pour le bon ordre – pour que l'on ne soit pas tenté de jaser – il souhaite même qu'elle épouse Rosmer. Mais brusquement, quand il apprend l'apostasie de Rosmer, le proviseur change d'attitude. Désormais il mène une veritable enquête, tantôt juge d'instruction, tantôt procureur passionné, il veut lui arracher des aveux complets, il demande presque sa condamnation, ou au moins qu'elle répare, qu'elle épouse. Certes il n'est ni calme ni impartial mais la passion le rend perspicace. Rebekka, froide et désormais honnête, répond avec une rigoureuse précision à la plupart de ses questions. Incontestablement Kroll aide Rebekka à faire le point, à voir clair à l'intérieur d'elle-même, si bien que Clara Stzuyver a pu écrire que Kroll était, pour Rebekka, comme l'incarnation de sa conscience.

Rebekka a donc mesuré son indignité. Elle a avoué ses fautes progressivement, sans humilité excessive mais sans provocation ni sans forfanteries. Et selle renonce à épouser Rosmer, donc à régner sur Rosmersholm. Faut-il chercher un lien de cause à effet entre cette prise de conscience d'une part et cette renonciation de l'autre? Renonce-t-elle seulement parce qu'elle se sent indigne? Faut-il faire de cette renonciation un acte de vertu, le résultat de cette conversion morale qu'elle vient de subir? Nous ne le pensons pas. D'abord parce que, lorsque Rosmer lui propose de l'épouser au début de l'action, déjà elle répond non, et pourtant à ce moment elle n'a pas encore révélé à Rosmer et à Kroll l'ensemble de ses fautes. Je crois que cette renonciation est aussi et surtout un constat d'échec.

Lucidement Rosmer proposé a Rebekka de l'épouser. Il avait déclaré publiquement, quoique d'assez mauvaise grâce, qu'il avait rompu avec l'Eglise. Il est donc désormais tout entier à sa merci, il échappe au parti adverse et Rosmersholm va reconnaître Rebekka comme l'épouse du maître de maison. Mais lucide encore une fois, Rebekka découvre qu'elle vient de remporter une victoire à la Pyrrhus. Quand elle entend parler Kroll puis Mortensgård, elle comprend qu'une vie commune avec Rosmer est pour elle impossible. Rosmer, ex-pasteur, ne peut plus séjourner à Rosmersholm, surtout s'il se marie avec un personnage suspect comme Rebekka. Le monde, à l'entour, est devenu trop nettement hostile. Et puis elle voit enfin Rosmer, ce somnambule que Kroll vient de réveiller brutalement, tel qu'il est réellement, faible, fin de race, incapable de résister aux attaques extérieures et plus encore de se mettre en valeur et d'affirmer hardiment sa foi nouvelle. Il a été trop longtemps habitué à être entouré de respect, à vivre dans le calme et le confort, lui, le descendant des Rosmer, le dignitaire de l'Eglise d'Etat. Rebekka ne se sent guère le courage d'affronter avec Rosmer la vie irrégulière et difficile de la bohême qu'elle ne connait que trop, ou, pis encore, les angoisses et les avanies de l'exil. Dans un prèmier temps elle décide donc de partir seule, sans attendre davangage. Ainsi elle échappera aux adieux difficiles et aux commentaires irritants des voisins et des amis. Et Rosmer, séparé de son mauvais génie, pourra sans doute faire figure honorable dans la petite ville.

Fanatique, Kroll jette sur ses proches un regard sans indulgence. Puisque Rosmer a quitté l'Eglise, il ne respecte certainement plus les commandements de Dieu et Rebekka est depuis lontemps sa maîtresse.

Et cette fois Kroll se trompe. Pourtant, si elle s'était rapprochée de Rosmer par intérêt, très vite elle est tombée amoureuse du pasteur et très tôt aussi, si on l'en croit, chez elle, l'ardeur des sens est tombée. Elle a renoncé a faire physiquement la conquête du pasteur. Rebekka et Rosmer ont fini par vivre dans un climat d'amitié passionnée dont la pureté n'est mise en doute tout d'abord par personne. Les aspects sexuels du drame *Rosmersholm* ne manqueront pas de surprendre les jeunes lecteurs ou les jeunes spectateurs d'aujourd'hui. Freud les a examinés mais il ne nous apporte pas toutes les réponses aux questions que nous nous posons.

Ecoutons l'aveu brutal de Rebekka. D'abord elle reconnaît que, dans les premiers temps où elle habitait Rosmersholm, elle était en possession de son indomptable volonté, elle ne reculait devant aucune perspective et pouvait échafauder les projets les plus hardis:

REBEKKA. . . Et puis elle a commencé à se développer, cette force qui a brisé ma volonté et qui m'a causé une si grande frayeur. . .
ROSMER. Et ensuite? Parle, je ne comprends pas. . .
REBEKKA. C'est à ce moment qu'il s'est emparé de moi, cet irresistible désir . .
ROSMER. Un désir, de qui?
REBEKKA. De toi.
ROSMER /*veut se lever*/.
REBEKKA /*arrête son mouvement*/. Reste assis. Ecoute la suite.
ROSMER. Tu veux dire que tu m'as aimé à ce point. . .
REBEKKA. Je croyais qu'il fallait appeler cela aimer. C'est ce que je pensais en ce temps-là. Je pensais que c'était cela l'amour. C'était, comme je t'ai dit, un irrésistible désir.[9]

Rosmer est effaré, il voudrait qu'elle revienne sur ses paroles. Mais non, elle maintient, elle insiste. Elle compare même ce desir à un de ces orages qui se déchaînent sur la mer, dans le Nord de la Norvège, un orage à quoi nul ne peut resister. Selon Rebekka, c'est cette même force obscure, irrésistible, qui l'a poussée vers le crime, le crime psychique dont elle s'est rendue coupable en éliminant Beate.

Ambitieuse, passionnée et habile, Rebekka a devant elle la voie libre. Pourquoi ne cherche-t-elle pas à triompher aussi sur le champ de bataille de l'amour? Est-elle arrêtée par des scrupules? Kroll est sceptique: ce que l'homme pieux admet comme principe, l'athée le considère tout de suite comme un antique préjugé. En français aussi le mot *libertin* a deux sens étroitement associés. Le libertin qui s'est affranchi de la loi

[9] 426.

divine ne résiste pas aux tentations de la chair. Dans le *Chevaux blancs,* Gylling, l'ancêtre de Kroll, explicite sa pensée très brutalement.

GYLLING. Je veux dire qu'il n'existe aucun gouffre, aucun abîme infranchissable entre la libre pensée. . .
ROSMER. Et quoi?
GYLLING . . . Et l'amour libre.
ROSMER. Et tu oses me dire cela . . . a moi! Tu n'as pas honte de ce que tu es en train de penser.[10]

Mais non, ce désir va se sublimer, se muer en une sorte d'amour platonique. Pour nous rendre sensibles à cette étonnante évolution, Rebekka use d'une métaphore empruntée encore une fois á la météorologie, aux sautes de temps du Grand Nord. Au moment où Rebekka se prépare au sacrifice, où elle va accompagner Rosmer dans la mort, elle dit clairement qu'elle est passée d'un désir brutal et mal dominé à une sorte d'amour calme et comme gratuit qui transfigure l'esistence:

REBEKKA. Quand j'ai pu vivre avec toi ici − dans le silence et le solitude − et que tu as fait passer a moi tes pensées, chacune de tes impressions au fur et à mesure quelles te venaient, c'est alors que s'est produit le grand revirement. Petit à petit tu comprends, presque insensiblement. Mais sans qu'il m'ait été possible de résister. C'était une transformation complète de tout mon être.
ROSMER. Que me racontes-tu encore, Rebekka?
REBEKKA. Et cette autre force, − ce mauvais désir des sens −, il a disparu; il est loin, loin de moi. Toutes les forces déchaînées se sont calmées, sans provoquer le moindre désordre. Un grand calme s'est emparé de moi. Un calme qui me fait penser à la tranquillité qui règne sur les montagnes aux oiseaux, chez nous, dans le Grand Nord, quand brille le soleil de minuit.[11]

Rosmer s'etonne et s'émerveille. Rebekka précise: «Cela veut dire tout simplement que le grand amour est né en moi. Le grand amour, l'amour renonçant, celui qui se contente de la vie en commun, telle que nous la menons ici.» En somme ice encore, il s'agirait bien d'une véritable conversion. La noblesse d'âme, si facile à découvrir chez Rosmer, aurait été contagieuse. Le désir vulgaire éprouvé par la fille du Docteur West se serait affiné au contact de Rosmer. Tout le merite de cette transformation serait-il imputable au seul Rosmer ou au cadre imposant et respectable de Rosmersholm?

Nous voulon bien admettre que Rebekka, au moment solennel oú

[10] 473 et s.
[11] 428.

elle fait cette confidence, est complètement sincère. On peut évidem-
ment conserver ses doutes, quand il s'agit d'un personnage aussi habile
à manier la parole. En tout cas, elle dit ce que Rosmer souhaite enten-
dre. Le plus longtemps possible Rosmer cherche à se duper. C'est le
type même du *selvbedrager* que Sigurd Hoel poursuit de ses sarcasmes. Il
veut à tout prix se dissimuler qu'il est amoureux de Rebekka et que Rebekka l'aime. Il cherche toutes sortes d'expressions pour caractériser
leurs rapports. Mais il se refuse à admettre qu'il s'agit tout simplement
d'un commerce amoureux. Car il tient à se considérer comme innocent, pur de toute faute. Il parle de «notre belle et pure amitié». Il
s'indigne quand Kroll et ses amis se permettent de les suspecter. A la
fin du drame, il reconnaît quand même qu'il s'est très tôt posé des
questions à ce sujet: s'agissait-il vraiment d'une amitié entre Rebekka
et lui ou bien d'un véritable amour? D'ailleurs Rosmer ne souffre apparemment pas de cette discrétion qu'il s'impose dans ses rapports
quotidiens avec Rebekka. Ce n'est bien sûr pas un tempérament sen-
suel. En est-il de même pour Rebekka que Henrik Ibsen caractèrise
comme «varmblodig» (tempérament ardent)[12] dans sa premiere es-
quisse de la piece?

Mais nous pouvons peut-être pousser l'analyse plus loin et plus libre-
ment que ne l'a fait Rebekka ellemême. Si elle n'attaque pas Rosmer
hardiment sur le terrain amoureux, c'est sans doute parce qu'elle ne
pas confer de tout perdre en prenant des initiatives unilatérales. Ne
remettrait-elle pas en question sa propre position à Rosmersholm
et cette harmonie précaire dans ses rapports avec le pasteur? On sent
qu'elle est à la fois proche et fort éloignée de Rosmer. Proche de lui par
l'amitié. Mais séparée de lui par sa position sociale. Rosmer est encore
appelé Monsieur le Pasteur par Madame Helseth. Son comportemant
reste celui d'un homme d'Eglise. Il impose le respect. Il reste d'ailleurs
éminemment respectable. Il est aussi le chef du prestigieux manoir de
Rosmersholm. Il n'a jamais connu les joies de la paternité. Mais sa figure s'apparente a celle du Pére. Rebekka demeure toujours un peu fi-
gée par le respect quand elle l'aborde, quand elle lui parle, quand elle
pense à lui. Essayer de prendre l'initiative dans le domaine amoureux,
ne serait-ce pas perdre le sens du respect? Ne s'agirait-il pas même d'un
véritables sacrilège?

Ici intervient le motif de l'inceste qui a déjà été mis en valeur par O.
Rank et auquel Siegmund Freud a consacré un long développement
dans une étude célèbre. On se rappelle que le Docteur West, intime ami

---

[12] 444.

de Madame Gamvik, la mère de Rebekka, est devenu sur le tard le père adoptif de la jeune fille. Celle-ci va habiter chez lui et elle cède aux avances de ce vieux débauché. Kroll ignore que Rebekka a été la maîtresse de West quand il entame son enquête. En revanche il découvre que, si West est devenu le père adoptif de Rebekka, c'est qu'il était très probablement aussi son père naturel. Et cela, Rebekka ne le soupçonnait même pas. Dans le but d'humilier Rebekka, Kroll lui jette à la figure qu'elle n'est sans doute que la fille naturelle du West. Et il est lui-même assez surpris de voir le désarroi de la jeune femme. Elle découvre − et elle seule en devient consciente − qu'elle a peut-être péché d'inceste et violé le plus grave de tous les interdits.

Freud est tout heureux de retrouver ici, dans une de ses variantes, le mythe d'OEdipe. Mais s'agit-il ici d'un motif central dans ce drame? Sans doute que non, puisqu'il est traîté ici avec une grande discrétion. L'esprit du temps ne permettait d'ailleurs pas à Ibsen de s'expliquer plus clairement. D'ailleurs il ne s'agit pas non plus d'une certitude (Où se cache d'ailleurs la certitude en matière de paternité?) *Il n'est pas impossible* que Rebekka soit la fille naturelle de West, *dans ce cas,* elle aurait commis un inceste. Il faut bien noter le moment où lui est fait cette révelation: au milieu du 3ᵉacte. [13] Ce n'est donc pas à cause de cette decouverte que Rebekka décline l'offre faite par Rosmer pour la première fois, puisque cette offre est faite à la fin du second acte.[14]

Cependant il ne s'agit pas non plus d'un motif superfétatoire dont Ibsen aurait fort bien pu faire l'économie. Car, même après avoir reçu ce choc, Rebekka fait front aux attaques de Kroll, avec qui elle se débat en tête-a-tête, puis quand Rosmer est revenu, elle conserve assez d'energie pour obliger Kroll à rester et à s'expliquer avec eux deux. Sa froide résolution surprend même Rosmer. Rebekka a pris sa décision. Elle n'acceptera aucune nouvelle offre. Qu'a-t-elle donc encore décidé? De partir en coupant les ponts derrière elle. Elle veut s'interdire toute tentation d'épouser Rosmer. Elle passe aux aveux les plus complets. Elle révèle sans faiblesse l'étendue de sa faute. Puis elle fait descendre sa malle. Elle prendra le prochain bateau.[15] C'est donc peut-être à cause de cet, inceste qu'elle aurait éventuellement mis sur sa conscience, qu'elle renonce − irrévocablement cette fois. Ici c'est encore l'action du scrupule ou du remords. Quelque chose comme l'horreur sacrée. Une dernière fois Rosmer l'invite à réfléchir et lui pose définitivement

13 411.
14 369.
15 420.

la question: Ne veut-elle donc pas devenir sa femme?[16] Lui-même se sent plus que jamais libre de sa personne et de son comportement. Pourquoi n'accepte-t-elle pas? Elle lui donne à deviner tout ce qui a changé en elle du fait de Rosmersholm et de Rosmer lui-même. Elle a perdu toute son audace, toute son effronterie d'antan dans un milieu aussi sage. L'atmosphère de Rosmersholm ennoblit l'âme mais en même temps elle la paralyse. Tout ceci ne nous apprend pas grand chose de nouveau. Mais elle ajoute qu'elle a derrière elle un passé. Ce passé, Rosmer croit pourtant le connaitre.

REBEKKA. Ah! bien cher, ne reviens jamais sur cette proposition! C'est tout-à-fait impossible! – Il faut que tu le saches, j'ai derrière moi un passé.
ROSMER. Quelque chose de plus que ce que tu m'as déjà raconté-
REBEKKA. Quelque chose de plus, quelque chose d'autre.[17]

Rosmer s'interdit toute curiosité malsaine. Il se doutait bien que Rebekka élevée dans les principes de la bohème, avait dû avoir quelques amis ou quelques amants. Cela n'aurait rien changé à sa détermination (Il veut dire: «Tout cela, c'est ton passé, Rebekka. Le passé est mort. Tu n'as plus aucun rapport avec ton passé».) Mais Rebekka semble vouloir dire qu'elle ne peut plus retrouver son innocence. Elle a commis une faute qui sort de l'ordinaire, elle a commis l'acte sacrilège. Elle pense sans nul doute à son inceste. «Quelque chose d'autres, quelque chose de plus.» Et l'union avec Rosmer, autre image du père, ne serait-ce pas comme une récidive, une autre faute inexpiable?

Il reste peut-être à nous étonner devant cette crainte qui semble s'être emparée de nos deux héros devant l'accomplissement physique de leur amour. On est surpris de voir que Freud n'ait pas monté en épingle l'étonnante déclaration de Brendel, lors de son second et dernier passage à Rosmersholm:

BRENDEL. Ne construis pas ta forteresse sur des sables mouvants. Et prends bien toutes les précautions voulues avant d'édifier ta vie sur cette charmante créature qui te rend la vie si agréable.
REBEKKA. C'est de moi que vous voulez parler?
BRENDEL /s'approchant d'un pas/. Je me suis laissé dire que mon ancien disciple avait une cause qu'il entendait faire triompher.
REBEKKA. Et alors?
BRENDEL. Sa victoire est assurée, mais – attention – à une condition . . . sine qua non.

[16] 426.
[17] 433.

REBEKKA. Laquelle?

BRENDEL. */la prenant délicatement par le poignet/.* Que la femme qui l'aime se rende joyeusement à la cuisine et coupe son joli petit doigt rose et blanc. De même que ladite dame aimante − se coupe à elle son oreille gauche aux courbes incomparables. *(il la relache et se tourne vers Rosmer)* Adieu, mon victorieux Johannes. [18]

Ulrik Brendel veut-il dire qu'un homme d'action n'aboutira jamais à ses fins, s'il se laisse retarder par de subalternes intrigues fèminines? De notre côté devrons-nous à tout prix chercher une explication psychanalytique du comportement prêté par Ibsen à ses héros? Rebekka a'arrête-t-elle simplement parce qu'elle craint de retomber dans une sorte d'inceste? Ou bien nous trouvons-nous en présence d'un phénomène lié à une certaine époque? *Rosmersholm* paraît en 1886. C'est aussi l'année ou Hans Jaeger publie *Fra Kristiania Bohêmen.* Le romancier et ses amis font en ce temps fort bruyamment l'éloge de l'amour libre. Face à eux Ibsen, qui n'est en aucune manière partisan de l'abolition du mariage, proclame bien haut que liberté de pensée et amour libre ne sont en aucune manière étroitement liés. Et les deux personnages principaux du drama chantent à voix alternées un hymne à l'amitié entre homme et femme, surtout si elle se place sous le signe de l'intellectualité ou du prosélytisme politique ou social. On se demande même à un moment si Rosmer ne s'oriente pas vers le mariage blanc (pourtant il parle de «stille op mod den, en ny levende virkelighet»[19] S'agirait-il quand même d'un *véritable* mariage?) Dans certains milieux émancipés et féministes, le mariage risque parfois d'être considéré ici comme une sorte de paravent derrière lequel s'abriterait l'amitié entre homme et femme et l'association de deux consiences engagées et militantes. Plus de mariage-passion, seul le mariage-association doit triompher. La femme ne doit pas être pour l'homme un objet de désir mais une compagne selon l'esprit, aux côtés de laquelle il aime à travailler et militer. Rebekka ne peut passer pour une suffragette mais c'est quand même une «femme émancipée», elle appartient à l'avant-garde féminine et Rosmer de son côté cherce à se «libérer.» Le cas de Rosmer et de Rebekka n'est pas isolé dans la littérature du temps. Les ennemis du féminisme se moquent de ces couples aux amours platoniques, de ces «associés» des rêveries métaphysiques ou politiques qui font communier dans un même ideal deux amis qui se prétendent «frère» et

[18] 433; − On peut aussi penser à Hedda Gabler et au fossé qui la sépare de l'accomplissement physique de ses intrigues amoureuses.

[19] 396.

«soeur». Que l'on relise les *Dames modernes* de John Paulsen ou la comédie *Maraudeurs-Camarades* d'August Strindberg. Plus près de nous Gerhard Hauptmann a repris dans *Ames solitaires (Einsame Menschen)* le thème de l'amitié amoureuse unissant deux intellectuels: leur aventure tourne mal, mal compris et mal supportés par leur entourage, tous deux iront se jeter dans les eaux du lac voisin.

L'eau coule aux pieds même de Rosmersholm. Sur le thème, qu'il a choisi, Ibsen aurait pu écrire un simple drame bourgeois. Grâce à l'intervention du Cheval blanc, grâce à l'évocation constante de motifs empruntés à la «tryllevise», Ibsen a donné a sa pièce des dimensions mythiques.[20]

Mais *Rosmersholm* est surtout une tragédie. Un homme et une femme sont enfermés dans un piège. Ils ont pris conscience de leurs limites, de leurs imperfections, voire de leurs fautes. Ils entendent échapper à ces limites, devenir autres. Ils croient subir une mutation, ils son prêts à travailler, à supporter des épreuves pour évoluer avec leur temps et se mettre au service de la société contemporaine. Rosmer, fils de militaire, petit-fils de pasteur, a beau se lancer sur la piste des pionniers, renoncer aux prejuges de son clan, chercher à créer l'élite de demain, vouloir travailler pour construire une société plus juste et meilleure, il ne réussit pas à se libérer vraiment, pas davantage à passer de la rêverie stérile à l'engagement public et à l'action concrète. Fin de race, timoré, dès la naissance épuisé sans avoir accompli aucun exploit, il se sent incapable de provoquer le scandale, de rompre par lui-même avec les hommes de sa classe, de s'engager dans la lutte nouvelle aux côtés de ceux qui passaient naguère pour ses ennemis. Sa conversion reste celle d'un faible et d'un rêveur. Elle est manquée.

Rebekka, être asocial, bête de proie, fille à la lourde hérédité et au trouble passé, arrive à Rosmersholm où son charme l'impose. Mais nul n'a encore découvert qu'il s'agit là d'une extraordinaire force destructive. Dangereuse et dissimulée, elle est avide de régner. Tout de suite elle va tendre des embuscades à ceux qui sont devenus ses maîtres. Beate tombe la première, victime des machinations de Rebekka. Quant à Rosmer, elle veut le capturer vivant, pour en faire son esclave. A cette fin elle entend le convertir, c'est à dire en faire un radical. Et Rosmer se laisse en effet émanciper. Mais ici intervient le miracle. Rosmer et Rosmersholm civilisent la sauvageonne. Se laisse-t-elle métamorphoser

---

[20] – Voir notre étude «Le drame d'Ibsen et la ballade magique» présentée à l'International Ibsen Seminar de Cambridge.
Contemporary Approaches to Ibsen T.II, pp. 140—160.

de bonne grâce? Collabore-t-elle même à l'oeuvre de salut? Ibsen ne nous le dit pas. Mais Rebekka reconnaît elle-même que ses griffes deviennent moins acérées, que sa hardiesse n'est plus aussi insolente. Elle sait de nouveau ce que peut être un scrupule et, quand Kroll l'aide a prendre conscience de ses fautes, elle est prête à se repentir. Même si elle n'a pas elle-même contribué à son salut moral, elle s'est sérieusement amendée, grâce au commerce avec Rosmer et à l'action bienfaisante de Rosmersholm. Elle est un instant heureuse à la pensée que bientôt, aux côtés de Rosmer, elle va faire son entrée dans le monde de l'harmonie et de la morale. Mais non, cette fille d'une médecin bohème et débauché se verra interdire l'entrée de la terre promise. Est-ce le poids des fautes personnelles, l'héritage moral laissé par ses tristes parents, l'action malveillante du clan conservateur? Peu importe. Rebekka sent tres bien qu'elle n'aura jamais sa place dans le monde où évolue normalement Rosmer. Vaine aura été sa conversion, vaine sa tentative l'évasion.

Nul n'échappe à son destin, nul ne peut rejeter le fardeau de l'hérédité ni la malédiction de ses propres fautes. Bel effort que celui de la conversion, ou belle patience. Mais quelle est la conversion qui véritablement délivre? Conversion de Rosmer, conversion de Rebekka, toutes deux complexes et toutes deux émouvantes comme les incertitudes de leurs deux vies. Mais toutes deux malheureuses et ne débouchant sur aucune issue.

* Nous citons d'après le texte norvégien, les références renvoient à *Hundreårsutgave,* Bind X, Oslo 1932.

Anagnorisis in *John Gabriel Borkman*

CHARLES LELAND

Anagnorisis is a term used by Aristotle in *The Poetics* to describe the moment of recognition in a play, the moment when ignorance gives way to knowledge. Ideally this moment coincides with the *peripeteia,* a reversal of fortune which, in tragedy, brings suffering and often death to the hero. So it can be said that *anagnorisis* follows in the wake of suffering. Also, since Aristotle exemplifies his concept with reference to Oedipus, later critics have often seen *anagnorisis* as self-recognition. In other words, tragic heroes experience a recognition of the true circumstances in which they exist and of how they must act in view of these circumstances. But even more fundamentally, they come to a knowledge of their true identity, as Oedipus did, of who they really *are.* This notion of *anagnorisis* as self-recognition has been a seminal idea in much later thinking about tragedy. It is the final beat of the tragic rhythm perceived by R. P. Blackmur and Francis Fergusson – purpose, passion, and then perception. Closer to home, Daniel Haakonsen, in his article for the *Festshrift til Jens Kruuse* makes «erkjennelse» one of the three cardinal virtues in Ibsen's heroic world: «erkjennelse, ansvar, og troskap mot den ideale inspirasjon i ens liv.»[1]

In Aristotle, Blackmur, and Fergusson the *anagnorisis* comes only at the end of the tragic rhythm: the hero moves through passion to perception; he moves from spiritual blindness to sight or insight. Such a «recognition» can, perhaps, be seen fairly close to the end of the tragic action of *John Gabriel Borkman.* At the end of Act III Borkman senses that the time is ripe for his «oppreisning;» he senses also what, precisely, that «oppreisning» will involve: it cannot be through another, it cannot be through a servile striking of the breast, it cannot be through dreams or a barren meditation on the past; the «oppreisning» must come through ceaseless work in the present, and all the work of reconstruction must be done by himself alone:

[1] «Fins det en moral i Ibsens skuespill?» (Aarhus, 1968), 182.

Det er ikke gjennem noen annens livsførelse at en mann kan finne oppreisning for sitt fall. . . Oppreise meg selv, vil jeg. . . Det er bare gjennem sin nutid og sin fremtid at et menneske kan sone fortiden. Gjennem arbeide – gjennem ustanselig arbeide for alt det som i ungdommen sto for meg som selve livet.[2]

There is irony here: at the very time that Borkman is insisting that he can redeem himself and his past all by himself, he is begging Erhart to help him.[3] The *anagnorisis* at the end of Act III does not extend to a recognition of Erhart's need for independence. (As John Northam has pointed out,[4] it is often part of the tragedy of Ibsen's heroes that they fail to understand the person with whom they are dealing.) It might even be argued that on a deeper level a yet more important element of *anagnorisis* is lacking at the end of the play in that Borkman never recognizes the radical *dependence* of his being and creative activity. Just as man is not the source of his own being, it is not given to him «to renew the face of the earth» by his own efforts alone, as Borkman felt called to do. Nor is it given to him to achieve his own redemption, «å oppreise meg selv,» as Borkman insists he can do. The *anagnorisis* within the frame of the play itself is a faulty and uncertain one.

I think, however, it could be argued – and I am going to argue – that Borkman's true *anagnorisis*, his true «erkjennelse», comes not at the end but at the beginning of his career and that it is as complete as it ever will be at that time. Borkman understood who he was, the nature of his calling or vocation, and what the consequences would be long before the beginning of the action of the play itself. The action of the

---

[2] *Ibsen: Nutidsdramaer 1877—99* (Oslo: Gyldendal, 1968), 552—553. All subsequent quotations from *John Gabriel Borkman* will be taken from this edition, but they will not be footnoted, since I presume that readers of this essay will know the text of the play very well.

[3] *Ibsen,* 552. In his fascinating study of the play in *Henrik Ibsens Realisme,* Daniel Haakonsen observes that all Borkman's frantic appeals to his son («å forene sin skjebne med hans, – forene ungdommens kraft og pågangsmot med sin egen drøm om skapende gjenoppreisning») accomplish are to tear Erhart loose from mother and aunt and offer him as a sacrifice to Mrs. Wilton. («Det Borkman oppnår, er å rive Erhart løs fra mor og tante for godt og overgi ham som et offer til fru Wilton» p. 152.) Poor Erhart is never under his own will, but to be dominated by Mrs. Wilton and her «joy of life» may indeed be better than to be subject to Ella, Gunhild, or John Gabriel!

[4] «The Substance of Ibsen's Idealism,» *Contemporary Approaches to Ibsen* (Oslo, 1965), 18.

play does not so much lead to *anagnorisis* as it reveals an *anagnorisis* and its ultimate consequence. I hope to show, then, that Ibsen's famous «retrospctive technique» in the play not only reveals past action which is determining present action, but also gradually uncovers the extraordinary dimensions (both – may I say? – existential *and* psychological) of Borkman's understanding of himself. What gradually comes to light is not only the nature of Borkman's psyche, but the existential depths of his unique act of being, an act of being shared, as he insists, by no other person. From the beginning he recognizes this, and we are gradually enlightened as to the nature of this recognition. Those around him fail to be so enlightened, fail to understand – hence his tragic isolation. However Ella, the loving, suffering, dying woman, at the very end, is granted some insight through connatural knowledge (that is, the knowledge born of love), insight into the essential uniqueness of Borkman's being.

So Ella herself experiences a kind of *anagnorisis,* and her experience is, in a sense, ours. As we, partially through Ella, see the reality and consequences of Borkman's unique being and vocation, we, like Ella, come to a realization, clearer for some than for others, of the kind of man Borkman is. Finally, the ultimate consequence of his vocation is brought before us in a stunning dramatic image (the long-estranged sisters stretching out their hands towards one another) – the image with which the play ends. This image, it seems to me, is a Joycean epiphany, suddenly manifesting the positive aspect of Borkman's single-minded and sacrificial pursuit of his vocation to create «forbundsliv. . . lys og varme over sjelene.» Borkman's action is a sacrifice in one basic sense of tht word – an offering of self, effecting reconciliation, and thus establishing at least the beginnings of a «forbundsliv.»

So then, it might be said that this play does not move towards a recognition but gradually *reveals* a recognition which has taken place long before the curtain rises. The gradual revelation of the true nature of the hero's initial *anagnorisis* is a most interesting subtextual action in the play. When the revelation of the *anagnorisis* is complete, a brief glimpse of a new order is given us and the play ends. There is, as I see it, a movement from dialectic (the opposed values of Borkman and Ella), to a resolution of sorts, and then to a vision – a vision of unity and reconciliation. In other words there is a movement from conflicting values (the sense that there are «andre hensyn»), to a recognition of hierarchy of values (that there are, indeed, «høyere hensyn»), to a vision revealing in a kind of epiphany the ultimate worth of Borkman's choosing to pursue these higher values in responding to his unique, painful, lonely, humanly-destructive calling.

I present these ideas with considerable diffidence. One obvious difficulty is that I am accepting Borkman's own evaluation of himself. This is heresy in much valuable criticism, in which the man is seen to be self-deceived. After all, Borkman considers this very possibility towards the bitter conclusion of his conversation with Foldal in Act II: «Vi har bedradd hinannen gjensidig altså. Og kanskje bedradd oss selv – begge to.» (We all remember Foldal's marvelous reply to this, a reply worthy of a Jonathan Swift: «Men er da ikke *det* i grunnen vennskap, John Gabriel?») But is not the man who considers seriously the possibility of being self-deceived less likely to be genuinely so than one who cannot be so objective? I consider Borkman's statement – «Kanskje bedradd oss selv» – just one of several expressions of anguish and doubt in the play, a doubt about the validity of his vocation and the propriety of his course of action, a doubt which does much to humanize a man who is neither Napoleon nor a sick wolf but a man with a huge, ungainly idea – a «kingly thought,» if you will, not Håkon's of course, but Borkman's own unique thought. That this idea *could* be part of a «comprehensive personal myth,» that it *may* constitute «self-administered mythopoeic therapy,» as James McFarlane put it in the «Introduction» to Volume VIII of *The Oxford Ibsen,* cannot be denied. However, *must* it be seen in this way? Granted that most of us need a bit of «self-administered mythopoeic therapy» at times, an unusual vocation need not *ipso facto* be classified as such therapy. Since judgment is so difficult in these cases (in life as in the play), I think that one legitimate critical approach is simply to accept the Ibsen hero at his own evaluation and to see where this acceptance will lead. This is, I insist, just *one* approach, but it can be an interesting and fruitful on. After all, there are those who take seriously Brand's assessment of himself and *his* vocation; I think Ibsen did. And there is more than a little of Brand in Borkman! Manders and Kroll, unsavory though they be, are, I think, too often lightly dismissed as simply deluded or hypocritical. Both these «professionals» represent value-systems which must be taken seriously. Both should be played as real forces to be contended with and not merely as weak, slightly-comic ineffectuals. So Borkman might be something more than a power-mad megalomaniac or a lonely schizophrenic living in an *entirely* self-created mythical universe.

First let us consider Borkman's sense of self and his vocation. I think there might be a key to it, a key which is in the existential order.[5] The key is in the realm of *elle* («to be») – the individual, unique act of being.

141

This being determines the nature of his actions, for «action follows upon being» (*operatio sequitur esse*), as the mediaeval existentialists put it: I act according to the way I am. Now, although my act of being is uniquely mine, it is, nonetheless, not as totally self-sufficient as I might wish, because it is derived from and unltimately sustained by another Act of Being, which *is* completely self-sufficient. In other words, I am not a self-created being and certainly not a necessary being. Since this is so, I cannot create my own physical and moral universe. This Ibsen's greatest heroes (from Brand and Peer Gynt to Solness and Borkman) do not quite understand. Here we might say that the characters are deceived – by the most universal creaturely deception, The basic deception of the creature is to think that he is self-created and thus a self-sufficient creator in his own right. As I have noted already, Borkman wants to renew the face of the earth all by himself, just as Brand wants to restore the image of God in man all by himself. From this point of view they are misguided and follow the troll ethic – «å være seg selv nok» – without really understanding what they are doing. Nevertheless these heroes *do* understand – or at least Borkman does – far better than those around them the uniqueness of their act of being, the special calling flowing from that uniqueness, and the actions necessary to realize that calling.

Let ut turn again to the text of the play. Early in Act II Foldal complains that people do not understand him. Borkman concurs: «Nei, *det* er saken. Det er forbannelsen som vi enkelte, vi utvalgte menneske har å bære på.» Early in Act III, in an attempt to explain himself to his wife, he refers to «den ubetvingelige kallelse inneni meg.» Borkman considers himself one of the «chosen,» one of the «utvalgte,» and being chosen involves an «irresistible calling,» an «ubetvingelig kallelse.» We

[5] It is obvious that I am not referring here to the existentialism represented by Jean-Paul Sartre, Simone de Beauvoir and their followers. Nor am I referring to the modern Christian existentialiam of Gabriel Marcel. It is to Thomas Aquinas and his radical concern with *esse,* the act of being, that I have turned. Aquinas also has been called an «existentialist» by his modern followers. See the following books:

Aquinas, St. Thomas. *On Being and Essence.* Translated with an Introduction and Notes by Armand Maurer. Second Revised Edition, The Pontifical Institute of Mediaeval Studies, Toronto, 1968.

Gilson, Etienne. *Being and Some Philosophers.* The Pontifical Institute of Mediaeval Studies, Toronto, 1949.

Maritain, Jacques. *Existence and the Existent.* Pantheon Books, New York, 1948.

cannot escape the Biblical overtones of these words: kall, kallelse, utvalgte. As John Northam has alerted us to the words of St. Johns' Gospel lying behind the text at the end of *Rosmerholm* (in his two articles in Ibsenårbok, 1977), so the words of Christ and St. Paul can be heard behind Ibsen's text here. In John's Gospel Our Lord says: «Ikke om eder alle taler jeg; jeg vet hvem jeg har utvalgt.» And here is Paul to Timothy: «Derfor tåler jeg alt for de utvalgtes skyld, forat også de skal vinne frelsen.» And to the Romans, in a famous passage: «Dem som han forut bestemte, dem har han også kalt; og dem som han kalte, dem har han også rettferdiggjort.»

Now Professor McFarlane does not mention Paul with reference to Borkman in his «Introduction» to Volume VIII of *The Oxford Ibsen*. But he does mention Nietzsche and the «Ausnahmemensch.» It is certainly true that Borkman considers himself an exceptional man. In answer to Foldal's observation that there is no precedent for his friend's actions, Borkman simply says: «Behøves ikke for unntagelsesmennesker.» The word is obviously a translation af «Ausnahmemenschen.» We can be fairly certain that Ibsen read Brandes's important monograph *Aristokratisk Radikalisme* (1889), a work which introduced Nietzshe to Scandinavian intellectual circles. But we also have Ibsen's undoubtedly exaggerated statement in the famous letter to Bjørnson that he was an inveterate Bible-reader: «Jeg leser bare Bibelen. Den er kraftig og sterk.» Borkman's strong sense of the uniqueness of himself and his vocation is, to my mind, more Pauline than Nietzschean. He feels deeply that he is chosen, called, and the «kallelse» for which he is «utvalgt,» is to release «de bundne millioner,» which «ropte på meg, skrek til meg om befrielse!» The call is made frighteningly concrete. A loud, insistent, shrieking call it is. No «wee small voice» but one thundering from Sinai. Sign of a serious neurosis perhaps, but perhaps not. After all, the shrieking turns into a song:

Der nede synger malmen. . . Når den blir løsnet. . . Derfor synger malmen – av glede – på sin vis.

But the loud call and the song, Borkman and Borkman alone hears. Is he, then, just «hearing things?» Are the songs he hears and the visions he sees merely the strange fruits of a disturbed psyche? Many good critics think so. I prefer to withhold judgment. It is, after all, nothing new to suggest that reality may have dimensions which can be grasped only through fantasy, only through imagination, only through the dream. It is interesting, by the way, to remember that in the most apocalyptic book of the Old Testament it is Gabriel who alone enables Daniel to understand his extraordinary vision. In the New Testament, we remember, Gabriel is the bearer of marvelous news – to Zanchery about the conception of John the Baptist and to Mary about the conception of Jesus. In each case the extraordinary event foretold is realized. The name Gabriel, incidentally, means «hero of God» – Gabrî'él. Whether Ibsen knew this or not, we shall never know. We know that he failed Greek in his *examen artium*. I don't think he even got a chance to fail Hebrew. Nevertheless we do know that his choice of names was usually quite deliberate. There must bave been some good reason for choosing such an un-Norwegian name as Gabriel! Be that as it may, John Gabriel Borkman feels that his call is unique to him: «Men ingen av alle de andre hørte det. Bare jeg alene.» The vocation sets him apart; he considers himself to be, as has been noted already, «et unntagelsesmenneske.» And Borkman's uniqueness is felt in terms of being, the uniqueness of the individual act of being: «Jeg er meg selv. . . Det er meg selv.» This uniqueness in being is the source of the uniqueness, eccentricity if you will, of action. (The principle again – *operatio sequitur esse.*) If another had done exactly what Borkman had done, the action itself would, nevertheless, have been different:

De hadde ikke evner som jeg. Og hadde de gjort det, så hadde de ikke gjort det med *mine* formål for øyne. Handlingen var da blitt en annen.

No one can perform *exactly* the same action as another. It is metaphysically impossible. I think there is profound truth here!

Most critics are hard on Borkman for using his uniqueness to justify himself and the destruction he spreads around him. He has little sense of the evil he has wrought – to those like Foldal, whose money he has misappropriated; to Ella, whose love he betrayed; and to Erhart, to whom he has been no father and whom he now only wants to use. Of his own son he says, «Ham kjenner jeg ikke» – terrible words, especially in light of the scriptural reference, this time to Peter's denial of Christ: «I know not the man.» (Peter fornektet ham og sa «Jeg kjenner ham ikke.» – Luke 22.57.) Gunhild seems to speak for most critics when she says: «Du har aldri elsket noe utenfor deg selv, – det er kjernen i det hele.» Yet Mrs. Borkman had already heard her husband maintain in words that may indicate either the most outrageous pride or the deepest charity that his «self» includes both her and Erhart: «Du og han kommer in under det jeg mener når jeg sier meg selv.» So Borkman sees every reason to exonerate himself: «Kort og godt – jeg har frikjent meg selv.» He is one chosen, set apart, predestined to a great work which he alone can accomplish; yet in his uniqueness he does not reject, but somehow includes in a strange other modality, those closest to him. Nevertheless, there is the appearance, certainly, of monstrous megalomania; and the reality of the destruction he causes: most believe that he richly deserves the prophecy and moral judgment which Ella ritually pronounces at the end:

Du har myrdet kjærlighetslivet i den kvinne som elsket deg, og som du elsket igjen. . . /med oppløftet arm/ Og derfor så spår jeg deg det, – John Gabriel Borkman, – du vinner aldri den pris du krevde for mordet. Du får aldri holde noe seiersinntog i ditt kolde, mørke rike.

The actions of a number of Ibsen's heroes are tragically destructive. It is almost as if the author senses that man's being itself is somehow flawed and the actions flowing from that being, no matter how high the ideals prompting them, are thus bound to be deeply flawed too. Again the principle – *operatio sequitur esse.* Yet act man must and act according to ideals. So the ultimate realization of these ideals can only be through flawed human actions, which cause suffering, destruction, and even death. But only after death is a new creation possible.

I think, at this point, two other considerations ought to be brought forward, and, finally, something should be said about Ella's last words. First – Borkman's calling, in the strict Pauline sense, provided his inescapable destiny. He was, if you will, predetermined by his vocation, and this vocation was a saving, freeing, ultimately joy-bestowing one. Borkman realizes this from the beginning; it is another aspect of his *anagnorisis.* In the course of the play the same recognition gradually dawns on us. Second – Borkman realizes, also early on, that his vocation involves the giving up, the sacrifice of human love. Since the flight is so precarious, there cannot be two up in the balloon, as he explains to Ella. The «forbundsliv – og lys og varme over sjelene,» which he seeks, is to be gained only at the cost of great suffering. Finally, I find Ella's conception at the end of the play of what is «best» for John Gabriel unequivocal enough at one level. Looked at more closely, however, it appears ambivalent. But at the deepest level, I think, it moves clearly towards the «epiphany» with which the play ends.

First then, Borkman's call, his vocation, was irresistible, «ubetvingelig:»

Den tvingende nødvendighet var over meg, Ella. . . Hadde ikke noe valg.

This is his answer to Ella's accusation of «selling her love for a directorship in a bank.» It is understandable that this is usually read as evidence of the man's being in the grip of uncontrollable passion, not sexual passion of course, but a lust for power: «Maktlysten var så ubetvingelig i meg, ser du! Og så slo jeg til. Måtte slå til.» The word «must» is used often by Borkman to describe the dynamism of his actions. Not free choice («valg») but some irresistible force impels him. «All the world knows,» says Gunhild in the Third Act, «how you have misbehaved.» Her husband replies:

Men den kjenner ikke *hvorfor* jeg har forgått meg. Menneskene skjønner ikke at jeg måtte det fordi jeg var meg selv, – fordi jeg var John Gabriel Borkman, – og ikke noen annen. Og det er *det* jeg vil prøve på å gi deg in forklaring over.

But this irresistible force, this moral imperative, is somehow not external to Borkman. He is not, I think, blindly following Schopenhauer's «Wille in der Natur.» The moral imperative comes from the very core of his being, and it is intimately related to his vocation, that is, the realization and connatural activity of his unique act of being. He tries desperately to explain all this, to get others to understand the existential foundation of his action, to explain that «higher considerations» (høyere hensyn») have taken over his life – dreadful and love-killing from one point of view but ultimately providing light and warmth for all mankind. There are, indeed, «høyere hensyn» which have taken over Borkman's life from the time he first heard the iron-ore calling after him and thus discovered his vocation, but these forces controlling his action do not remain external. They are internalized to become part of his very being, just as «the helpers and servers» become part of Solness's being and the commandment against adultery becomes part of Manders's being. But although internalized, these forces remain related to some external, albeit ideal, reality.

Now let us turn to a consideration of Borkman and Ella's love and the difference in perspective between their vision of things. Certainly they have different conceptions of serious sin. For Borkman «det infameste er venns misbruk av venns tillit.» For Ella, of course, it is closer to the heart: «Den store nådeløse synd. . .er å myrde kjærlighetslivet i et menneske.»

But even more to the point is the exchange between Borkman and Ella which follows the reference to «den store nådeløse synd:»

ELLA. Jeg spøkte med dine planer og spurte om du ville vekke alle gullets slumrende ånder.

BORKMAN /nikker/. Jeg kan huske det uttrykk. /langsomt/ Alle gullets slumrende ånder.

ELLA. Men du tok det ikke for spøk. Du sa: ja, ja, Ella, det er nettop *det* jeg vil.

BORKMAN. Det *var* det også.

We see that this exchange ends with another basic difference in point of view. Ella had mentioned jokingly «alle gullets slumrende ånder,» but they are no joke to Borkman. He latches on to Ella's metaphorical expression and, as it were, «literalizes» it. For Ella «gullets slumrende ånder» are symbols, dreams, metaphors; for Borkman they are real.[6] This is dramatized most effectively at the end of the play when Borkman tries to get Ella to see again the reality, the concrete details of the «drømmeland,» from their seat high above the fjord. For Ella the «drømmeland» is far in the past, and no detail of it can be distinguished any more, obliterated as it is with a blanket of snow; it is as dead as the old tree is dead:

Vårt livs drømmeland var det, ja. Og nu er det land snedekt. – Og det gamle tre er dødt.

But Borkman, entranced by his vision, does not hear the nay-sayer beside him:

BORKMAN /uten å høre på henne/. Kan du skimte røken av de store damp-skibene ute på fjorden?

ELLA. Nei. . .

BORKMAN. Jeg kan høre det.

ELLA /engstelig/. Jeg tror du tar feil, John.

Ella sees what there is to see – a dead tree and snow covering and thus obliterating all the distinctive features of the landscape. The woman is the realist, and her love, like her vision, is linked to the physical, to the

[6] Inga-Stina Ewbank (most recently in «Translating Ibsen for the Contemporary English Stage, *Theatre Research International,* Vol. II, No. 1, p. 50) has noted as one of the characteristics of Ibsen's mature style «the tendency to leap from everyday to visionary, from literal statement to metaphor.» Here it is even more: the concurrence of metaphor and literal statement. The «medium» conveys an important «message» about the characters.

dead tree and the dying man. Borkman recognizes the real, the physical world too, especially in his genuine love for Ella: «Som kvinne var du meg det dyreste i verden.» Ella agrees that she is moved only by feelings of the heart («bare din egen hjertesak», as Borkman says). «Bare den! Bare den! Det har du rett i,» Ella replies. Borkman confesses too that his feelings for Ella were really quite special; she could not at all be replaced by another woman, not by Gunhild or anyone else: this also is a suffering which must be borne. He must surrender the kind of life and the kinds of values embodied in Ella; these values, which he recognizes and loves, must be surrendered in view of «høyere hensyn.» But, as he says, «mine oppgaver i livet hjalp meg til å bære *det* også.» What were his «oppgaver i livet» for which he gave up so much?

Alt hva jord og fjell og skog og hav rommet av rikedomme − det ville jeg underlegge meg og skape herredømme for meg selv og derigjennem velvære for de mange, mange tusen andre.

Is it merely the dream of a proud man, of a megalomaniac? I have already cited Neitzsche. I need not again cite Christ's temptations in the wilderness, as other have done. But can we clearly distinguish, at least for another, between a Satanic temptation and a utopian dream? Borkman's is a dream of power, of course, and we know these dreams to be exceedingly dangerous. But it *does* take power to build a new world. Must we condemn all dreams of renewal, all utopian visions, every kingly thought? Thomas More, who gave us the word «Utopia», has been canonized. Borkman's great mistake (it is one he shared with Brand; one he did *not* share wit Thomas More) was his belief that he could «renew the face of the earth» all by himself. Radical renewal, like radical creation, does not belong to man, who must, in the words of Paul Tillich, have «the courage to accept his own finiteness.» Ibsen perceived this and gave us tragic heroes like Brand, Solness, and Borkman, whose *anagnorisis* never extended this far.

Borkman's dream has little to do with this earth. It does not materialize in the world of the living, as Ella recognizes. It somehow materializes a bit in the final vision of the steamships and the factories and in his death, when an ice hand becomes an iron-ore hand to take him. Metaphors like «all the sleeping spirits of gold» were real for him. For Ella, in the end, a metaphor becomes real too: «Det var en isnende malmhånd som tok ham i hjerte.»

Borkman does not doubt that the dream must be pursued even unto death. And in pursuing his dream, it should be remembered, he did not forget Ella. He still loved her. There are fleeting moments in the text when Ibsen, with great mastery, intimates their continuing understanding of and love for one another:

ELLA. . .Så mangen aften som vi talte om dine formål –
BORKMAN. Ja, med deg kunne jeg tale, Ella.

Then there is that unforgettable moment in the last act when Ella, despite her illness, decides to go out into the snow with Borkman:

ELLA /besluttet, kaster kåpen om seg/. Jeg går med deg, John.
BORKMAN. Ja, vi to, vi hører jo også sammen, vi, Ella.[7]

The quality of Borkman's tenderness is beautifully and delicately conveyed in the simple reply to his beloved: the thrice-repeated «vi's» the «ja» and the «jo» (strong words of affirmation), the «Ella» answering to the «John.» The ordinary words, so arranged in these lines, have the simplicity and power of the greatest poetry. (It is almost as good as the words of Ruth to Naomi; «Whither thou goest, I will go, and where thou lodgest, I will lodge. . . Where thou diest, will I die.») Borkman's language is not the language of a man who has sold his soul. He and Ella may belong together, but somehow the utter uniqueness of his vocation did not ultimately allow the lovers a shared vision and a shared life. He could not take his beloved on board the balloon for the perilous venture. Singlemindedly to pursue his dream and to set aside his deepest and irreplaceable human love was a «passion» which must be borne. «Mine oppgaver i livet hjalp meg til å bære *det* også.» The verb «å bære» is one Ibsen frequently uses to indicate the suffering, the passion, of his tragic heroes. Mrs. Alving's «dette bæres ikke» is repeated in many plays and in many contexts. Bjørn Hemmer sees Ibsen's early heroes – Svanhild and Falk, Skule, Brand, Peer Gynt, and Julian – as individuals choosing to follow a special calling at the expense of human fellowship. As he writes: «De kan ikke, åndelig sett, gå inn i et varig fellesskap.»[8] The same, I maintain, applies to Borkman. and his isolation from this world and its joys and its loves, involves incredible suffering; the isolation is a real «passion,» in the root meaning of the word.

[7] Ibsen, 561. Ingá-Stina Ewbank has written well of the difficulty in translating Borkman's line in the article referred to in Footnote 6.
[8] *«Brand,» «Kongs-emnerne,» «Peer Gynt»: En Studie i Ibsens Romantiske Diktning* (Oslo: University Press, 1972), 18.

But deeply involved in Borkman's passion is Ella's. For Ella, as we have seen above, the «hjertesak» is all-important. And now that loving heart has been crushed, even worse, sold for «the kingdom, the power, and the glory.» «Ja, *det* mener jeg,» says Ella. «Du har myrdet kjærlig-hetslivet i den kvinne som elsket deg. Og som du elsket igjen. . .» The famous prophecy follows:

Og derfor så spår jeg deg det, – John Gabriel Borkman, – du vinner aldri den pris du krevde for mordet. Du får aldri holde noe seiersinntog i ditt kolde, mørke rike.

Part of the tragedy, surely, is that both Ella and John Gabriel are right. They adhere to irreconcilable, but nonetheless real, values. Borkman, with genuine feeling, recognizes this: «Å, Ella – jeg vet snart ikke lenger hvem har rett – enten jeg eller du.» (Again, hardly the words of a devil or a megalomaniac.) Like Brand, Borkman is humanized throughout the play with many temptations to doubt. He does not pur-sue his extraordinary calling without many misgivings; if this were not so, he would cease to be human. He also fully recognizes the danger of self-doubt. «Vær da aldri så gal å tvile på Dem selv,» he admonishes Frida Foldal. It is obvious here that he is also admonishing himself.

Man's moral thinking and the actions flowing from this thinking can exist on more than one level, as Kierkegaard, among others, has taught us. We have the story of Abraham and Isaac. We have Christ making hatred of father, mother, wife, and children a condition for following him. A hunger strike is a sin against nature, suicidal, but for a cause it can become an heroic act. So also with sexual desire and romantic love. Obviously one can have the deepest experience of both and recognize their great value, but voluntarily set them aside, for a time or forever, in order that another set of values be realized. However, when a man does this, he is bound to suffer some frustration, discouragement, and doubt as to the reality of the values he is seeking. He will suffer the temptation to believe that he is, in fact, self-deceived, as others so readily judge him to be. This is part of his passion and must be borne. Borkman is certainly not deaf to the judgment his beloved Ella passes on him. He reacts to it both physically and verbally. As the stage direc-tion has it: «Han vakler hen til benken og setter seg tungt ned.» He then says: «Jeg frykter nesten at du får rett i den spådom, Ella.» This is Bork-man's final doubt, his last temptation against his vocation.

Ella answers significantly: «Du skal ikke *frykte* for *det,* John. Just *det* ville være det beste som kunne times deg!» It is best, then, that John Gabriel «never enter triumphant into his cold, dark kingdom.» Why does Ella say this? I am not sure. Is it that Borkman will have a chance to become more human if he is denied *triumphant* entry into his cold, dark kingdom? It is the mode of entry, not the fact of entry that is in question; he *must* enter his kingdom – there is no doubt about that. And enter it he does. Borkman lets out a cry and falls back exhausted. «Nu slapp den meg,» he gasps. The hand-of-ice-cum-hand-of-iron-ore lets him go, presumably into death. At first Ella intends to seek help in an effort to save him. She moves away for a moment; then she stops, comes back to Borkman, and feels his pulse. She knows that he is dead. Then, again, the word «best» is heard – softly but distinctly:

ELLA /*sakte og fast*/. Nei. Best så, John Borkman. Best så for deg.

The instinctive «nei» shows the very human reluctance to accept the fact of the death of a person one loves. As to the rest, is Ella simply repeating what she has said earlier? or has she now seen a certain triumph in Borkman's death? Does she realize that he has *had* his «seiersinntog» after all? Best not to call for help; best to let him die through the «isnende malmhånd.» I have the impression that Ella's final judgment on the man she loved («Best så, John Borkman. Best så for deg!») is, in a sense, a reversal of the first judgment. It *is* best that he die now, not that he live to love her, best that he die «for rikets – og maktens – og ærens skyld.» Ella now sees his death as a «seiersinntog.» This would be, then, *her* final *anagnorisis;* she sees at last that her broken heart *had* to be. And Borkman's death, now in a way triumphant, effects a reconciliation, a «soning,» more dramatically real than brought about by the death of little Eyolf. First come the simple words of reconciliation. As Inga-Stina Ewbank has pointed out, Gunhild and Ella can again use the first person plural – «vi.» And this pronoun signifying unity is repeated five times in the last four speeches of the play in «a veritable ritual of we's!»[9] Then the curtain falls as the twin-sisters, alienated for so long, reach out their hands towards one another. The conclusion of the play gives us a quiet, unforgettable dramatic image of peace, reconciliation, even love.

To conclude – Borkman's *anagnorisis,* as I see it, lies in his realization of the absolute demands of his vocation. He recognized these demands early in his career, at the time he rejected Ella, whom he loved, for

[9] Henrik Ibsen, *John Gabriel Borkman,* English Version by Inga-Stina Ewbank and Peter Hall, «Introduction,» (University of London, Athlone Press, 1975), 7.

Gunhild, who was merely useful to him. He realized that he could not share his vocation, as he could not share his being, with another. Although Ella was close to Borkman, belonging to him as it were and standing for very real human values, she could not share wholeheartedly his vision, as she could not share wholeheartedly his life. By the end, however, she had some intimation of Borkman's uniqueness, the absoluteness of his vocation, and the reality of his triumph. Borkman was faithful to his vocation in his attempt to realize his extraordinary vision, faithful to the end. The worth of his death is confirmed by its sacrificial aspect; in other words, it effects a reconciliation in which both deserted wife and deserted beloved share, reconciliation being the ultimate purpose of sacrifice. Borkman's dream was to bring «forbundsliv hele jorden rundt» thereby to create «lys og varme over sjelene i mange tusen hjem.» Ella says quietly, «And it remained a dream.» For her the dream is an unreality. Borkman repeats the same words, but gives them, it seems to me, quite another sense: «Det ble ved drømmen, ja.» «It remains a dream, yes,» but the dream itself has some reality of its own – an existence in the mind, and what exists in the mind can be realized outside the mind, as all artists know; a dream can be realized. Borkman hears the wheels of the factory turning, actually hears them; «Fabrikkene går.» He died once before the dream was realized, before he had taken possession of the inexhaustible riches of the earth; he dies this second time hearing and seeing «alle de som jeg ville skapt.» The dream is now becoming real for him. Indeed, all he sees and hears is just the beginning, «de utenverkene omkring riket.» He becomes more and more aware of the reality of this kingdom: «Jeg fornemmer dem, de bundne millioner, jeg føler malmårene, som strekker sine buktede, grenede, lokkende arme ut efter meg.» Here again the metaphors are *realized* in the mind of Borkman. The other aspect of the dream, the inner part of his kingdom – are «ære,» the «forbundsliv,» the «lys og varme over sjelene» – is entered into only at the end, in and through his death. At this point we have the final and most significant revelation of Borkman's *anagnorisis.* For us it amounts to a Joycean epiphany. For we see the beginning of the «forbundsliv,» the true «ære» of the kingdom in the reconciliation of Gunhild and Ella as they stretch out their hands towards one another over the dead body of John Gabriel Borkman. The evil done will be long a-mending; the human wreckage will not soon be restored; Ella may die before the restoration is complete; Erhart may not hurry back from the south to be reconciled to his mother. There is no brave Fortinbras from Norway standing in the wings to take over the kingdom, no Edgar immediately at hand to unify and bring peace to the realm. But Ella has surrendered her claim to Erhart, and Ella and Gunhild at last appear reaching out towards one another. The play ends, as do many great tragedies, with a distant sense of a new beginning. Best så. . . Best så.

The utter necessity

ARNE RØED

I

When Ibsen returned to Norway in 1891, he was a very famous man. His plays were translated into all civilized languages and performed all over the world; books and articles about him abounded; and he himself became a tourist attraction in Kristiania. He could be seen on most days at the Grand Café, and when he arrived, everybody stood up and remained standing, in deep silence, till the great man had sat down at a table permanently reserved for him,[1] on a chair that carried a silver plaque engraved Dr. Henrik Ibsen.[2] In fact, he was treated like royalty – even by the King himself. 'We are two kings here tonight', Oscar II is reputed to have said on one occasion.[3]

During this decade Ibsen wrote the four gloomiest plays of his career.

In these plays he seems to say that worldly success, fame, money, influence, admiration, were worth precisely nothing. And this applied not only to fame and the trappings of fame, but also to artistic achievment as such. In *When We Dead Awaken* Rubek says: '(....) all the talk about an artist's vocation and so on began to strike me as empty and hollow – as fundamentally meaningless.'[4]

Almost from the day of their publication it was felt that in these plays Ibsen was speaking about himself and the problems he had found himself faced with, as a man and an artist, towards the end of his career. This conclusion seems reasonable enough as regards Solness and Rubek – both of them artists – but Borkman seems a less likely candidate for an Ibsen self-portrait. While Ibsen's own biography in the end

[1] *Le Gallienne, Richard, quoted by Meyer, Michael: Henrik Ibsen*, vol. III, *The Top of a Cold Mountain*, London. 1971, pp. 257—8.

[2] A newspaper article about the Grand Hotel, Oslo, which I read many years ago. I have not been able to find any other reference to the information given.

[3] Koht, Halvdan: *Henrik Ibsen. Eit diktarliv*, I—II, Oslo 1954, p. 238; Meyer III, p. 293.

[4] *When We Dead Wake* in *Ghosts and Other Plays*, transl. Watts, Peter; Penguin Classics. London 1976, p. 259.

turned out to be an over-whelming success story, Borkman's ended in dishonour and a long prison sentence for fraud.

And yet, if we think of Borkman, not just as a businessman, but the businessman as an artist, we find that the three men have one thing in common: they all have committed some kind of treason against their own work. The question that arises must be: why was Borkman so much more harshly treated than the two others? And next: in what way does this utter condemnation reflect Ibsen's attitude to himself and his own work?

II

As a realistic play *John Gabriel Borkman* is deceptively simple: A rich banker and industrialist embezzles a fortune, is found out and sent to prison for a number of years, and after his release keeps himself imprisoned in his home, until he finally walks into the snow and dies.

A very simple story indeed, which has usually been interpreted, either as a comment on Nietzsche's superman philosophy, or as a study in frozen emotions, symbolized by the snow outside. Or both.

On closer inspection, however, this story soon ceases to be simple. There are some very strange circumstances attached to it.

We learn that as a young man Borkman was in love with one young woman, but then suddenly deserted her and married her *twin sister* instead. The reason, we are told, is that his friend and business partner, on whom his future as a businessman depended, also wanted to marry this girl, and demanded her in return for a directorship in the bank. So, in fact, he sold the woman he *loved* for a career.

But this is not all. When he, some years later, embezzled all the money he could lay his hands on, he left his former fiancée's money intact, whereas he staked his own and his wife's and the bank's money on his hazardous venture.

Stranger things still are revealed. It is his business partner who reports Borkman to the police, apparently as an act of revenge. According to Borkman the two had been so intimate that he had had no secrets from his friend, Hinkel, who must consequently have known everything about Borkman's embezzlement already at the planning stage, in which case he should have prevented it – or else been sent to prison along with his friend.

Another strange thing is Ella Rentheim's extraordinary idea that she is, somehow, the mother of Borkman's son; more so, in fact, than his mother in the flesh. She seems to regard this as more than a metaphor. Both women thus claim that they are the mother of the same child by the same father. The strangeness of the situation is enhanced by the fact that they are not only sisters, but twins.

Yet another strange thing is the fact that Borkman's only friend is an unproductive, barren poet, who wrote a tragedy in his youth, and after that never another word. He only tinkers with the old text in the vain hope that one day the play may be performed. He earns his living as a minor civil servant, but in Ibsen's draft he is a pharmacist, which seems interesting in view of the fact that Ibsen himself started his career as a dramatist by writing a tragedy when he, as a young man, was a pharmacist's apprentice.

Finally we have in this play a sub-plot that seems to have little to do with the main action. Borkman's son runs away from his depressing surroundings in the company of a rich and beautiful woman whose lover he seems to have been for some time. And they are bringing with them a young girl, a gifted pianist, who turns out to be no other than the daughter of Borkman's friend, the barren poet. Since Ibsen was a superb craftsman, the possibility must be considered that this is more than a subplot loosely tacked on to the tragedy of a businessman who broke the law.

III

The following analysis of *John Gabriel Borkman* is based on two assumptions:

1. That it is not just a realistic play, but a fusion of realistic play and allegory, both at the same time, and the two complement each other; and

2. that its theme is Ibsen's conviction, at the end of his working life, that he, too, had betrayed his own work. It is an intensely personal play, part of Ibsen's spiritual autobiography, yet another session in his perpetual judgment day.

In the *Ibsen Yearbook 1977* I have set out, with a fair amount of documentation, my reasons for believing that Ibsen made extensive use of allegory in his last four plays.[5] There is not time to repeat them here. I only want to make one point:

A literary analysis cannot be *proved* correct. Nor does it prove anything, but it *can* be made to seem more or less *probable,* and the most probable interpretation is the one that takes into account most of the details contained in the text, and answers the largest number of questions the text gives rise to.

[5] *Ibsenårbok 1977,* pp. 123—126.

Ibsen 's last four plays contain a great many strange details that, so far at any rate, do not seem capable of being convincingly integrated in a coherent purely realistic interpretation. Critics have therefore tended to pass them by in silence, or else assigned to them a vague and unspecified symbolic function. However, these details do take on very precise meaning within a fully developed allegorical framework.

A suitable starting point for our analysis of *John Gabriel Borkman* is a scene in the play that seems to cry out for an allegorical interpretation. It is, quite appropriately, the climax of the play in the third act, where Erhart turns up with Mrs Wilton and announces that they are going away together. Here Borkman, too, emerges from his isolation, so for the first time all the major characters confront each other face to face. This, as one would expect, causes a considerable stir, but the important thing is the altercation that immediately flares up between the two sisters. To Gunhild only one thing matters: not for a moment has she doubted that Erhart's only task in life is to restore the family honour and undo the disgrace his father has brought on their name. So at this moment she takes it for granted that all she has to do, is to remind him:

Are you forgetting what you have pledged your life to?

(348)

But Ella Rentheim believes that he belongs first and foremost to her:

Erhart, I can't bear to lose you. For I tell you, I am solitary and dying. (. . .) Will you be with me till the end? Join yourself to me entirely? Be for me as if you were my own child?

(347)

At this stage Borkman stakes his claim:

I've tried to help myself out of it with dreams and hopes (. . .) all these years. But (. . .) I'll have done with dreams (. . .) Lift myself up again, that's what I'll do. Begin from the bottom again (. . .) by work (. . .) Erhart, will you join me and help me with this new life?

(349—50)

What we are witnessing here is not just a clash between two possissive women who want him for their own, specific purposes, and Borkman, when he finally speaks, does not change the situation in any way: he just joins the battle as a third contestant for his son's allegiance.

This scene represents an allegorical confrontation: Almost as in a fairy-tale a young man is offered the choice of three different tasks to which he is invited to dedicate his life, but characteristically chooses a fourth – the arms of the woman with whom he is in love.

If this interpretation is further investigated, the two twin sisters become more than two unhappy women fighting for the love and loyalty of a selfish young man who runs away from them both. Since each of them claims to be the mother of the same child by the same father, they can be seen as influences in Borkman's life, the inspirations that formed his destiny, and the struggle between them is the struggle as to which of them was going to be behind what Borkman created.

They are sisters because they both demand to have the same function, viz. to be the inspiration that determined the character of Borkman's work; and they are two different personalities because they stand for two diametrically opposed attitudes to life. They are twins because the demarcation line between these attitudes, in spite of all, is far from easy to draw. They cannot be kept wholly apart: somehow they intertwine, and that is what constitutes the tragedy inherent in the whole situation.

The characters in the play can, allegorically, be seen as aspects of Borkman's personality – its various strivings and conflicting aims. In *The Master Builder* Ibsen used this device for the first time in its fully developed form, but in *Borkman* he finds it necessary to produce an even more complex version of it. The persons reflecting Borkman's personality do not just do so singly; they are members of groups, in themselves comprising different aspects of the basic attitudes that represent the sad chaos of Borkman's personality.

There are three such groups.

The first consists of Gunhild and Hinkel, who, though he does not appear on the stage, must, like Captain Alving in *Ghosts,* and Beate in *Rosmersholm,* be considered a character in the play. They represent the two components of ambition – Hinkel the power urge, and Gunhild the vanity without limits.

The second group comprises Ella and Foldal. They stand for Borkman the artist, the lover of music, the visionary, the young man with his altruistic dreams, the awareness of spiritual values. But Frida, too, is a member of this group. She, the daughter of the barren poet, is a gifted, a *real* artist. And that links her to the third group, Erhart and Mrs Wilton. These three stand for the future generation, for Ibsen's stubborn desire and undying dream that his artistic vision would one day come true.

Ella represents the spiritual values that Borkman – and Ibsen – betrayed, and can thus be seen as a reincarnation of Aline Solness. She stands for Borkman's desire to achieve something that would benefit everybody, not only himself. But here the fatal problem arises. Even the ambition to do good is ambition. And – most important – there can be no clear distinction between selfish ambition and altruistic ambition. Both ambition and the desire for power are necessary qualities in a person who wants to serve mankind on a large scale. That is why Gunhild and Ella are twins: the twin faces of ambition. When Borkman married Gunhild, he was captured by selfish ambition.

Everybody who wants to create something, even such a seemingly prosaic thing as a business, must have something of the artist in him. Without the artist's imagination and urge to create he gets nowhere. This aspect of Borkman's personality manifests itself in his love of music, but above all it is represented by Foldal. This barren poet is also one of Borkman's victims. Not only did he lose his savings in Borkman's bankruptcy; something much worse happened to him on the allegorical plane.

Here he is Borkman's double, representing the dead artist in him, the part of Borkman that died when he exchanged one woman for another, thereby also exchanging one inspiration for another.

On this decisive evening their carefully constructed dreamworld comes to and end. 'Haven't you sat here, putting hope and faith and trust in me?' Borkman asks. – 'They weren't lies as long as *you* believed in *my* vocation', says Foldal. 'As long as you believed in me, I believed in you.' (324)

These very strange words may be construed thus: as long as the man of action believes in the ideals the poet stands for, so long the poet has the power to inspire. It all depends on whether the man of action accepts the ideals. If not, the poet loses his power to inspire, and with it his faith in the man of action – all of which means that if the man of action destroys the artist in himself, he also destroys himself as a man of action.

IV

Borkman, as we meet him on the last evening of his life, is a man who has committed two crimes: one – the desertion of the woman he loved, and, two – a crime in the legal sense of the word, for which the law could, and did, punish him.

The way Ibsen handles these two crimes, however, they seem to merge into one. And that, in a way, is what they are – their common denominator is treason, and the punishment for both is the same: isolation. Isolation is the essence of prison life, but when Borkman sold the woman he *loved,* he also isolated himself from *both* the deep emotional contact with a live human being, *and* the intellectual contact with the source of his inspiration. That is why he is such an utterly lonely man – a loneliness that manifests itself in his inability to go back into the world after his release. All that is left is his insane daydream that the world will in the end have to come to him and beg him to return.

V

But if Ibsen had himself in mind when he created Borkman, what is the connection between the two? Strangely enough the answer seems clear if we remember that Ibsen's career is sharply divided into two very different periods.

The great break in Ibsen's career was the publication of *The Pillars of Society* in 1877, which introduced what is known as his realistic period. It came after a long struggle with *Emperor and Galilean,* which had resulted in a pause of four years, during which he made the momentous decision to adopt a new technique and devote himself to new themes.

By the early 'nineties Ibsen had come to look on this break with the past as a betrayal of his calling as a creative writer. He felt that behind his early work he had had a grand, coherent vision of life, which was to be given its final and complete expression in *Emperor and Galilean.* But during his work on this drama something went wrong. The ultimate vision escaped him, and he lost his faith in God. As a consequence of this he abandoned his attempt to get his grand vision into focus, and used the bits and pieces he could salvage from it as themes for separate 'problem plays' in a contemporary setting.

In my analysis of *The Master Builder* [6] I have tried to identify the ingredients of this vision, and shall not repeat them here. Suffice it to mention the main point: Ibsen felt equally strongly drawn to two opposed ideas of life. On the one hand the one embodied in the strong character who would devote himself to a cause and make any sacrifice for that cause, in fact a purely spiritual attitude, which can loosely be called puritanism because it must be based on self-discipline and self-sacrifice. It is most clearly exemplified in Brand. On the other hand Ibsen could never abandon the dream of an earthly paradise whose inhabitants were able to enjoy the life of the senses fully and without guilt feelings

---

[6] Ibid. pp. 122—179.

of any kind in a free and uninhibited abandonment to hedonism –
'the beautiful pagan sin'[7], as the young Julian calls it.

The conflict between the two runs through most of Ibsen's mature
drama from *Brand* to *When We Dead Awaken*. The important point, however, is that Ibsen refused to see this as an insoluble and essentially
tragic conflict which could only lead to disaster. Ibsen wanted to see
both attitudes reconciled in a human being strong enough to embrace
both in a synthesis between body and soul, God and the world, Emperor and Galilean, hedonism and puritanism.

When Ibsen failed to create this synthesis in *Emperor and Galilean*, he
began, after a pause of four years, to write his realistic modern plays,
but he felt that this switch was a betrayal of the dream that had been
with him for so long, and in his last four plays he returns to it. In *The
Master Builder* he is mainly concerned with his attempt to recapture it, in
Little Eyolf he explores the dream itself. In *John Gabriel Borkman* his theme
is the betrayal as such, its nature and underlying causes. It is the most
merciless of the group.

VI

Ibsen's 'crime', as he himself felt it, was, like Solness's and Borkman's,
embezzlement. Unable to use his grand vision the way providence had
intended, he had appropriated it for more mundane purposes: he had
divided it up and staked the pieces in a totally different gamble.

Unlike Borkman's, Ibsen's gamble came off as far as his career was
concerned, but his feeling of having failed in a deeper sense must have
been complete, leaving him with a sense of guilt so overwhelming, that
it can only be explained by assuming that to him poetry was more than
art. It was a calling in a religious sense. The poet should be a seer, a
prophet, his task should be to change the world, even human nature.
When he wrote to Brandes that what was needed was a 'menneskeåndens revoltering', he was in deadly earnest: he meant it literally. The
revolution of the human spirit. Nothing less would do.

One of the central characters in Ibsen's work, if not *the* central character, is the person who feels it as his duty and vocation to change the
world – the 'world-improver', the 'world betterer'. This character returns again and again in Ibsen's work. Vaguely present in *The Preten-
ders,* he erupts in *Brand* and fails pathetically in *Emperor and Galilean*. In
The Wild Duck he becomes a bitter, satirical portrait – many think a
self-portrait of the author. In *Rosmersholm* he occurs twice: in Rosmer,

[7] *Emperor and Galilean*, the Oxford Ibsen, vol IV, p. 241.

who wanted to create – yes, *create* – 'noblemen of the spirit', and in Ulrik Brendel, who is a tragic-satirical caricature of a prophet who at the critical moment discovers that the ideas he thought he had in him simply did not exist – but a would-be world-betterer all the same. But above all: Ibsen regarded himself as a world-betterer. That was his vocation. That or nothing.

It is against the background of this vast ambition the deep gloom of Ibsen's last period must be seen. He felt that he had, not so much failed as an artist, as betrayed his calling.

When he abandoned his grand vision of the ideal human existence he committed the unforgivable sin, he gave up his struggle for man's soul, and found himself reduced to taking up separate aspects of his activities in their social context. To Ibsen this was his fall from grace, for man without his soul has no meaningful function in any society. Whatever he does is completely trivial, seen in relation to what has been lost. Henrik Ibsen's enormous sense of failure and guilt, which he at this stage felt he could only express adequately in the portrait of an insane and powerless megalomaniac who thought he had a right to do anything he found necessary in order to further his own ends, *and* in the portrait of this megalomaniacs double, a barren poet who has only one theme, which he rearranges endlessly because he is unable to think new thoughts.

Borkman has betrayed not only the woman he *loved,* but everything she stood for – his altruistic dream, his inspiration. In the same way Ibsen felt that he had betrayed what *he* loved most, the thing that meant most to him, his grand vision, his calling as a world-betterer.

Borkman tells Ella that she had been 'the dearest thing in the world' to him. Applied to Ibsen, this means that his vision, his calling, had been the most important thing in his life, and, like Borkman, he had sold it for a mess of pottage.

We now come to a very important point. The fact that Borkman did not touch Ella's money, means, allegorically, that Ibsen thought he had kept the core of his vision intact, put it in the deep-freeze, so to speak, for future use. The irony of the situation is palpable. Borkman, having rejected Ella's spiritual gift, ends up by owing his *material* welfare to her, whereas Ibsen becomes rich and famous on what he had stolen, while the core of his vision disappeared completely, just like Ulrik Brendel's unwritten works.

However, the strength of Ibsen's drama is still due to the fact that the bits and pieces also belonged to his elusive vision. What Ibsen found impossible to achieve, was to create people who could express his synthesis in convincing art. The bits and pieces, on the other hand, were far less elusive, and could form the substance of his realistic drama: will-power, obedience to a vocation, readiness to make sacrifices and, above all, honesty, especially intellectual honesty.

VII

No other character in Ibsen's work has been so utterly condemned by his creator as Borkman. Bearing in mind the identity between the two, we may ask why Ibsen saw himself in such a merciless light.

It is here necessary to take into account how severely Borkman is judged. According to Ella he has committed the sin for which there is no forgiveness, he has exchanged what was dearest in the world to him for a career; he has murdered his own soul and hers. When he tries to defend himself, he says he had done it for 'higher considerations' – though he immediately modifies this to 'other considerations'. What emerges out of their conversation is that the task Borkman had embarked upon, was something he rated more highly than life, something that constituted a higher consideration than love, and which, apart from everything else, represented a necessity from which there was no possible escape. 'Den tvingende nødvendighed' he calls it, 'the utter necessity.'

We are still not told what this utter necessity was, nor the character of the 'higher considerations' that had determined his choice.

One thing, however, is plain. A businessman need not solely be a person who wants to make as much money as possible. He may be an artist who is trying to create a firm, a business empire, riches that may benefit his country.

Borkman was the businessman as an artist, and it is this artistic side of Borkman that forms the link between Borkman and Ibsen himself. The tenseness of the dialogue sounds less hysterical and neurotic if we think, not of a tycoon, but of an artist. Only then will such expressions as 'higher considerations' and 'life is not always the dearest' etc. make full sense.

If we, instead of a businessman and the woman he deserted, see Ibsen and his grand moral-artistic vision, everything becomes plain and meaningful.

But now we are in for a shock. When told about the 'utter necessity', many of us will immediately expect to be taken back to *Emperor and Galilean*. In the third act of part one, Julian asks:

JULIAN. What is my calling?

A VOICE IN THE LIGHT. You shall establish the empire.
JULIAN. Which empire?
VOICE. The Empire.
JULIAN. And in what way?
VOICE. By way of freedom.
JULIAN. Tell me all! What is the way of freedom?
VOICE. The way of necessity.
JULIAN. And by what power?
VOICE. By *villing.*
JULIAN. *What* shall I will?
VOICE. What you *must.* [8]

Borkman, however, did not belong in these dizzy metaphysical heights. His 'utter necessity' was not a result of him being chosen to be the tool of Providence, destined to carry out a momentous and necessary act, as, for instance Judas Iskariot.

What we are told is quite simply this:

The desire for power was irresistible in me, and so I agreed. *Had* to agree.

(333)

Ibsen gives Borkman no other excuse. His betrayal had been a completely selfish act. Desire for power, that was all, that was his 'utter necessity'. It is the shallowness, the absolute emptiness of his explanation that makes Ibsen's condemnation of Borkman so final and so merciless. But what about Ibsen himself?

We do not know what was in Ibsen's mind when he, during his work on *Emperor and Galilean,* realized that the grand vision was beyond his grasp. It was probably a mixture of guilt and relief, but be that as it may, two things can hardly be disputed. Looking back from 1896 Ibsen knew that he had indeed wielded power. He had changed the whole course of world drama, and, also become rich and famous – everything, in fact, that Borkman had wanted, but failed to achieve. However, he may also very well have felt that these things were a poor substitute for his grand vision: he had exchanged the world of the spirit for worldly success. Instead of the prophet, the 'world-betterer', he had become a successful dramatist, and even though *A Doll's House* and *Ghosts* undoubtedly had contributed towards changing the world, they still fell short of what he had really set out to do. It is, to repeat what has already been

[8] Ibid. p. 258.

said, against Ibsen's vast ambition to be a moral influence, that the gloom of his last four plays must be seen and judged.

But in one respect Ibsen had a greater right to be forgiven by himself than Borkman had. 'The utter necessity' was in his case infinitely more compelling than in Borkman's. It was inescapable. Borkman was both an artist and a businessman, and perhaps first and foremost a businessman. But Ibsen was nothing but an artist, and he could never cease to be one. After his experience with *Emperor and Galilean* Ibsen was exhausted and at a loose end. It took him four years to reeover. But he *had* to get over it, for he *had* to go on creating. No real artist can stop his urge to create. This is the real 'utter necessity'. He had to go on, somehow. He did. The absolution he refused himself, posterity, equally compelled, has had to give him.

VIII

Strangely enough, this play is not all gloom. Ibsen was so obsessed with his vision that he could never give it up completely. Also here a certain hope for the future is held out.

There is a third group of characters, so far barely mentioned, consisting of Erhart, Mrs Wilton and Frida Foldal. Frida thus belongs to two groups and forms the link between the past and the future.

The play has in a way two final scenes; or rather, the second half of the last act can be regarded as an epilogue, whereas the real end of the play is to be found in the dramatic scenes in the third and first half of the fourth acts, where all the characters are finally confronted with one another, and even Foldal turns up again for a last, but significant appearance.

In this confrontation Erhart refuses to serve any of the three members of the older generation. He has found his own aim in life, which, on the face of it, may seem both banal and irresponsible. After a recent London revival one critic put it like this: 'He slips off to a warmer climate with the local siren.'[9] Mrs Wilton may well be the local siren, but there is much more to her than that.

Although she only appears in two brief scenes she is drawn with great care, and her function in the play prepared with the utmost precision even before she enters.

Ibsen takes great pains to establish that she is not a virtuous woman. Erhart has obviously been her lover for some time when the play begins; their relationship would be meaningless if we were to suppose

[9] Robert Cushman, *The Observer*, 2.2. 1975.

that he had not, and they have now decided to go abroad in order to live together in greater freedom. And they are bringing Frida with them.

We are also told that they have no intention of marrying, and she, at any rate, does not expect their relationship to last for a life-time. It is an affair, not a marriage. Allegorically Mrs Wilton stands for pure hedonism.

But the story does not end there. One may well ask what Frida is doing in this context, since Erhart and Mrs. Wilton undoubtedly could enjoy their affair without her. In fact, she is likely to be more of an encumbrance than a chaperone, which they are obviously not in need of anyway.

The answer is that she, too, is part of the allegorical structure. At the very end of the act a completely new perspective is opened up:

MRS BORKMAN /*with an evil smile*/. Mrs Wilton, do you think you are really acting wisely in taking that young girl with you?
MRS WILTON /*returning the smile, half ironically, half seriously*/. Men are so changeable, Mrs Borkman. And so are women. When Erhart is finished with *me* – and *I* with him – it will be as well for both that[10] he, poor dear, has someone to fall back on.
MRS BORKMAN. But what about yourself?
MRS WILTON. Oh, I shall manage all right, you know.

(355)

In other words, Mrs Wilton is only going to be a stage in Erhart's development. Her role will be that of preparing him for Frida. After his liberation, through Mrs Wilton's hedonism, from all ties and obligations forced upon him by his oppressive home atmosphere, and the ensuing guilt feelings, he will be ready for Frida and what she stands for.

Frida, as we have already seen, also belongs to a group consisting of her father, Ella Rentheim and herself. They represent the artistic and spiritual part of Borkman's character, which he had betrayed. It is going to blossom forth in the new generation: *his* son and Foldal's daughter: once again the synthesis of hedonism and puritanism.

The remarkable thing about these conversations is how definite it is all taken to be. Although none of it can very well be more than a possibility and a hope, the two women, especially Mrs Wilton, seem to take for granted that it will happen.

Secondly, what happens has a spectacular effect on Foldal. He is

[10] Ibsen's text has *at* (= that) not *hvis* (= if); a point missed by the translator.

brought back to life again for a brief moment. Almost incoherent with joy when he stumbles out of the snow after having been run over by Mrs Wilton's sledge he still manages to say the words that gather together the various strands of the action:

FOLDAL /*radiantly happy*/. Your son, John Gabriel! Is he to go with them?
BORKMAN. Yes. It's he who's to help Mrs Wilton to educate your little Frida.
FOLDAL. Now God be praised! Then the child is in the best of hands.

(368)

We also notice the complicated way the thing is put: 'help Mrs Wilton to educate your little Frida! For Frida, too, will have to be prepared for her life with Erhart. Mrs Wilton's sensualism will have to be an essen¹ial part of Frida's as well as Erhart's development.

There is a note of triump in this scene, and Borkman contributes to it. He assures Foldal that as to the sledge in which the three are driving away, 'everything is genuine. Both outside – and in' (363). The last, rather surprising word must be a reference to the people in the sledge. They will not come to grief, for they are honest in their enterprise, and Frida is a *real* artist.

IX

In addition to the allegorical elements there are two, let's call them 'ordinary', symbols used in the play: the snow, symbolizing the frozen emotions that destroy Borkman and the two women in his life; and metal ore. Unlike the English word, the Norwegian 'malm' is a weighty and sonorous word, well suited for symbolic use. But in the play it also occurs as both gold and silver. Gold stands for wealth and all the temptations wealth entails. As silver it represents spiritual values. It is significant that Ella's hair is silver white.

When Borkman dies, the hand that grips him is a metal hand, a *malmhånd*, the common denominator of both gold and silver, implying that both had determined his destiny. But when the younger generation drives away, it is the *silver* that can sing at last:

BORKMAN /. . ./ did you notice the silver bells?
FOLDAL /. . ./ Silver bells, you say? Were they silver bells? Real, genuine silver bells?
BORKMAN. You can be sure of that.

(Ibid)

In order that the fact may really sink in, the word is repeated three

167

times in three lines, and once more six lines further on. It is a pity that Rolls Royces,[11] however old, are not equipped with silver bells. They are obviously important, for now they make Foldal, the barren poet, feel that he has won his victory as last:

FOLDAL /*with quiet emotion*/. Isn't it wonderful, how happily things can work out for a person! It's my – my little gift for poetry that's turned to music in Frida. And so I haven't been a poet in vain, after all.

(Ibid)

This is not only an old man who has been overwhelmed with unexpected happiness. It is Borkman's artistic double. And that is brought out in a most spectacular way. During this brief scene, for a few minutes, Borkman becomes human again. The kind, altruistic Borkman is somehow released by the dramatist. It is he who introduces the silver bells into the conversation, and he treats his old friend with something approaching love. 'Gamle venn' – 'my old friend' are his last words to him.

Quotations are taken from Ibsen, Henrik: *John Gabriel Borkman* in *The Master Builder and Other Plays*, transl. *Una Ellis-Fermor, Penguin Classics, London 1958.*

[11] In Norwegian Television's *John Gabriel Borkman* (1978, director Per Bronken), which was shown at the Seminar, the action has been brought forward to the 1920's, and Mrs Wilton provided with a Rolls Royce.

Eight Ibsen Plays and a Modern Japanese Drama *A Vicarage*
A Study of Influence

TOSHIHIKO SATO

In the Twentieth Century, Ibsen has become so well known throughout the world that, without considering this dramatist, we hardly could study of modern drama in any country; indeed, Ibsen had much influence over modern European and American playwrights. But, how about that in Orient? In Orient, especially in Japan, after having been introduced as early as in 1892, he played an important role in the formation on modern Japanese theater, providing a model for Japan's new drama which was seeking a more intellectual drama with life coursing in its veins. This is the reason why Ibsen, as in the West, has been considered as «the father of modern drama» in Japan; and, many young playwrights of Japan have learned Ibsen's ideas and dramatic techniques which they utilized in their own productions. Among them was Kichizo Nakamura (1877—1941), the author of *A Vicarage* (1910), a modern drama dealing with modern Japanese religious corruption.

In this paper, I propose to study Ibsen's eight plays and Nakamura's *A Vicarage* and detect the influence of the former on the latter. Although there are many aspects and points for discussion, time and space are limited here and therefore I will examine only some parallels and resemblances in the characters and scenes of *A Vicarage* and Ibsen's *Brand, The Master Builder, A Doll's House, The Lady from the Sea, Ghosts, Little Eyolf, The Wild Duck* and *Rosmersholm*.

I

Bokushi no Ie (A Vicarage) is a three act play with seven characters. After his wife Toshiko dies, Fujiwara, a minister, decides to marry a wealthy lady Kaneko. Kaneko built Fujiwara's new church, helping him financially, as he had wished for many years, but right before the completion of the church, Toshiko's son Shinichi falls from the tower of the church and dies. Discovering that Shinichi's death was due to the urge of Mariko, Kaneko's daughter, and that his wife Kaneko whom Fujiwara had earnestly believed as a fine lady, was an exprostitute in America, Fujiwara becomes upset and comes to lose his faith in God. Since then, the church begins to look like a sphinx to Fujiwara. He cries out desparately, «I am a sphinx, too.»

Now I will analyze the characters of the Japanese play *A Vicarage* and Ibsen's eight plays and point out parallels and similarities:

a) Brand and Fujiwara. In *Brand,* Brand had the church built by spending all the money he had inherited from his mother, just as Kaneko, Fujiwara's wife in *A Vicarage,* spent all her savings for an identical purpose. Both churches were constructed without donations from other sources. There are another parallels between the two: In Act III of *A Vicarage,* Fujiwara says that he was an earnest Christian like Job and sacrificed all his fortunes and family in order to missionize Christianity, while Brand sought all or nothing, victimezing everything.

b) Fujiwara and Solness. In *A Vicarage* we find Fujiwara who wants to have a high tower for the new church, just as Solness in *The Master Builder* desired to have a spire on his new home.

c) Shinichi and Eyolf. Nakamura used a silent character Shinichi for the sake of economy. Although Shinichi, a boy with weak legs, born to Fujiwara by a previous marriage, does not appear on the stage, he nevertheless plays an important role in the action; he fell to his death from the newly constructed tower before the play begins. This reminds us of Eyolf in *Little Eyolf,* a cripple who plunged from the edge of a pier and drowned.

d) Kaneko and Mrs. Alving. Kaneko, Fujiwara's second wife, has built the towering church that Fujiwara wanted. She meant, by offering her money, to wash away her shameful past. This can be attributed to the fact that Nakamura had a character Mrs. Alving of *Ghosts* in his mind at the time of creation: Mrs. Alving in fact had an orphanage built, «Captain Alving's Foundation,» in attempting of cancelling out her miserable life with her debauched husband.

e) Mariko and Ellida, Rita, Hilda, and Hedvig. Mariko bears comparison with characters in *The Master Builder, The Lady from the Sea, Little Eyolf* and *The Wild Duck.* An illigitimate daughter of Kaneko, Mariko has a strong curiosity about and yearning for the ocean vastness. Thus she becomes interested in a ship captain Ushio since she regards him as a transfiguration of the mysterious sea itself, and finally goes away with him. Her fascination with the sea and interest in the seaman certainly are patterned after Ellida in *The Lady from the Sea,* who was obsessed by an idea that her fate was to join her old fiance a seamen, because she belonged to the sea.

However, Mariko's more substantial model is Hilda of *The Master Buil-*

der: the daemonic Hilda, delighted in diverting a husband's attention from his wife, insists on Solness's climbing a high tower to destruction, is recalled in Mariko when she drives Shinichi to his death in a similar way. She explains her motive as her wish to become Fujiwara's only child. Like Hilda who had just such an attachment and influence on a much older man, Solness, Mariko is in love with her step-father Fujiwara, and she does not hesitate to express it at the catastrophic moment. In fact Nakamura mentioned about her that she «is partly modeled after Hilda Wangel of *The Master Builder*. . . She was meant to be, as such, an incarnation of the liberalism, or personification of the individual, or individualization of the romantic spirit of man. She is half human and half symbol.»[1]

Furthermore, Mariko, in her jealousy of Shinichi, resembles Rita in *Little Eyolf* and Hedvig in *The Wild Duck*. Rita's husband Allmers, has a sister Asta, whom he loves a great deal. In their adolescence, he used to call Asta «big brother Eyolf,» pretending he had a boy chum in order to cover up his childish shame of having only a sister instead of a brother. When Rita is told by Allmers why he had named his pride, his precious baby Eyolf, Rita cannot help feeling jealous of her own child, as it was named in memory of Asta.

In *The Wild Duck,* Hedvig, a girl of fourteen with weak sight, throws additional light on Mariko. Hedvig's mother Gina once had an affair with a much older man Werle who subsequently married her off to Hjalmar Ekdal. When Hjalmar finds out that Hedvig is not his child, he drives Hedvig away with a hatred which Hedvig cannot understand. Desparately she tries to regain her father's love. Gregers, a good friend of Hjalmar, and like most of Ibsen's idealists, a bungler, suggests to Hedvig that she sacrifice her most precious possession – a wild duck. Unable to kill her duck, Hedvig shoots herself instead. As Shoyo Tsubouchi (1859—1935), a modern Japanese critic and playwright, said, «We may say that Mariko was created from Hilda of *The Master Builder,*»[2] Nakamura has obviously created in Mariko a character based on Rita of *Little Eyolf* and Hedvig of *The Wild Duck*.

f) Ushio and the Stranger and Krogstad. Kinpei Ushio is another character who has Nakamura's source in two Ibsen plays *The Lady from the Sea* and *A Doll's House*. The Stranger of *The Lady from the Sea,* a boatswain

---

[1] Nakamura Kichizo, «Jojosaretaru Shakaigeki,» *Kabuki,* quoted in Ochi Haruo, «Taishoki no Gikyoku,» *Kokugo to Kokubungaku,* vol. 38 (Oct. 1962), 29.

[2] Tsubouchi Shoyo. *Ibusen Kenkyu* (Tokyo: Okochi-Shoten, 1948), edited by Kawatake Shigetoshi, pp. 291—292.

to whom Ellida was once engaged, appears again to Ellida, now Mrs. Wangel. In Nakamura's play, Ushio, once a customer of the prostitute Kaneko, appears again to Kaneko, now Mrs. Fujiwara. Ushio also plays the same role as the villain Krogstad in *A Doll's House*, who threatens Nora.

g) Fujiwara and Hjalmar Ekdal. In the end of Act II in *A Vicarage*, when Fujiwara learns about his wife's past life and the source of the money with which they built the church, he is tormented by the fact that he was deceived. Here we find another Fujiwara among Ibsen models, Hjalmar Ekdal in *The Wild Duck* who discovered Gina's past; Hjalmar, trembling with rage, cries to his wife; «How could you keep a thing like that hidden from me!»[3]

h) Fujiwara and Kaneko, Rita and Allmers. After a night of torment and introspection, Fujiwara and Kaneko resolve that, since they have lost both his son and her daughter, they will be partners in operating a home for children of former prostitutes. Although this can be comparaed to the orphanage project in *Ghosts,* it is more than that; this is the decision that Rita and Allmers make at the end of *Little Eyolf.* At the loss of their Eyolf, Rita is determined to take all poor neglected children to herself to fill the gap left by Eyolf's death: Allmers volunteers to help in her task.

II

Now let us briefly look at scenes in *A Vicarage* and Ibsen plays for comparison; there are, roughly speaking, two kinds of parallels exist: 1) the beginning scenes in *A Vicarage* and *Ghosts;* and 2) four sets of confrontation scenes of the new and old generation in *A Vicarage* and *Ghosts, Brand, Rosmersholm* and *A Doll's House.*

a) the beginning scenes of the two plays *A Vicarage* and *Ghosts.* In *Ghosts* and *A Vicarage,* Act I begins with the completion of the new building: one on the day of celebration, and the other on the day before the celebration.

b) confrontation scene I: Fujiwara and Ueda vs. Brand and the Dean, and Rosmer and Kroll. The religious confrontation scenes between Fujiwara and Morito Ueda is similar to that between Brand and the Dean in *Brand* and Rosmer and Kroll in *Rosmersholm.*

The confrontation scenes of the new and old as seen in *Brand* are as follows:

[3] Henrik Ibsen. *Rosmersholm and The Wild Duck.* Translated by James W. McFarlane (London: Oxford University Press, 1960), p. 203.

172

THE DEAN. . . . They drew not in the common yoke /Grew Personalities, in short. That's half the twofold core that lies/. Embedded in this shell of fable; − /That all strength sever'd, is unstable, And deathdoomed who the world defies./ When God desires a man to fall/ He makes him an Original;. . .
BRAND. Yes, very likely; but what though? /In Death I see not Overthrow. And is your faith quite firm and fast/. That had those builders spoken still. /On speech, and acted with one will,/ They would have piled the pinnacle. /Of Babel up to heaven at last?
THE DEAN. To heaven? /No, that is where it lies: /No man gets quite to Paradise./ There, see, we have the second core, /Embedded in this shell of Fable; − /That every building is unstable/. Which to the starry heaven would soar.
BRAND. Yet, Jacob's ladder reach'd that goal. /Thither by longing soars the Soul.[4]

BRAND. Ay, indeed, That's the condition! First to bleed! /Your blooddless spirit to put on/. Man must first a skelton!
THE DEAN. I would not put the lancet through. /A very kitten − far less you: But yet I thought no harm were done/. In leaving just ajar the door/. That opens, where I went before.
BRAND. And do you know what you have sought? /This, that upon the Stat's cock-cry/. I that Ideal shold deny. /For which I until now have fought?
THE DEAN. Deny, friend? Who makes such request? /Duty is all I bid you follow: I ask you quietly to swallow/. That which you people can't digest. . .[5]

And from *Rosmersholm:*

KROLL. Rosmer. . .Rosmer! I shall never get over this. */looks sadly at him/* Oh, to think that even you should want to lend yourself to the work of corrupting and preverting this unhappy country.
ROSMER. It is the work of liberation I want to take part in.
KROLL. . . . But do you really think any sort of liberation can be expected from the doctrines now busy poisoning our whole social life?
ROSMER. I am no supporter of any prevailing doctrine, nor indeed of either side in the dispute. I want to try to bring men together from all sides. . . I will devote my life and all my strength to this thing; to create a true democracy in the land.[6]

In A Vicarage, Fujiwara, a minister who believed in the human conscience and social reform, but the other minister old Ueda, has a rigid orthodox belief centering around the Bible. The point of confrontation is

[4] Henrik Ibsen. *Brand.* Edited by William Archer (New York: C. Scribner's Sons, 1906), pp. 204—205.

[5] Ibid., pp. 206—207.

[6] Henrik Ibsen. *Rosmersholm and the Wild Duck.* Translated by James W. McFarlane (London: Oxford University Press, 1960), pp. 313—314.

found when Fujiwara reads books of William James and Nietzsche, which Ueda considers anathema to the true religion.

c) confrontation scene II: Fujiwara and Ueda vs. Manders and Mrs. Alving. The unyielding conservative old minister Ueda, who does not allow any compromise in his thought, reminds us of Manders in *Ghosts*. In *Ghosts,* we find in the early scene of Act I, a confrontation between Mrs. Alving and Manders: Mrs. Alving keeps several «radical» and «common» books which Manders is shocked to find, and he reproaches Mrs Alving: «Do you read this sort of literature?»[7] A long argument between the two ensues.

In *A Vicarage,* Ueda looks at the title of some of Fujiwara's books, and throws them down as if they were scorpions. However, the confrontation in *A Vicarage* does not further the action here as it does in Ibsen's plays.

d) confrontation scene III: Fujiwara and Ueda vs. Kroll and Rosmer. Another type confrontation scene in *A Vicarage* resembles one in *Rosmersholm;* it is found in dialogues between Fujiwara and Ueda and Kroll and Rosmer. In Act III, after learning about his wife's past, Fujiwara is told how Mariko tricked his son Shinichi, a pathetic crippled youngster, was encouraged to climb up the nearly completed tower his shock leads him to apostasy. Although he shakes hands with Ushio and permits Mariko to marry Ushio as she wants, he curses and renounces God completely. Then, Fujiwara's blasphemy scandalizes old Ueda. Now he gives up his faith, and Ueda announces an end to his friendship with Fujiwara. This incident is paralleled in *Rosmersholm,* when Kroll, Rosmer's brother-in-law and Rosmer are arguing. Let us compare the dialogues between Ueda and Fujiwara with those between Kroll and Rosmer:

UEDA. You had better quit your clergyman's job immediately!
FUJIWARA. I am not only quiting that, but I have given up Christianity, as I said just now. I no longer believe in God.
UEDA /*angrily*/. That is not so. You must say God has given you up![8]

FUJIWARA. . . You have lost your beloved son and daughter as well as your grand-child, and you're entirely alone, aren't you?
UEDA. No, God is with me. I am not lonely by being alone.

---

[7] Henrik Ibsen. *A Doll's House and Ghosts.* Translated by William Archer (New York: C. Scribner's Sons, 1917), p. 178.

[8] Nakamura Kichizo. *Bokushi no Ie* (Tokyo: Shunjusha-Shoten, 1910), pp. 262—263.

KANEKO. . .

UEDA. I hate to see a man who abandons God. You shall no longer set foot in my house. Goodbye![9]

In *Rosmersholm:*

KROLL. */rises/.* Are these words that befit a clergyman?
ROSMER. I am no longer a clergyman.
KROLL. Yes, but. . . the religion you were brought up to . . .?
ROSMER. It is no longer mine.
KROLL. No longer!
ROSMER */rises/.* I have given it up. I had to give it up, Kroll.[10]

KROLL. No, let us not talk about it. Ugh! Forgive me. Goodbye!
ROSMER */following him/.* Kroll! Things must not end like this between us. I'll look in on you tomorow.
KROLL */in the entrance hall, turns/:* You shall not set foot in my house.[11]

e) confrontation scene IV: Ushio and Kaneko vs. Krogstad and Nora. In Act II of *A Vicarage,* Ushio blackmails Kaneko. Unless she will give him the money he wants, he will expose her to her husbond. Kaneko, believing her sin will be forgiven by true repentance, tells Fujiwara her past and her relationship with Ushio. But Fujiwara cannot forgive her. Here a peaceful family's happiness, as in *A Doll's House,* is suddenly overshadowed by a blackmailer who knows the secret of the wife. The wife, after long hours of distress, decides to confess all to her husband, but when she does, the husband is so enraged that he will not forgive her. At this the wife realizes the false foundation of their marriage and plans to leave home. These borrowings from *A Doll's House* imply something more significant than a simple imitation in *A Vicarage.*

III

Bokushi in Japanese means «a minister,» and *Ie,* «a house,» whilw *no* is a postposition (possessive or genetive) equivalent to the Englich preposition «of». Accordingly, in literal translation, the title is *A Vicar's House,* not *A Vicarage.* While the Japanese language does have a word «vicarage» («bokushikan»), Nakamura preferred «Vicar's House» to «Vicarage»

[9] Ibid., pp. 285—286.

[10] Henrik Ibsen. *Rosmersholm and The Wild Duck.* Translated by James W. McFarlane (London: Oxford University Press, 1960), p. 315.

[11] Nakamura Kichizo. O-bei Inshoki (Tokyo: Shunjusha-Shoten, 1910), p. 137.

undoubtedly since Ibsen's *A Doll's House* was in his mind at the time of the creation.

Nakamura went to the United States to study theology, but later he changed his mind and studied drama after he became interested in Ibsen. He writes of how he became interested in Ibsen, when he was reading at Central Park in New York in the following manner:

It looks like a picture-postcard. I am now a person in the postcard and read Ibsen's plays which I carried here with me. When my eyes are tired, I look at the pond, enchanted by the intense sunlight gleaming with ripples. And suddenly I resume reading as if I recalled what I was reading.[12]

Before too long Nakamura was stimulated and deeply impressed of Brander Matthews's (1852—1929) book *The Development of the Drama* (1903) and enrolled in Columbia University in order to attend his lectures. At Columbia his interest in Ibsen was strengthened when he heard the lectures of William Archer (1856—1924), a British drama critic and English translator of Ibsen's works. It was about this time when Nakamura decided to become a playwright.

Upon his return to Japan in 1909, he wrote plays utilizing what he had learned abroad, among which was *A Vicarage (Bokushi no Ie,* 1910). He also wrote a book concerning Ibsen's life and work which was entitled *Ibusen* (1914 and 1926). Because of these works that he wrote, he was nicknamed Henrik Nakamura, when he called *The Master Builder* «the Bible of modern literature.»[13]

Considering the above common elements that I have found by the textual study, it is possible for me to conclude that technically Nakamura applied a retrospective method to have Kaneko's past revealed through dialogues of other characters. This is what he had learned from Ibsen. Besides, for his own production, he has borrowed Ibsen's materials – the scenes and characters – of *The Lady from the Sea, A Doll's House, Rosmersholm, The Master Builder, Little Eyolf, Ghosts, The Wild Duck* and *Brand.* These plays [14] are what Nakamura had seen in New York, Lon-

[13] Nakamura Kichizo. *Ibusen* (Tokyo: Toho Shuppan Kabushiki Gaisha, 1926), p. 395.

[14] As for performances of Ibsen plays which Nakamura saw abroad, they are as follows:
Love's Comedy, Peer Gynt, Hedda Gabler, The Master Builder, A Doll's House (thrice) and Rosmersholm (twice) in New York in the summer of 1907 to June 1908; *Hedda Gabler* in London in the summer of 1908; *A Doll's House, Ghosts, The Wild Duck, Rosmersholm, The Lady from the Sea, Little Eyolf, John Gabriel Borkman* and *When We Dead Awaken* in Berlin from 1908 to 1909.

don and Berlin while he was abroad from 1907 to 1909. He had been obsessed with his study of Ibsen since 1907, and as Nakamura himself wrote in the Preface of *A Vicarage,* «My work *A Vicarage* is an Ibsenian product,»[15] this was in the true sense the fruit of Nakamura's Ibsen study in the United States, England and Europe.

[15] Nakamura Kichizo. *Bokushi no Ie* (Tokyo: Shunjusha-Shoten, 1910), p. 15.

Ibsen bibliography 1977 – 1978

CECILIE WIBORG BONAFEDE

Aaron, Jules. The Master builder. By Henrik Ibsen. American Conservatory Theatre, Geary Theatre, San Francisco December 24, 1977. – Educational theatre journal 30/1978, 424 – 425. Anmeldelse.

Alique, José-Benito. Prólogo. – Ibsen, H. . Peer Gynt. Madrid 1978. S. 7 – 31.

Allphin, Clela. Women in the plays of Henrik Ibsen. N.Y. 1975. 117 s.

Almgren, Carl Eric. Ibsens «både – och». – Dagens Nyheter 1978, 2/7, 4.

Alnæs, Karsten. Footlights to film. – Scandinavian review 66/1978:4, 67 – 71. Av: Film og kino 1978:1.

Alnæs, Karsten. På filmreise gjennom Ibsens verker. – Film og kino 1978:1, 8 – 11.

Andersen, Helge. På visitt i Helmers stue. – Frisprog 1978, 11/3, 4. Anmeldelse av Svenska Teaterns (Helsingfors) gjestespill på Det Norske teatret, Scene 2.

Anderssen, Odd-Stein. Akklimatisering i skogbrynet. (Nationaltheatret: Fruen fra havet.) – Aftenposten 1977, 27/12, nr. 598, 7.

Anderssen, Odd-Stein. Amfiscenen: «Lille Eyolf»: Når et barn blir i veien. Anmeldt av . . . – Aftenposten 1978, 12/5, nr. 213, 48.

Anderssen, Odd-Stein. «Brand» – som ideologenes uttogsmarsj? (Nationaltheatret: Jubileets femte Ibsenforestilling.) – Aftenposten 1978, 12/6, nr. 260, 44.

Anderssen, Odd-Stein. Dur fra møllefossen – med sordin. Trøndelag Teater: «Rosmersholm». Anmeldt av . . . – Aftenposten 1978, 4/2, nr. 59, 36.

Anderssen, Odd-Stein. Hedda – med eller uten Gabler. Festspillåpning i Bergen. Anmeldt av . . . – Aftenposten 1978, 25/5, nr. 230, 64.

Anderssen, Odd-Stein. I solskinn den gamle ørn. Amfiscenen: Ibsenprogrammet «Tvert imot!» anmeldt av . . . – Aftenposten 1978 1978, 19/6, nr. 272, 5.

Anderssen, Odd-Stein. Våkenatt med fru Inger. (Riksteatret: første bidrag til Ibsen-jubileet.) – Aftenposten 1977, 5/12, nr. 563, 44.

Andersson, Gunder. Borkman och Sartorius. Två representanter för 1800-talets borgerlighet. – Dramaten 7/1976 – 77: 60, 10 – 11.

Andreas-Salomé, Lou. Una favola. – Ibsen, H. . L'anitra selvatica. Genova 1977. S. 51 – 61. (Teatro di Genova. N.26.) Av: Henrik Ibsens Frauengestalten nach seinen sechs Familien-Dramen, 1892. Overs. av Anna Maria Meriggi Felgentreff.

Anker, Øyvind. «Digteren Henrik Ibsen lider nød i Rom». – Aftenposten 1978, 1/6. Kronikk.

Anker, Øyvind. Henrik Ibsen-brev som ikke kom med i Hundreårsutgaven. – Ibsenårbok 1977, 7 – 21.

Anker, Øyvind, vide *(Ibsen, Henrik)* Henrik Ibsen's brev. Oslo 1978.

Anzai, Tetsuo. Mittau no dramaturgy – Shakespeare, Ibsen, Shaw. – English literature and language (Tokio) 10/1973, 33 – 46.

Askeland, Gunnar. Ole Bull inviterer Henrik Ibsen til Bergen. – Verdens Gang 1978, 20/3, 34. (Den ukjente Henrik Ibsen.)

Astaf'eva, Marina. Ibsen kak sozdatel' social'noj dramy. «Šou ob Ibsene.» [Ibsen som skaper av det sosiale drama. Shaw om Ibsen.] – Problemy zarubežnogo teatra i teatrovedenija. Sbornik trudov. Moskva 1977. S. 161 – 175.

Bajić, Stanislav. Predgovor. – Ibsen, H., Narodni neprijatelj. Beograd 1975. S. 5 – 18.

Balice, Vincent J. Chesterton and Ibsen: A misunderstanding. – The Chesterton review 2/1976, 215 – 225.

Balvetti, Mario. Festa grande per papà Ibsen. In Norvegia si celebrano con impegno i 150 anni dalla nascita del padre del dramma moderno. – Paese sera (Roma) 1978, 15/3.

Bang-Hansen, Kjetil. Vi må tolke Ibsen ut fra vår tids teatersyn. – Aftenposten 1978, 20/3, nr. 133, 7. Intervju.

Barranger, M. S. Ibsen's «Little Eyolf» and modern tragicomedy. – Quarterly journal of speech 63/1977: 2, 180 – 187.

Barranger, M. S. «The lady from the sea»: Ibsen in transition. – Modern drama 21/1978: 4, 393 – 403.

Barrie, J. M. Ibsen's ghost. A play in one act. Ed. by Penelope Griffin. Pref. by Roger Lancelyn Green. Lond. 1975. X, 110 s.

Bergen skal få Ibsen-monument. – Aftenposten 1977, 28/12, nr. 600, 7.

Berke, Jacqueline. Silver, Lola. The «awakened» woman in literature and real life. – Proceedings of the sixth national convention of the popular culture association, Chicago 1976. Comp. by M. T. Marsden. Bowling Green 1976. S. 1165 – 1179. (Microfilm.)

Berlin, Jeffrey Bennett. The treatment of truth in the dramatic work of Henrik Ibsen and Arthur Schnitzler. Diss. State university of New York at Binghamton 1976. 603 s.

Bernhardt, Rüdiger. Ibsens Polaritätsgedanke. – Weimarer Beiträge 1978: 6, 85 – 111.

Beyer, Edvard. Etterord. – Ibsen, H. Samlede verker. B. 4. 6. Oslo 1978. S. 399 – 434, 501 – 518.

Beyer, Edvard. Henrik Ibsen. Oslo 1978. 169 s. ill. Bibliografi, 164 – 170. Kfr. Norges litteraturhistorie, bd. 3, kapitlet om Ibsen. Også i engelsk utgave, oversatt av Marie Wells, London 1978.

Beyer, Edvard. Henrik Ibsen 1828 – 1906 – 1978. – Norway information. Publ. by the Royal Norwegian Ministry of foreign affairs. UDA 425/77. 15 s.

Beyer, Edvard. Henrik Ibsen – lys levende 150-årsjubilant. – Forskningsnytt fra NAVF 23/1978: 2, 9 – 12.

Bhalla, Brij. M. The feminine self in Ibsen. – Journal of the School of languages 3 (1975 – 76): 2, 22 – 31.

Bibliografi over norsk litteraturforskning 1975. 1976. 1977. Ibsen. – Norsk litterær årbok 1976, 237 – 238. 1977, 238 – 240. 1978, 256 – 258.

Bien, Horst. Nachwort. – Ibsen, H. Dramen. Berlin 1977. S. 815 – 40.

Bigley, Bruce. Praxis and stasis in Ibsen's «Bygmester Solness» – or what ever happened to plot and character? – Scandinavian studies 5/1978, 195 – 210.

Billington, Michael. The ghost in the machine. – The Guardian 1978, 18/3, 2.

Bly, Robert, vide *Ibsen, Henrik.* Three poems translated by . . .

Bonafede, Cecilie W. Ibsen-bibliografi. – Ibsenårbok 1977, 218 – 231.

Boyer, Régis. Elisabeth – Laura – Nora. – Internasjonale studiekonferanse om nordisk litteratur. 11. Gent 1976. Literature and reality: Creatio versus Mimesis. Ed. by A. Bolckmans. Ghent 1977. S. 181 – 194.

Brandes, Georg. Henrik Ibsen. A critical study. Authorised translation by Jessie Muir. Rev., with an introduction by William Archer. With a 42 page essay on Bjørnstjerne Bjørnson. N. Y. 1977. XVI, 170 s.

Brandrud, John, vide *Grøndahl, Carl Henrik.* Ibsen-instituttet bør holde til på UB. (Intervju.)

Bredsdorff, Elias. Fra Andersen til Scherfig. Kbh. 1978. 240 s. Ibsen, 73 – 115. Tr. første gang 1962.

Bredsdorff, Elias. Henrik Ibsen. Verso «L'anitra selvatica». – Ibsen, H. L'anitra selvatica. Genova 1977. S. 27 – 38. (Teatro de Genova. N. 26.)

Brigg, Øivind. Ibsensk «mageplask» i Trondheim – det skulle vært verre! – Verdens Gang 1978, 7/2, 35. Anmeldelse av «Rosmersholm».

Bronson, D. Consuming struggle vs. killing time: preludes to dying in the dramas of Ibsen and Beckett. – Aging and the elderly. Ed. by S. F. Spicker m.fl. Atlantic Highlands, N. J. 1978. S. 261 – 281.

Bruns, Alken. Übersetzung als Rezeption. Deutsche Übersetzer skandinavischer Literatur von 1860 bis 1900. = Skandinavistische Studien. 8. Neumünster 1977. (Zur Rezeption skandinavischer Literatur in Deutschland 1870 bis 1914. Teil 2.) Ibsen im Zeichen des Poetischen Realismus, 120 – 136.

Brustein, Robert. Artist and the citizen. – New Republic 1978, no. 178, 24/6, 23, 26 – 27.

Brustein, Robert. The evolution of a woman: A doll's house. – Brustein, R. The culture watch. Essays on theatre and society, 1969 – 1974. N. Y. 1975. S. 79 – 81.

Brustein, Robert. The fate of Ibsenism. – Scandinavian review 66/1978: 4, 7 – 19.

Brynhildsvoll, Knut. Über Rolle und Identität und ihr gegenseitiges Verhältnis in Peer Gynt. – Edda 1978: 2, 95 – 105.

Brøymer, Bjørn. Ibsen – inngangsport for nye teatergjengere. (Nationaltheatret står i Ibsen-jubileets tegn.) – Morgenbladet 1977, 29/12, 1,10.

Bugge, Erle Moestue. «Et dukkehjem» – nå som italiensk tegneserie. – Aftenposten 1978, 7/8, 6.

Bugge, Niels Magnus. En død i skjønnhet. [«Rosmersholm».] Fjernsynsteatret anmeldt av... – Morgenbladet 1978, 15/11, 5.

Bugge, Niels Magnus. Fabelaktig «gjengangere». Fjernsynsteatret anmeldt av... – Morgenbladet 1978, 30/8, 1, 8.

Bugge, Niels Magnus. Inn i Ibsen-året med John Gabriel Borkman. − Morgenbladet 1978, 11/1, 5. Anmeldelse av Fjernsynsteatrets forestilling.

Bugge, Niles Magnus. Maisolen i et septemberliv. Om Henrik Ibsen og Emilie Bardach. − Morgenbladet 1978, 15/2. Kronikk.

Bugge, Ragne. Ibsen i Italia sett med norske øyne. Fremførelsen av «Byggmester Solness» på Teatro Valle i Roma, april 1976. − AION. Annali dell'Istituto universitario orientale di Napoli. Sezione germanica. Vol. XIX, 1976. Studi Nederlandesi − Studi Nordici. S. 216−219.

Bukdahl, Jørgen. Arricia og Rom (Kierkegaard, og Ibsens gennembrud med Brand). − Bukdahl, J. De to spor. Kbh. 1976. S. 114−137.

Bull, Francis, Ibsen − the man and the dramatist. − Norway information. Publ. by the Royal Norwegian Ministry of foreign affairs. UDA 426/78. 4 s.

Bø, Olav, vide Per Gynt stemnet. 14. Vinstra 1978.

Bøyg, Hedda Gabler − Ibsen's svar på Ulrike Meinhof. − Dagbladet 1978, 3/7, 5.

Calmeyer, Bengt. Flott − men hvor er løkens kjerne? − Arbeiderbladet 1978, 18/8, 13. Anmeldelse av Rogaland Teaters gjestespill med Peer Gynt på Oslo Nye Teater.

Calmeyer, Bengt, Frihetskjemperen Brand. − Arbeiderbladet 1978 12/6, 12. Anmeldelse av Nationaltheatrets forestilling.

Calmeyer, Bengt, Gjest i Helmers hjem. − Arbeiderbladet 1978, 3/3, 12. Anmeldelse av Svenska Teaterns (Helsingfors) gjestespill på Det Norske Teatret, Scene 2.

Calmeyer, Bengt, Historien om Hedda. (Fortalt av Hedda Gabler, Marowitz, Henrik Ibsen og Janny Hoff Brekke.). − Arbeiderbladet 1978, 25/5, 19. Anmeldelse av forestillingen på Den Nationale Scene.

Calmeyer, Bengt. Ibsens muntre avling. − Arbeiderbladet 1978 7/2, 14. Anmeldelse av «De unges forbund» på Nationaltheatret.

Calmeyer, Bengt. Lyriker Ibsen frigjort på Amfi. − Arbeiderbladet 1978, 19/6, 14. Anmeldelse av Nationaltheatret, Amfiscenens forestilling.

Calmeyer, Bengt. «Peer Gynt» som dukkespill. − Arbeiderbladet 1978, 4/11, 13. Riksteatrets forestilling.

Calmeyer, Bengt. På terskelen til noe stort? − Arbeiderbladet 1977, 27/12, 13. Anmeldelse av «Fruen fra havet» på Nationaltheatret.

Calmeyer, Bengt. Tett og nært, iskaldt og mørkt. − Arbeiderbladet 1978, 11/1,15. Anmeldelse av «John Gabriel Borkman».

Carén, Lisi. Hedda stadig på ny. − Dagbladet 1978, 13/10, 4. Anmeldelse av Operaballettens «Hedda».

Carlson, Harry S. «Fruen fra havet» sett med amerikanske øyne. − Aftenposten 1978, 10/4, nr. 162, 5.

Carlsson, Anni. Andersenspuren in Ibsens Vildanden. − Ibsenårbok 1977, 46−51.

Carlsson, Anni. Ibsen, Strindberg, Hamsun. Essays zur skandinavischen Literatur. Kronberg/Ts 1978. 103 s. ill.

Carlsson, Anni. Nachwort. − Ibsen, H. Baumeister Solness. Stuttgart 1977. S. 91−95.

Carr, Joan. «The forest's revenge»: Subconscious motivation in «The Wild Duck». – The Modern Language review 72/1977, 845 – 856.

Cedrup, Lennart. Helslakt for McQueen som Ibsens Folkefiende. – Verdens Gang 1978, 6/9, 35. Anmeldelse av filmpremieren i Montreal.

Chaillet, Ned. Rosmersholm. – Plays and players 25/1977: 3, 24 – 25. Anm. av forestillingen på Theatre Royal, Haymarket.

Chamberlain, John S. «Gengangere» and «Emigrantlitteraturen». – Scandinavica 16/1977, 1 – 10.

Ciesielski, Zenon. Zbliżenia skandynawsko-polskie. Szkice o kontaktach kulturalnych w XIX i XX wieku. [Relations between Poland and Scandinavia. Outline of cultural contacts in the XIXth and XXth centuries.] Gdańsk 1972. 275 s. Summary. Ibsen, 209 – 20, 248 – 49 o.a.

Clurman, Harold. Ibsen. N. Y. 1977. London 1978. XII, 223 s. (Masters of world literature.)

Crowo, John. Delte meninger om britisk «Brand». – Aftenposten 1978, 2/5, nr. 197, 7. Referat av britiske anmeldelser av forestillingen på The National Theatre.

Curtis, Anthony. Rosmersholm. – Drama 127/1977-78, 58. Anm. av forestillingen på Haymarket.

Cycle Ibsen. – Le Nouveau Carré. 3e saison 1976 – 1977. Paris 1976.

Davidsen, Elisabeth. Hedda Gabler. – Ibsenårbok 1977, 107 – 120.

Den levende Ibsen. Analyser af udvalgte Ibsen-forestillinger 1973 – 78. Red. af Ulla Strømberg og Jytte Wiingaard. Kbh. 1978. 167 s. ill.

Den ukjente Henrik Ibsen. – Verdens Gang 1978, 20/3, 33 – 36.

D'Heurle, Adma. Lost children: The role of the child in the psychological plays of Henrik Ibsen. – Psychoanalytic review 63/1976: 1, 27 – 47.

Dittmann, Reidar. Edvard Munch, a personal reflection. – Edvard Munch and Henrik Ibsen. Northfield, Minn. 1978. S. 5 – 10.

Dobijanka-Witczakowa, Olga. Posłowie. – Ibsen, H., Dramaty. Poznań 1977. S. 495 – 506.

Durbach, Errol. The dramatic poetry of Ibsen's «Ghosts». – Mosaic 11/1978: 4, 55 – 66.

Durbach, Errol. Temptation to err: The denouement of Rosmersholm. – Educational theatre journal 29/1977, 477 – 485.

Duve, Arne. Den fremmede i Ibsens diktning. – Stavanger Aftenblad 1977, 9/11, 2, 4.

Duve, Arne. Den store Bøygen. – Nationen 1978, 16 – 17/1. Kronikk.

Duve, Arne. Drama-forfalskninger hos Ibsen. – Frisprog 1978, 11/3, 4.

Duve, Arne. En dårekiste i Cairo. – Morgenbladet 1977, 11/1, 4.

Duve, Arne. Et avlastende skuespill – Lille Eyolf. – Frisprog 1977, 29/10, 4.

Duve, Arne. Et fødselsdrama hos Ibsen. – Stavanger Aftenblad 1978, 3/1, 2.

Duve, Arne. Et nytt Ibsen-image. – Morgenbladet 1978, 22/4. Kronikk.

Duve, Arne. Forviklinger mellom Ibsen og Bjørnson. – Nationen 1975, 10/1. Kronikk.

Duve, Arne. Fredrikke Nielsen og Henrik Ibsen. – Nationen 1977, 11/5. Kronikk.

Duve, Arne. Fødselsdager hos Ibsen. – Stavanger Aftenblad 1978, 19/4, 12.

Duve, Arne. Gjengangere og det som fulgte. – Grimstad Adressetidende 1978, 27/4, 5.

Duve, Arne. Henrik Ibsen i skriftestolen. – Frisprog 1977, 26/11, 4, 6.

Duve, Arne. Henrik Ibsen og Bardach-affæren. – Frisprog 1978, 15/4, 4.

Duve, Arne. Henrik Ibsen og John Paulsen. – Bergens Tidende 1975, 10/2. Kronikk.

Duve, Arne. Henrik Ibsen og Søren Kierkegaard. – Nationen 1978, 26/4. Kronikk.

Duve, Arne. Henrik Ibsens hemmelighet? – Telemark Arbeiderblad 1978, 27/5, 23.

Duve, Arne. Henrik Ibsens hemmeligheter? Oslo 1977. 112 s., ill. Ny utvidet utg. 1979.

Duve, Arne. Henrik Ibsens verden i tall. – Morgenbladet 1978, 28/6. Kronikk.

Duve, Arne. Hvem diktet Ibsen på? – Bergens Tidende 1976, 21 – 22/7. Kronikk.

Duve, Arne. Hvem var «Fruen fra havet»? – Morgenbladet 1978, 4/1, 4-5.

Duve, Arne. Hvorfor kalte Ibsen seg Brynjolf Bjarme? – Nationen 1974, 27/9. Kronikk.
Feilaktig registret under *Heide* i bibliografien 1975 – 76.

Duve, Arne. Ibsen, Borkman og loven. – Morgenbladet 1976, 21/9. Kronikk.

Duve, Arne. Ibsen, Grimstad og Skien. – Grimstad Adressetidende 1978, 13/4, 7.

Duve, Arne. Ibsen og julen. – Bergens Tidende 1977, 24/12. Julenummeret.

Duve, Arne. Ibsens drama-mønster. – Bergens Tidende 1977, 18 – 19/7. Kronikk.

Duve, Arne. Ibsens legeskikkelser. – Tidsskrift for den norske lægeforening 1975: 32, 1872 – 1873. En kommentar til Kristian Rees artikkel s.s. nr. 27.

Duve, Arne. Ibsens «norske mysterier». – Frisprog 1978, 27/5, 5.

Duve, Arne. Ibsens synderegister i «Peer Gynt». – Nationen 1977, 10/11. Kronikk.

Duve, Arne. Julen i Henrik Ibsens diktning og virkelighet. – Nationen 1976, 23 – 24/12. Kronikk.

Duve, Arne. Med Henrik Ibsen på ball i Grimstad. – Grimstad Adressetidende 1978, 14/3, 1, 4.

Duve. Arne. The real drama of Henrik Ibsen? Oslo 1977. 30 s.

Duve, Arne. Rebekka Wests bekjennelser. – Nationen 1977, 14/10. Kronikk.

Duve, Arne. Tvillinger i Ibsens skuespill. – Frisprog 1978, 11/2, 4.

Ebbing, Elisabeth. Hedda Gabler, En kvinderøst og Henrik Ibsen. – Edda 1978: 6, 341 – 343.

Edvard Munch and Henrik Ibsen. Steensland Gallery, St. Olaf College, Northfield, Minn., March 16 to April 23, 1978. Introd., transl. and ed. by Reidar Dittmann. The essays, Munch and Ibsen, by Paal Hougen. Northfield, Minn. 1978. 69 s. ill. (American catalogue edition.).

Edwards, Sheila. Father of the modern drama. Norway ant the world observe 150th anniversary of birth of Henrik Ibsen. – The Norseman 1978: 1, 2 – 6.

Egeberg, Egil. Ibsen og Tolstoj. – Ergo 1978, 96 – 103.

Egeland, Erik. Ibsen og Bronkens John Gabriel Borkman. – Aftenposten 1978, 11/1, nr. 17, 44. Anmeldelse av Fjernsynsteatrets forestilling.

Egeland, Erik. Lysende «Gengangere». – Aftenposten 1978, 30/8, nr. 396, 6. Anmeldelse av Fjernsynsteatrets fremførelse.

Egeland, Erik, «Rosmersholm» i Fjernsynsteatret: Bronken-symboler i Ibsens univers. – Aftenposten 1978, nr. 528, 15/11,7.

Eide, Elisabeth. Ibsen som sosialreformator i Kina i årene etter 1917. – Forskningsnytt fra NAVF 23/1978: 2, 13 – 16.

Ellingsen, Thor. «Gengangere» på slagen landevei. – Dagbladet 1978, 30/8, 4. Anmeldelse av Fjernsynsteatrets fremførelse.

Ellingsen, Thor. Livfullt og friskt «dukkehjem». – Dagbladet 1978, 2/3, 7. Anmeldelse av gjestespill av Svenska Teatern, Helsingfors på Det Norske Teatret, Scene 2.

Ellingsen, Thor. Sterk TV-åpning på Ibsenåret! – Dagbladet 1978, 11/1, 4. Anmeldelse av John Gabriel Borkman.

Elsom, John. Brand. – The Listener 1978, 4/5, 579 – 580. Anmeldelse av forestillingen på Olivier Theatre.

Engelstad, Carl Fredrik. Henrik Ibsen and the modern Norwegian theatre. – Norway information. Publ. by the Royal Norwegian Ministry of foreign affairs. UDA 431/78. 2 s.

Engelstad, Carl Fredrik. Ibsen-forskningen – stadig fornyelse. – Aftenposten 1978, 23/2. Kronikk. Anmeldelse av Ibsenårbok 1977.

Engelstad, Carl Fredrik. Peer Gynts vei over scenen. – Aftenposten 1978, 2/5. Kronikk. Anmeldelse av Hans Midbøe: Peer Gynt, teatret og tiden.

Engelstad, Carl Fredrik, vide *Grøndahl, Carl Henrik.* Vi trenger Ibsen-institutt (Intervju.)

Ennemoser, Günther. Gossensass 1850 – 1914. Beiträge zur Geschichte der Gemeinde Gossensass mit besonderer Berücksichtigung der Zeit von 1850 – 1914. Diss. Univ. Padova, Seksjon Brixen (Syd-Tirol) 1975. Ibsen, 149 – 161.

Ertsaas, Karl Robert. Fakkeltog for falentens sønn. – Dagbladet 1978, 21/3, 5.

Ewbank, Inga-Stina. Translating Ibsen for the contemporary stage. – Theatre research international N. s. vol. 2/1976: 1, 44 – 53.

Fallenstein, Robert. Hennig, Christian. Rezeption skandinavischer Literatur in Deutschland 1870 – 1914. Quellenbibliographie. = Skandinavistische Studien. 7. Neumüster 1977. (Zur Rezeption skandinavischer Literatur in Deutschland 1870 bis 1914. Teil 1.) Henrik Ibsen, 162 – 253.

Firkins, I. T. Henrik Ibsen. A bibliograhy of criticism and biography, with an index to characters. Norwood, Pa 1976. 80 s. Repr. of 1921 ed.

Fjelde, Rolf. Introduction. – Ibsen, Henrik. The complete major prose plays. Bergenfield, N. J. 1978. S. 1 – 8.

Fjelde, Rolf. «The lady from the sea»: Ibsen's positive world-view in a topographic figure. – Modern drama 21/1978: 4, 379 – 391. Av: Ibsen sesquicentennial symposium, New York 1978.

Fletcher, John. McFarlane, James. Modernist drama: origins and patterns. – Modernism. 1890 – 1930. Ed. by Malcolm Bradbury and James McFarlane. Harmondsworth 1976. S. 499 – 513. (Pelican guides to European literature.) Ibsen.

Foss, Birthe. «Hedda Gabler» som ballett. – Arbeiderbladet 1978, 7/10, 12.

Friese, Wilhelm, vide *Ibsen auf der deutschen Bühne:* Texte zur Rezeption. Tübingen 1976.

From Ibsen's workshop: notes, scenarios and drafts of the modern plays. Transl. by A. G. Chater, ed. and with an introd. by William Archer, new foreword by John Guare. N. Y. 1978. 528 s. (Da Capo Press book.)

Fuchs, Elinor. O'Neill's poet: Touched by Ibsen. – Educational theatre journal 30/1978: 4, 513 – 516.

Fujiki, Hiroyuki. Ibsen. – Obei Sakka to Nihon Kindai Bungaku. Eds.: Fukuda, M., Kenmochi, T., Kodama, K., Vol. 3. Russia, Hokuo, Nano Hen. Tokio 1977. S. 210 – 247.

Gabrieli, Iselin Maria. Haugan, Jørgen. Henrik Ibsens metode. Den indre utvikling gennem Ibsens dramatik. Kbh. 1977. – AION, Annali dell'Istituto universitario orientale di Napoli. Sezione germanica. Vol. XXI, 1978. Studi Nederlandesi – Studi Nordici. S. 458 – 460. Anmeldelse.

Gabrieli, Iselin Maria. Rilettura di Ibsen. Napoli 1977. 157 s. (Quaderni degli annali dell 'Istituto universitario orientale di Napoli. Sezione germanica. 14.)

Gentikow, Barbara. Skandinavien als präkapitalistische Idylle. Rezeption gesellschaftskritischer Literatur in deutschen Zeitschriften 1870 bis 1914. = Skandinavistische Studien 9/1978. (Zur Rezeption skandinavischer Literatur in Deutschland 1870 bis 1914. Teil 3.) Rezeption früher gesellschaftskritischer skandinavischer Dramen in Deutschland: Bjørnstjerne Bjørnsons «Ein Fallissement» und Henrik Ibsens «Stützen der Gessellschaft», 28 – 92. Rezeption skandinavischer Texte zum Eheproblem und zur Frauenfrage: Ibsens «Nora» und Ellen Keys «Missbrauchte Frauenkraft», 92 – 170.

Gerlach, Hans Egon. Nachwort. – Ibsen, H., Rosmersholm. Stuttgart 1978. S. 105 – 109. (Universal-Bibliothek. 2280.)

Gerlach, Hans Egon. Nachwort des Übersetzers. – Ibsen, Henrik. Schauspiele. Hamburg 1977. s. 1079 – 1082.

Girdzijauskaite, Audrone. Ibsenas Valstybes teatro scenoje (1920 – 1940). – Muzika ir teatras (Vilnius) 9/1973, 135 – 145.

Glass, Dudley. Ibsen in music. – Scandinavian review 66/1978: 4, 51.

Gording, Elisabeth. Gjestespill med «Hedda Gabler». – Norges Handels- og Sjøfartstidende 1978, 3/11, 15. Anmeldelse av forestillingen på Den Nationale Scene.

Gording, Elisabeth. Riksteatret: «Peer Gynt» som marionett-teater. – Norges Handels- og Sjøfartststidende 1978, 2/11, 8.

Gording, Elisabeth. Svensk gjestespill med «Et dukkehjem». – Norges Handels- og Sjøfartstidende 1978, 2/3, 13. Anmeldelse av forestillingen til Svenska

Teatern, Helsingfors, på Det Norske Teatret, Scene 2.

Gosse, Edmund William. Henrik Ibsen. Norwood, Pa. 1978, 244 s. ill. pl. Cop. 1907.

Gossensass im Zeichen von Henrik Ibsen. – Dolomiten 1976, 16/7, nr. 160, 12.

Gram, Nina. «Brand» i London. Fra ros til ris. – Verdens Gang 1978, 28/4, 39. Anm. av forestillingen på National Theatre.

Gramsci, Antonio. La morale e il costume. («Casa di bambola» di Ibsen al Carignano). – Ibsen, H., Casa di bambola. Roma 1978. S. 109 – 112. (Cultura politica. 160. Sez. femminismo. 6.)

Grant, Steve. Hedda Gabler. – Plays and players 24/1977: 11, 22 – 23. Anmeldelse av forestillingen på Duke of York's.

Gravier, Maurice. Etudes Ibseniennes. – Etudes germaniques 32/1977: 4, 403 – 406.

Gray, Ronald. Ibsen: a dissenting view. A study of the last twelve plays. Cambridge 1977. 231 s.

Green, Allan. Förebilder i Ibsens Brand. – Bohusläningen 1977, 2/4, 4.

Green, Allan. Han var eldsjäl – och tände eldar. – Bohusläningen 1978, 22/4, 4.

Grimstad bymuseum, vide *Ibsen-jubileet* i Grimstad 1978.

Grøndahl, Carl Henrik. Henrik Ibsens rovdyr og prinsesser. – A-magasinet 1978: 16, 18 – 20.

Grøndahl, Carl Henrik, Ibsen-instituttet bør holde til på UB. – Aftenposten 1978, 31/3, nr. 145, 5. Intervju med overbibliotekar John Brandrud.

Grøndahl, Carl Henrik. Ibsen-året er ringt inn. – Aftenposten Radio/TV 1978: 1, 5.

Grøndahl, Carl Henrik. Lek og tekst med dukker i Riksteatret: «Peer Gynt». Anmeldt av ... – Aftenposten 1978, 3/11, nr. 508, 6.

Grøndahl, Carl Henrik. Skien feirer Henrik Ibsen. – Aftenposten 1978, 11/3, nr. 119, 4.

Grøndahl, Carl Henrik. Spekeskinke og romantikk. «Sancthansnatten» i Skien. – Aftenposten 1978, 20/5, nr. 222, 6.

Grøndahl, Carl Henrik. Ved denne korsvei, Henrik. – Aftenposten 1978, 18/3, nr. 131, 2.

Grøndahl, Carl Henrik. Vi trenger Ibsen-institutt. Intervju med Carl Fredrik Engelstad og Daniel Haakonsen. – Aftenposten 1978, 30/3, nr. 143, 6.

Guare, John, vide *From Ibsen's workshop.* N. Y. 1978. (Da Capo Press book.)

Gulbrandsen, Kjell. Drømmen om livsglede. – Friheten 1978, nr. 22, 16/3, 6.

Gulbrandsen, Kjell. Ibsen og Oktoberrevolusjonen. – Friheten 1978, nr. 23, 20/3, 9.

Gulbrandsen, Kjell. Ibsen – vår medkjemper. – Friheten 1978, nr. 23, 20/3, 9, 14.

Gullhon, Ingunn. 1977 er Ibsen-år på franske scener. – Aftenposten 1977, 7/12, nr. 567, 6.

Gaare, Jørgen. Ibsen og Bjørnson: «Lemmene av en lemlestet dikter». – Morgenbladet 1978, 11/9, 4. (Ibsen og Morgenbladet.)

Gaare, Jørgen. Ibsen og Bjørnson: Teaterfeiden. – Morgenbladet 1978, 12/9, 4,5. (Ibsen og Morgenbladet.)

Gaare, Jørgen. Morgenbladet tilsluttet de unges forbund? – Morgenbladet 1978, 21/11, 4. (Ibsen og Morgenbladet.)

Gaare, Jørgen. «Sandheden har mer end en Side». Ibsens «kunstneriske Hvorledes». – Morgenbladet 1978, 5/10, 5.

Gaare, Jørgen. Teater for åpen scene: Ibsens første samtidsroman. – Morgenbladet 1978, 3/10, 4. (Ibsen og Morgenbladet.)

Gaare, Jørgen. Teater for åpen scene: Ändelig føde med sproglige fordommer. – Morgenbladet 1978, 4/10, 4.

Gaare, Jørgen. Til Catilinas anonyme forfatter: «Bliv ved paa den betraadte Bane». – Morgenbladet 1978, 23/8, 4. (Ibsen og Morgenbladet.)

Hageberg, Otto. Etterord. – Ibsen, H. Samlede verker. B. 5. Oslo 1978. S. 413 – 460.

Hamberg, Lars. Forskandets petitesser. – Nya Argus 71/1978: 3 – 4, 39 – 41.

Hamberg, Lars. Ibsen och de ungas krav. – Vasabladet 1978, 13/7, 2. 26/7, 2.

Hansen, Jan Erik. Ibsen ser – og blir sett. – Morgenbladet 1978, 13/3, 4. Anm. av M. Schulerud «Ibsenbilder».

Hansen, Karin Synnøve, vide *Norsk Filminstitutt.* Henrik Ibsen 1828 – 1978. En filmografi.

Harris, Joseph. The masterbuilder tale in Snorri's Edda and two sagas. – Arkiv för nordisk filologi 91/1976, 66 – 101.

Hartmann, Alf. Et funn i Stavanger. «Peer Gynt» på Rogaland Teater. Anmeldt av... – Verdens Gang 1978, 27/2, 35.

Hartmann, Alf. Lengslenes evighet. – Verdens Gang 1977, 27/12, 35. Anmeldelse av Fruen fra havet.

Hartmann, Alf. Låghalt Ibsen. – Verdens Gang 1978, 4/2, 47. Anmeldelse av «Rosmersholm» på Trøndelag Teater.

Hartman, Alf. Peer Gynt på snarvisitt. – Verdens Gang 1978, 18/8, 30. Anmeldelse av Rogaland Teaters forestilling.

Hartmann, Alf. På søk etter Ibsen i Roma. Et gjenferd i Amalfi. – Verdens Gang 1978, 20/3, 35 – 36. (Den ukjente Henrik Ibsen.)

Hartmann, Alf. Strålende Dukkehjem. – Verdens Gang 1978, 2/3, 6. Anmeldelse av forestillingen til Svenska Teatern, Helsingfors, på Det Norske Teatret, Scene 2.

Haslund, Fredrik Juel. En torpedo under ekteskap og seksualmoral. Om Ibsens Gengangere – et familiedrama i 3 akter. – Forskningsnytt fra NAVF 23/1978: 2, 23 – 32.

Haugan, Jørgen. Efterskrift. – Ibsen, H. Gengangere. Kbh. 1976. S. 87 – 132.

Haugan, Jørgen. Henrik Ibsen og den vitenskapelige selvrefleksjon. – Forskningsnytt fra NAVF 23/1978: 2, 17 – 22.

Haugan, Jørgen. Henrik Ibsens metode: Den indre utvikling gjennom Ibsens dramatikk. Dr.avh. (Københavns universitet). Kbh., Oslo 1977. 330 s. Engelsk sammendrag. Anmeldelser, vide *Poul Houe, Gunnar Ollén, Iselin Maria Gabrieli.*

Haugan, Jørgen. The riddle of the Ibsen sphinx. – Scandinavian review 66/1978: 4, 35 – 39.

Haugen, Erik Anker. Antaùparolo. – Ibsen, H. Brand. Antverpeno 1978. S. 11 – 15.

Hećimović, Branko. Vojnović izmedju Vodopića i Ibsena. – Republika 32/1976, 825 – 834.

Hegna, Trond. «En storartet striptease». – Profil 1978; 2/3, 12 – 15. Intervju.

Heiberg, Hans. «...født til kunstner»: et Ibsen portrett. Stabekk 1978. 280 s. ill. (Den Norske bokklubben. Ekstrabok.) 1.utg. 1968.

Heiberg, Hans. Ibsen, grunnlegger og gesandt. – Programbladet 32/1978: 1, 6.

Hellberg, Lars. Velvillig interesse for «Fru Inger til Østråt». (Riksteatrets gjestespill i Stockholm.) – Aftenposten 1978, 18/3, nr. 132, 3.

Hellstrøm, Ulf Peter. Søkelys på «Et dukkehjem». – Aftenposten 1978, 31/3. nr. 145, 5. Anmeldelse av jubileumsutstillingen i Universitetsbiblioteket i Oslo.

Hemmer, Bjørn. Etterord. – Ibsen, H. Samlede verker. B. 2. 3. Oslo 1978. S. 481 – 527, 429 – 439.

Hemmer, Bjørn. Ibsen og Bjørnson: essays og analyser. Oslo 1978. 266 s. (Metaserie.) Ibsen, 15 – 209, 237 – 259.

Hemmer, Bjørn, vide *Peer Gynt stemnet.* 13. Vinstra 1977.

Hennig, Christian, vide *Fallenstein, R. Hennig, C.* Rezeption skandinavischer Literatur in Deutschland 1870 – 1914. Quellenbibliographie.

Henrik Ibsen. Hg. von Fritz Paul. Darmstadt 1977. VIII, 400 s. (Wege der Forschung. 487.)

Henrik Ibsen – jubilee year 1978. A brief survey of events in Norway during jubilee year 1978. – Norway, UDX 033/78. 7 s.

Henrik Ibsen og Universitetet. – Nytt fra Universitetet i Oslo 1978: 5, 1 – 2.

Henrik Ibsen og Universitetet: «Man må blues på landets vegne». – Aftenposten 1978, 20/3 nr. 133, 5.

Henrik Ibsens Norske Stilebog fra 1848. Oslo 1977. 30 s. faks. (Gyldendal norsk forlag. Julebok 1977.)

Hoff, Thorstein. Livredder Bjørnson. – Verdens Gang 1978, 12/5, 38.

Hoff, Thorstein. På suksess-topp etter harde tak. Rogaland teater satset og vant med Ibsens «Peer Gynt». – Verdens Gang 1978, 4/3, 46.

Hoghe, Raimund. Höhere Tochter scheitert: Ibsen «Hedda Gabler» in Paderborn. – Theater heute 18/1977: 4, 61.

Holmboe, Thorolf. En billedserie og dens opphavsmann. – Byminner 1978: 2, 23 – 36.

Hornby, Richard. Script into performance: A structuralist view of play production. Austin, Tex. 1977. 215 s. Om et dukkehjem.

Houe, Poul. Kunst og metode: om Henrik Ibsen. – Højskolebladet 103/1978: 23 – 24, 360 – 365, 377 – 382. ill. Om Jørgen Haugan, Henrik Ibsens metode.

Hougen, Pål. Edvard Munch og Henrik Ibsen. – Norsk Teaterårbok 1975, 166 – 174. (Fra utstillingskatalogen Edvard Munch og Henrik Ibsen, Vestlandske kunstindustrimuseum 1975.)

Hougen, Pål. Munch and Ibsen. – Edvard Munch and Henrik Ibsen. North-field, Minn. 1978. S. 11 – 29.

Hougen, Pål. Munch und Ibsen. – Munch und Ibsen. Kunsthaus Zürich 29. Februar bis 11. April 1976. S. 9 – 22.

Houm, Philip. Helene Alving og vi. – Houm, P. Gleder og gremmelser. Oslo 1977. S. 56 – 60.

Hsun, Lu. Che cosa accade dopo che Nora se ne è andata. – Ibsen, H. Casa di bambola. Roma 1978. S. 113 – 119. (Cultura politica. 160. Sez.femminis-mo. 6.)

Høst, Else. Hedvig. – Ibsen, H. L'anitra selvatica. Genova 1977. S. 79 – 101. (Teatro di Genova. N. 26.) Av: Vildanden av Henrik Ibsen, 1967.

Høst, Else. Veiledning. – Ibsen, H. Vildanden. Oslo 1976. S. 114 – 122. (Gyldendals skoleutgaver.)

Høst, Else, vide *Ibsenårbok* 1977.

Haakonsen, Daniel. «L'anitra selvatica» ovvero il realismo di Ibsen. – Ibsen, H. L'anitra selvatica. Genova 1977. S. 63 – 77. (Teatro di Genova. N. 26.) Av: Henrik Ibsen's realisme, 1957.

Haakonsen, Daniel. En beveget Ibsen-stil. – Aftenposten 1978, 20/12, nr. 588. Kronikk. Fruen fra havet på The Royal Exchange Theatre, Manchester.

Haakonsen, Daniel. En engelsk «Fruen fra havet». – Aftenposten 1978, 15/12, nr. 580. Kronikk. Fruen fra havet på The Royal Exchange Theatre, Manchester.

Haakonsen, Daniel. Hvordan skal Ibsen egentlig spilles? – Aftenposten 1978, 18/12, nr. 584. Kronikk. Fruen fra havet på The Royal Exchange Theatre, Manchester.

Haakonsen, Daniel. Kvinneskikkelser i Ibsens diktning. – Kirke og Kultur 83/1978: 8, 472 – 480. Også i Nytt fra Universitetet i Oslo 1978: 16, 12/9, 1 – 3.

Haakonsen, Daniel, vide *Grøndahl, Carl Henrik.* Vi trenger Ibsen-institutt. (Intervju.)

Haakonsen, Daniel, vide *Ibsenårbok* 1977.

Haaland, Arild. Hvem var Bøygen? – Aftenposten 1978, 17/4. Kronikk.

Haaland, Arild. Ibsens verden: en studie i kunst som forskning. Oslo 1978. 243 s.

Ibsen, Hedvig. La soffitta di Venstöp. – Ibsen, H. L'anitra selvatica. Genova 1977. S. 113 – 117. (Teatro di Genova. N. 26.) Av en artikkel i Varden, Skien, 16/5-1903.

Ibsen, Henrik. L'anitra selvatica. Trad. di Marcella Rinaldi. Con una raccolta di saggi e pagine critiche a cura di Marcella Rinaldi. Genova 1977. 239 s. (Teatro di Genova. N. 26.) Stykket oppført 1977 i Genova (Teatro di Genova) og i Roma (Teatro Argentina). Regi: Luca Ronconi.

Ibsen, Henrik. At a wedding. Henrik Ibsen: «Ved et bryllup». Overs. av John Northam. – Ibsenårbok 1977, 216 – 217.

Ibsen, Henrik. Baumeister Solness. Schauspiel in 3 Akten. Aus d.Norw.übertr.von Hans Egon Gerlach. Mit e. Nachw. v. Anni Carlsson. Stuttgart 1977. 95 s. (Universal-Bibliothek. 3026.) Nachdr.

Ibsen, Henrik. Brand. Tradukinta el la norvega de Erling Anker Haugen. Antverpeno 1978. 320 s.

Ibsen, Henrik. The burnt ship. Henrik Ibsen «Brændte skibe». Overs. av John Northam. – Ibsenårbok 1977, 77.

Ibsen, Henrik. Casa di bambola. Un dramma sulla condizione della donna. A cura di Gabriella Ferruggia. Trad.di Maria Emma Raggio-Salvi e Lucio Chiavarelli. In appendice due lettere di Ibsen sui diritti della donna e interventi critici di Gramsci e Lu Hsün. Nuova ed. Roma 1978. 119 s. (Cultura politica. 160. Sezione femminismo. 6.)

Ibsen, Henrik. The complete major prose plays. Transl. and introd. by Rolf Fjelde. N. Y. 1978. 1143 s.

Ibsen, Henrik. Dramen. Aus d.Norweg.übers.von Bernhard Schulze. Mit e.Nachwort von Horst Bien. Berlin 1977. 841 s. (Bibliotek der Weltliteratur.)

Ibsen, Henrik. Et dukkehjem. Udg. af Danskelærerforeningen ved Lars Nielsen. 9. opl. Kbh. 1978. 140 s. 1. opl. 1945.

Ibsen, Henrik. Gengangere. Udg. af Dansklærerforeningen ved Jørgen Haugan. Kbh. 1976. 132 s. 2. opl. 1979.

(Ibsen, Henrik). Henrik Ibsen i scenisk belysning. Udg. af Jytte Wiingaard. Kbh. 1978. 169 s. ill. = Teatervidenskabelige studier. 6.

(Ibsen, Henrik). Henrik Ibsen's brev. Kronologisk registrant med Adressatregister m.v. Ved Øyvind Anker. Oslo 1978. 153 s. faks. (Universitetsbiblioteket i Oslo. Skrifter. 6.)

Ibsen, Henrik. In a composer's visitors book. Henrik Ibsen: «I en komponists stambog». Overs. av John Northam. – Ibsenårbok 1977, 121.

Ibsen, Henrik. Narodni neprijatelj. [En folkefiende.] Forord av Stanislav Bajić. 2. utg. Beograd 1975. 125 s.

Ibsen, Henrik. Om Vigtigheden af Selvkundskab. – Verdens Gang 1978, 20/3, 33. (Den ukjente Henrik Ibsen.)

Ibsen, Henrik. The Oxford Ibsen. Vol.VIII. Little Eyolf, John Gabriel Borkman, When we dead awaken. Ed. and transl. by James Walter McFarlane. Oxford, London, N. Y. 1977. XIII, 390 s. Introduction, 1 – 34. Appendices, 309 – 381. Select bibliography, 383 – 390.

Ibsen, Henrik. Peer Gynt. Versión, prólogo y notas: Jose-Benito Alique. Madrid 1978. 210 s. port. (Colección Novelas y cuentos. Seccion literatura. Serie Literatura Noruega Teatro siglo XIX. 227.)

Ibsen, Henrik. Peer Gynt. Russisk overs. av Alla Šarapova. Moskva 1978. 269 s.

Ibsen, Henrik, Rosmersholm. Schauspiel in 4 akten. Aus. d. Norweg. Übertr.u.mit..Nachw.von Hans Egon Gerlach. Stuttgart 1978. 109 s. (Universal-Bibliothek. 2280.) Nachdr.

Ibsen, Henrik. Samlede verker. 16. utg. Oslo 1978. 6 b. + tilleggsbind. Etterordsforfattere: B. 1. Åse Hiorth Lervik. B. 2. Bjørn Hemmer. B. 3. Bjørn Hemmer og Paulus Svendsen. B. 4. Edvard Beyer. B. 5. Otto Hageberg. B. 6. John Northam og Edvard Beyer. Tilleggsbind: Ibsen-bilder. Ved Mentz Schulerud. Anmeldelser, vide *Erik Pierstorff, Jan Erik Hansen.*

Ibsen, Henrik. Schauspielle. Ubertr.von Hans Egon Gerlach. Mit e.Vorw.von Joachim Kaiser. 3.Aufl. Hamburg 1977. 1085 s. (Campe-Klassiker.) 1.Aufl. 1968.

Ibsen, Henrik. Die Stützen der Gesellschaft. Nora. Schauspiele. Aus d.Norw.übertr.von Georg Schulte-Frohlinde. Nachwort, Zeittaf.u. bibliograph. Hinweise: Hans Georg Meyer. München 1978. 191 s. (Goldmann-Klassiker. 7569.) (Ein Goldmann-Taschenbuch.)

Ibsen, Henrik. Three poems by Henrik Ibsen, translated by Robert Bly: Burnt ships, The Murder of Abraham Lincoln, The Power of memory. – Scandinavian review 66/1978: 4, 46 – 50. Orig. tit. Brente skibe, Abraham Lincolns mord, Minnets makt.

Ibsen, Henrik. Vildanden. 2. utg. ved Else Høst. Oslo 1976. 126 s. (Gyldendals skoleutgaver.)

Ibsen, Henrik. Vildanden. Udg. af Dansklærerforeningen ved Folmer Jensen. 2. udg. 2. oplag. Kbh. 1977. 178 s. 2. udg. 1973.

Ibsen, Henrik. De wilde eend. Hedda Gabler. Vertaling Cora & Sybren Polet. Amsterdam 1977. 215 s. (BB Toneel.) Nawoord: Amy van Marken.

Ibsen and Munch. – Scandinavian review 66/1978: 4, 40 – 45.

Ibsen auf der deutschen Bühne: Texte zur Rezeption. Hg.von Wilhelm Friese. Tübingen 1976. 150 s.

Ibsen for alle pengene på National denne våren. – Aftenposten 1978, 9/1, nr. 13, 6.

«Ibsen senza fine» con il prof. Lampl al Cca (Circolo della cultura, Trieste). Referat av foredrag 30/11-1978. – Il Piccolo (Trieste) 1978, 27/12.

Ibsen som dansende bjørn til sin egen geburdsag. – Dagbladet 1978 20/1, 5.

Ibsenhuset, vide *Ibsen-jubileet* i Grimstad 1978.

Ibsen-jubileet braker løs i mars. – Aftenposten 1977, 5/12, nr. 563, 7.

Ibsen-jubileet i Grimstad 1978. Utg. av Ibsenhuset og Grimstad bymuseum. Grimstad 1978. 12 s.

Ibsenukens høydepunkt: Urfremførelsen av «Terje Vigen». (Musikk av Guttorm Guttormsen.) – Morgenbladet 1978, 20/3, 10.

Ibsen-utstilling åpnet i New York. – Aftenposten 1978, 25/5, nr. 230, 7.

Ibsenårbok 1977. Red.komité: Daniel Haakonsen, Else Høst, Einar Østvedt, John Northam. Oslo 1977. 234 s. port. Anmeldelse, vide *Carl Fredrik Engelstad.*

Iwaszkiewicz, Jaroslav. Szkice o literat1977. 375 s. ill.

Jacobsen, Ruth Sommerfeldt. Hva med oss og Henrik Ibsen? – Nationen 1977, 28/9. Kronikk.

Jansson, Sigurd. Ibsen 150 år. Nordens främste dramatiker. – Blekinge Läns Tidning 1978, 10/1, 2.

Jenkins, Martin, vide *Meyer, Michael. Jenkins, Martin.* «Brand» and «Peer Gynt» – two plays for the imagination. – The Listener 1978, 14/12, 787 – 790.

Jensen, Folmer. Dramaturgisk analyse. – Ibsen, H. Vildanden. Kbh. 1977. S. 129 – 171.

Johanssen, Kjell Chr. Vildanden mellom mørke fjell. – Arbeiderbladet 1978, 9/2, 15. Anmeldelse av Telemark Teaters forestilling.

Johnson, Kari. The symbolic child: a study of transformation in Henrik Ibsen's late plays. Diss. Univ. of California, San Diego 1977. 205 s.

Johnsrud, Even Hebbe. Grimstads Ibsen. – Aftenposten 1978, 20/3, nr. 133, 6.

Johnston, Brian. The mediocre angels of De unges Forbund. – Scandinavian studies 50/1978, 304 – 317.

Jones, David Richard. The virtues of Hedda Gabler. – Educational theatre journal 29/1977, 447 – 462.

Jorgenson, Theodore. Henrik Ibsen: a study in art and personality. London 1978. 550 s. Cop. 1945.

Julian, Ria. Ibsen in Manchester. – Plays and players 26/1978: 3, 10 – 13. Anm. av «The Lady from the Sea» på Royal Exchange Theatre.

Jølting, Per. Henrik Ibsen i Rosenes by. – Jølting, P. Inne i fjordene. Molde 1976. S. 17 – 27.

Kabell, Aage. Ibsen og Norden. – Nordisk tidskrift för vetenskap, konst och industri 55/1979: 1, 12 – 21.

Kaiser, Joachim. Vorwort. – Ibsen, H. Schauspiele. Hamburg 1977. S. 7 – 26. (Campe-Klassiker.)

Kalocsay, K. Postparolo. – Ibsen, H. Brand. Antverpeno 1978. S. 301 – 319.

Kanter, Robert, vide *Kildal, Birger.* Tre ganger Ibsen i Paris. – Morgenbladet 1978, 10/1.

Kauffmann, Stanley. A doll's house. – Kauffmann, S. Persons of the drama: theatre criticism and comment. N. Y. 1976. S. 125 – 129.

Kauffmann, Stanley. A doll's house/Hedda Gabler. – Kauffmann, S. Persons of the drama: theatre criticism and comment. N. Y. 1976. S. 120 – 123.

K. B. Amputert Ibsen i NRK? – Morgenbladet 1978, 12/1, 4.

Keller, Werner. Gewissen und analytische Form in Ibsen's Gesellschaftsdrama. – (Beissner, Friedrich) Festschrift für... Hg.: Ulrich Gaier, Werner Volke. Bebenhausen 1974. S. 180 – 196.

Kildal, Birger. Tre ganger Ibsen i Paris. – Morgenbladet 1978, 10/1, 4. «En folkefiende» på Edward VII-teatret, «Hedda Gabler» på Cité internationale og «Byggmester Solness» på Bio-Théâtre Opera. Kommentarer ved Robert Kanter i L'Express.

Kirke- og undervisningsdepartementet. 150 år. Ideer, stoff- og programtilbud for undervisningen i 1978. Oslo 1978. 17 s.

Kjetsaa, Geir. Henrik Ibsen og Oscar von Knorring. – Ibsenårbok 1977, 22 – 45.

Kjøller Ritzu, Merete. In margine a una rappresentazione italiana del Peer Gynt. – AION. Annali dell'Istituto universitario orientale di Napoli. Sezione germanica. Vol. XIX, 1976. Studi Nederlandesi – Studi Nordici. S. 145 – 154.

Klett, Renate. Schickeria-Theater: Ibsen «Vildente» in Genua. – Theater heute 18/1977: 8, 56.

Knispel, O. M. Ibsens håndskrift: Forandringen helt usedvanlig. – Aftenposten 1978, 18/3, nr. 131, 6.

Kott, Jan. Ibsen na nowo odczytany. W 150-lecie urodzin Ibsena (1828 – 1978). – Wiadomošci. Tygodnik. (London) XXXIII, 1978, nr. 1702, 12/11, nr. 1703, 19/11, nr. 1704, 26/11, nr. 1705, 3/12. (Ibsen lest påny.)

Krag, Helena. Ny Nora i Stockholm. – Arbeiderbladet 1978, 13/11, 12. Stockholms Stadsteaters forestilling.

Kristensen, Sven Møller. Literary sociology: Four lectures. Brugge 1975. 47 s. (U-niv.te Gent. Faculteit van de letteren en wijsbegeerte: Inaugurale reden en lezingen. 2.)

Kruntorad, Paul. Palitzsch inszeniert in Wien «Hedda Gabler», C. H. Meyer Hor-váths «Italienische Nacht». (Das neue Burgtheater.) – Theater heute 19/1978: 7, 16 – 17.

Krøvel, Eva. «Hedda» med nerve og drama. Anmeldt av... – Aftenposten 1978, 7/10, nr. 462, 5.

Kvaal, Tor Kaare. Dikteren som tiet når han talte. «Tvert i mot» på Amfiscenen anmeldt av... – Morgenbladet 1978, 19/6, 1.

Kvaal, Tor Kaare. Et dryss av vidd, fart og spenning. De unges Forbund anmeldt av... – Morgenbladet 1978, 6/2, 1, 10.

Kvaal, Tor Kaare. Nye rystelser i dukkehjemmet. Gjestespill på Scene 2 anmeldt av... – Morgenbladet 1978, 3/3, 8. Svenska Teatern, Helsingfors. Forestilling på Det Norske Teatret, Scene 2.

Kvaal, Tor Kaare. Regnbuen mellom havet og fjellet. «Lille Eyolf» anmeldt av... – Morgenbladet 1978, 12/5, 1, 10.

Kvaal, Tor Kaare. Scenen som omvei. «Brand» anmeldt av... – Morgenbladet 1978, 12/6, 1, 10.

Kvaal, Tor Kaare. Unge sørgende bruder. «Fruen fra havet» anmeldt av... – Morgenbladet 1977, 27/12, 1, 10.

Lampl, Hans Erich. Nova über Henrik Ibsen und sein Alterswerk. Das Tagebuch der Emilie Bardach (1889 – 90). Oslo/Trieste/Zürich 1977. 94 s. ill.port.faks.

Lampl, Hans Erich, vide *«Ibsen senza fine».*

Lange-Nielsen, Sissel. «Hedda Gabler». – Aftenposten 1978, 4/9, nr. 404, 6. Anmeldelse av Radioteatrets fremførelse.

Lange-Nielsen, Sissel. Ibsen i Finlands radio. – Aftenposten 1978, 18/1, nr. 29, 6. Anmeldelse av «En folkefiende».

Lange-Nielsen, Sissel. Kvinner presenterer Ibsen. – Aftenposten 1978, 10/1, nr. 16, 11. Anmeldelse av et TV-program 9/1 1978.

Larkin, Maurice. Hope and despair. – Larkin, M. Man and society in nine-teenth-century realism. London 1977. S. 163 – 174.

Larkin, Maurice. Society versus the individual. – Larkin, M. Man and society in nineteenth-century realism. London 1977. S. 152 – 162.

Lee, Jennette. The Ibsen secret. A key to the prose dramas of Henrik Ibsen. N. Y. 1976. 207 s. port. Repr. of 1907 ed.

Leino, Eino. Henrik Ibsen. – Leino, E. Maailmankirjailijoita. Helsinki 1978. S. 203 – 279. = Suomalaisen kirjallisuuden seura. 342.

Leirfall, Jon. Var Peer Gynt islending? – Syn og segn 84/1978: 3, 161 – 165.

Leland, Charles. Ibsen, Chesterton and Shaw: A misunderstanding all around: A response to Vincent Balice. – The Chesterton review 3 (1976 – 77), 35 – 42.

Leland, Charles. In defense of pastor Manders. – Modern drama 21/1978: 4, 405 – 420.

Lervik, Åse Hiorth. Etterord. – Ibsen, H. Samlede verker. B. 1. Oslo 1978. S. 409 – 443.

Lester, Elenore. Ibsen's unliberated heroines. – Scandinavian review 66/1978: 4, 58 – 66.

Levin, Mona. «Hedda» av Charles Marowitz i Bergen: – Norsk Ibsen-pietet hemmer nytenkning. – Aftenposten 1978, 24/5, nr. 228, 6.

Levin, Mona. «Ibsen in America» i mai 1978. Symposium, konsert og teater i New York. – Aftenposten 1977, 31/10, nr. 503, 7.

Lingard, John Christopher. The past in Ibsen's tragedies. Diss. Univ. of Western Ontario (Canada) 1976.

Ljubimov, N. Innledning. – Ibsen, Henrik. Peer Gynt. Russisk overs. av Alla Šarapova. Moskva 1978. S. 5 – 28.

L. L. Fot-noter til Ibsen-året. – Norsklæraren 2/1978: 2, 29 – 30.

Lundberg, Bengt. Henrik Ibsen – dramatiker med bestående världsrykte. – Östgöta Correspondenten 1978, 16/2.

Lunde, Johs. Ibsen – demon eller idealist? – Morgenbladet 1978, 20/2. Kronikk.

McCarthy, Mary. Il testamento di Ibsen. – Ibsen, H. L'anitra selvatica. Genova 1977. S. 103 – 112. (Teatro di Genova. N. 26.) Orig. tit. The Will and Testament of Ibsen, i Partizan Review XXIII, 1956. Overs. av Liliana Salvadori.

Macfall, Haldane. Ibsen: the man, his art and his significance. Ill. by Joseph Simpson. Folcroft, Pa. 1976. 326 s. port. Repr. of 1907 ed.

McFarlane, James Walter. Ibsen's poem-cycle «I Billedgalleriet»: a study. – Scandinavica 17/1978: 1, 13 – 48.

McFarlane, James Walter, vide *Fletcher, J.* McFarlane, J. Modernist drama.

McFarlane, James Walter, vide *Ibsen, Henrik.* The Oxford Ibsen. Vol. VIII. Oxf., Lond., N. Y. 1977.

Magris, Claudio. Ibsen, passioni al tramonto. Centocinquant'anni dalla nascita del drammaturgo. – Corriere della sera (Milano) 1978, 19/8.

Marken, Amy van. Nawoord. – Ibsen, H. De wilde eend. Hedda Gabler. Amsterdam 1977. S. 205 – 213.

Marker, Frederick J. Ibsen at Oxford. – Scandinavica 17/1978, 137 – 157.

Marker, Frederick and Lise-Lone. Early Ibsen performances in America. – Scandinavian review 66/1978: 4, 20 – 34.

Marker, Lise-Lone and Frederick. Ibsen's theatre: aspects of a chronicle and a quest. – Modern drama 21/1978: 4, 345 – 378. ill.

Marowitz, Charles. Schøyen, Liv. Hedda. Oslo 1978. 133 s. ill. (Aschehougs litteraturverksted. 5.)

Meyer, Hans Georg. Nachwort. – Ibsen, H. Die Stützen der Gesellschaft. Nora. München 1978. S. 169 – 178. (Goldmann-Klassiker. 7569.) (Ein Goldmann-Taschenbuch.)

Meyer, Michael. Askeladden i kongeriket. – Programbladet 32/1978: 1, 4 – 5, 32.

Meyer, Michael. Jenkins, Martin. «Brand» and «Peer Gynt» – two plays for the imagination. – The Listener 1978, 14/12, 787 – 790. Forhåndsomtale av radiofremførelsen i Radio 3, 12/12-1978.

Michaelis, Rolf. Luc Bondy inszeniert Ibsens «Gespenster» am Deutschen Schauspielhaus Hamburg. – Theater heute 18/1977: 8, 4 – 8.

Michaelis, Rolf. Rudolf Noelte in Berlin und Nicolas Brieger in Hamburg inszenieren Ibsens «Nora». – Theater heute 18/1977:. 5, 6 – 10.

Midbøe, Hans. Peer Gynt, teatret og tiden. Oslo 1976 – (Scandinavian university books.) 1. Ludvig Josephson og den «eldre» tradisjon. 1978. 192 s. pl.ill. 2. Hans Jacob Nilsen og den «antiromantiske» revolt. 1976. 194 s. pl.ill. Anmeldelse, vide *Carl Fredrik Engelstad.*

Miller, Arthur. Preface to an adaption of Ibsen's An enemy of the people. – Miller, A. Theater essays. N. Y. 1978. S. 16 – 21.

Mortimer, John. The drawingroom iconoclast. – Observer magazine 1978, 19/3, 36 – 37.

Munch til Minnesota. – Aftenposten 1978, 13/3, nr. 121, 6. Utstilling av grafikk over Henrik Ibsens skuespill ved St.Olaf College.

Nationaltheatret: «Fruen fra havet» innleder Ibsen-året. – Aftenposten 1977, 23/12, nr. 595, 6.

Neiiendam, Klaus. The second staging of Peer Gynt, 1886. – Theatre research international N. s. vol. 2/1976: 2, 104 – 117.

Nettels, E. Howells and Ibsen. – Texas studies in literature and language 20/1978: 2, 153 – 168.

Nicoll, Allardyce. The triumph of realism: Ibsen. – Nicoll, A. World drama from Æschylus to Anouilh. London 1976. S. 440 – 459.

Nielsen, Lars. Vejledning. – *Ibsen, H.* Et dukkehjem. Kbh. 1978. S. 103 – 135.

Nielson, Haakon B. Da Albert Engstrøm sang viser for Ibsen. – Aftenposten 1978, 19/4, nr. 178, 5.

Nielson, Haakon B. Ibsen – en kraft av første rang. – Aftenposten 1977, 23/11, nr. 544, 5.

Nigro, Kirsten F. The lady from the sea, by Henrik Ibsen. Brum Studio, Birmingham Repertory Theatre, November 1, 1977. – Educational theatre journal 30/1978, 263. Anmeldelse.

Nilsen, Wenche Thorunn. Vinternatt med vampyrer. [Intervju med Per Bronken om TV-versjonen av John Gabriel Borkman,] – Programbladet 32/1978: 1, 8 – 9.

Nordrå, Olav. Ibsen og kvinnene. – Aftenposten 1978, 20/3, nr. 133, 4.

Noreng, Harald. Bjørnson i Ibsens diktning – og Ibsen i Bjørnsons. – Verdens Gang 1978, 12/5, 36 – 37.

Noreng, Harald. Henrik Ibsen: Rimbrev til fru Heiberg. – (Steen, Ellisiv) Kvinner og bøker. Festskrift til ... på hennes 70-årsdag 4. februar 1978. Oslo 1978. S. 87 – 101.

Norsk filminstitutt. Henrik Ibsen 1828 – 1978: en filmografi. Utarb. av Karin Synnøve Hansen. Oslo 1978. 30 s. ill. Også utgitt på engelsk.

Northam, John. A note on the language of Rosmersholm. – Ibsenårbok 1977, 209 – 215.

Northam, John. Etterord. – Ibsen, H. Samlede verker. B. 6. Oslo 1978. S. 475 – 501.

Northam, John. Ibsen the poet. – Modern drama 21/1978: 4, 421 – 431.

Northam, John. On a firm foundation – the translation of Ibsen's prose. – Ibsenårbok 1977, 78 – 89.

Northam, John. Waiting for Prospero. – (Bradbrook, Muriel Clara) English drama: Forms and development. Essays in honour of ... Cambridge 1977. S. 188 – 202. Om Rosmersholm.

Northam, John, vide *Ibsen, Henrik.* «At a wedding». *Ibsen, Henrik.* «The burnt skip». *Ibsen, Henrik.* «In a composer's visitors book».

Northam, John, vide *Ibsenårbok* 1977.

Oberholzer, Otto. IV. Internationales Ibsen-Seminar. – Skandinavistik 8/1978: 2, 144 – 145.

Oellers, Norbert. Spuren Ibsens in Gerhart Hauptmanns früher Dramen. – (Rüdiger, Horst) Teilnahme und Spiegelung. Festschrift für... Hg.von Beda Allemann und Erwin Koppen. Berlin 1975. S. 397 – 414.

Ollén, Gunnar. Nytolkning av Ibsen? – Tidsspegel 1978: 4, 150 – 151. Om J. Haugan, Henrik Ibsens metode.

Page, Elin B. Jubileumsforestilling i London: «Samfundets støtter». – Frisprog 1977, 12/11, 4. Anm. av forestillingen på Aldwych med The Royal Shakespeare Company.

Palmer, Helen H. European drama criticism 1900 – 1975. Comp. by ... 2. ed. Dawson 1977. 653 s. Ibsen, 260 – 278.

The paradox of Ibsen. – Norway information. Publ. by the Royal Norwegian Ministry of foreign affairs. 1978: 426. (January). 4 s.

Paucker, Eleanor K. El Brand de Ibsen, y El sepulcro de don Quijote de Unamuno. – (Turnbull, Phyllis B.) Poemas y ensayos para un homenaje. Madrid 1976. S. 135 – 141.

Paul, Fritz, vide *Henrik Ibsen. Darmstadt 1977.*

Peer Gynt. Urpremiere 24. februar 1876. – Norsk Teaterårbok 1975, 3 – 6.

Peer Gynt stemnet. 12. Vinstra 1976. Frå Peer Gynt stemnet på Vinstra 8. – 15. august 1976. Folkekultur og eksistensialisme i Henrik Ibsens Peer Gynt. Ved Erik Østerud. Vinstra 1976. 31 s. ill. 4°. Også med etterord på tysk og engelsk.

Peer Gynt stemnet. 13. Vinstra 1977. Frå Peer Gynt stemnet på Vinstra 5. – 14. august 1977. Peer Gynts verden. Ved Bjørn Hemmer. Vinstra 1977. 39 s. ill. 4°. Også med etterord på tysk og engelsk.

Peer Gynt stemnet. 14. Vinstra 1978. Frå Peer Gynt stemnet på Vinstra 4. – 13. august 1978. Folketradisjonens Peer Gynt. Ved Olav Bø. Vinstra 1978. 35 s. ill. 4°. Også med etterord på engelsk og fransk.

Pierstorff, Erik. De unge med Ibsen-rekord. – Dagbladet 1978, 12/5, 4. Anmeldelse av Lille Eyolf på Amfiscenen, Nationaltheatret.

Pierstorff, Erik. Henrik Ibsen, anarkist og besteborger. – Dagbladet 1978, 25/4, 10.

Pierstorff, Erik. Henrik Ibsens «Peer Gynt» verdensmesterskap i Stavanger. – Dagbladet 1978, 28/2, 5. Anmeldelse av forestillingen på Rogaland Teater.

Pierstorff, Erik. Ibsen – oppstilt og til fots. Anmeldelse av I. s samlede verker utg. 1978. – Dagbladet 1978, 18/3, 20 og 20/3, 5.

Pierstorff, Erik. Ibsen snauhogd i Seljord. – Dagbladet 1978, 9/2, 5. Anmeldelse av «Vildanden» på Telemark Teater.

Pierstorff, Erik. Ibsen som filmmann. – Film og kino 1978: 1, 14 – 15.

Pierstorff, Erik. Ibsen – vår mann på National. – Dagbladet 1977, 27/12, 5. Anmeldelse av «Fruen fra havet».

Pierstorff, Erik. Om å musisere med Ibsen. – Dagbladet 1978, 11/12, 5.

Pierstorff, Erik. Peer Gynt i Beograd: billetter på svartebørs. – Dagbladet 1978, 25/9, 8.

Pierstorff, Erik. Peer Gynt med dukker og mennesker. – Dagbladet 1978, 3/11, 5.

Pierstorff, Erik. Rosmersholm i grått og svart. – Dagbladet 1978, 4/2, 4. Anm. av forestillingen på Trøndelag Teater.

Pierstorff, Erik. Valgte Ibsen side? – Dagbladet 1978, 19/10, 4. Anmeldelse av «Lærlingen» på Møre og Romsdal Regionteater.

Pierstorff, Erik. Veldig Ibsen – men veldig mye! – Dagbladet 1978, 12/6, 9. Anm. av «Brand» på Nationaltheatret.

Playwright as painter. – Scandinavian review 66/1978: 4, 52 – 57.

Pletanek, Vaclav. Ibsen presentert som Bresjnev-fan. – Morgenbladet 1978, 15/7, 5. Ibsen-jubileet i Praha, Tsjekkoslovakia.

Politzer, Heinz. Die Wunde Glück: Zu Henrik Ibsens «Baumeister Solness». – Politzer, H. Hatte Ödipus einen Ödipus-Komplex? Versuche zum Thema Psychoanalyse und Literatur. München 1974. S. 127 – 155. (Serie Piper. 86.)

Pollan, Brita. Ibsen 150 år efter. Og ennu for tidlig? – Aftenposten 1978, 20/3, nr. 133, 4.

Popovich, Helen. Shelf of dolls: A modern view of Ibsen's emancipated women. – CEA critic 39/1977: 3, 4 – 8.

Postlewait, Thomas Elwood. The design of the past: Uses of memory in the drama of Henrik Ibsen, Samuel Beckett and Harold Pinter. Diss. University of Minnesota 1976. 258 s.

Rathsman, Gunnela. Litteraturresa till Sörlandet och Ibsen. – Nya Wermlands-Tidningen 1978, 23/5, 2. 6/6, 2.

Ree, Kristian. Ibsens leger. Samt medisinske aspekter på dikteren og hans dikterverk. – Tidsskrift for den norske legeforening 1975: 27, 1507 – 1511.

Reed, Walter L. The Cherry orchard and Hedda Gabler. – Homer to Brecht. The European epic and dramatic traditions. Ed. by M. Seidel and E. Mendelson. New Haven, Conn. 1977. S. 317 – 335.

Řezniček, Ladislav. Ibsens italienske år. – Arbeiderbladet 1978, 18/7, 16. 20/7, 12.

Rieger, Gerd Enno. Noras Rollenengagement. – Orbis litterarum 32/1977, 50 – 73.

Rieger, Gerd Enno. Utopins dramaturgi hos Ibsen. – Internasjonale studiekonferanse om nordisk litteratur. 11. Gent 1976. Literature and reality: Creatio versus Mimesis. Ed. by A. Bolckmans. Ghent 1977. S. 311 – 322.

Rieger, Gerd Enno. Zur Dramaturgie des Utopischen bei Ibsen. – Literatur ist Utopie. Frankfurt am Main 1978. S. 245 – 265. (Suhrkamp. 935.)

Rinaldi, Marcella, vide *Ibsen, Henrik*. L'anitra selvatica. Genova 1977. (Teatro di Genova. N. 26.)

Rischbieter, Henning. Peter Palitzsch inszeniert Ibsens «Baumeister Solness» in Frankfurt. – Theater heute 19/1978: 10, 13 – 15.

Roberts, Richard Ellis. Henrik Ibsen: a critical study. Norwood, Pa. 1977. 205 s. Repr. of 1912 ed.

Rogers, Katherine M. A woman appreciates Ibsen. – The Centennial review 18/1974, 91 – 108.

Rosengarten, David. The Lady from the sea: Ibsen's submerged allegory. – Educational theatre journal 29/1977, 463 – 476.

Rovinsky, Robert T. Ibsen and Lagerkvist revisited. – Scandinavian studies 50/1978, 39 – 49.

Rudler, Roderick. Ibsen som rolleinstruktør. – Samtiden 87/1978 : 4, 243 – 255. Også i Ergo 1978, 1 – 11.

Rudler, Roderick. Ibsen vår første moderne teatermann. – Aftenposten 1978, 20/3, nr. 133, 7. Intervju.

Rudler, Roderick. Uroppførelse av Gildet paa Solhoug og Fru Inger til Østeraad. – Ibsenårbok 1977, 52 – 76.

Rühle, Günther. Niels-Peter Rudolph und Peter Zadek inszenieren «Hedda Gabler» von Ibsen in Berlin und Bochum. – Theater heute 18/1977: 4, 8 – 14.

Røed, Arne, «Right to the top» – ? – Ibsenårbok 1977, 122 – 179.

Røed, Liv Herstad. Av perfekt merke. TV starter Ibsen-året med oppsetning. – Verdens Gang 1978, 11/1. 31. Anmeldelse av «John Gabriel Borkman.

Røed, Liv Herstad. Forloren and. Bidraget fra Telemark Teater til Ibsen-året. – Verdens Gang 1978, 9/2, 31. Anmeldelse.

Røed, Liv Herstad. Ibsen-året er over oss. – Verdens Gang 1978, 9/1, 41.

Røed, Liv Herstad. Visuell dominans over «Rosmersholm». – Verdens Gang 1978, 15/11, 35. Anmeldelse av Fjernsynsteatrets forestilling.

Rønning, Helge, «Gengangere» – et familiedrama. – Drama-analyser fra Holberg til Hoem. Red. av Leif Longum. Oslo 1977. S. 54 – 64.

Saari, Sandra E. Hedda Gabler: The past recaptured. – Modern drama 20/1977, 299 – 316.

Saari, Sandra E. Of madness or fame: Ibsen's Bygmester Solness. – Scandinavian studies 50/1978, 1 – 18.

Sanborn, Torunn Ystaas. «Byggmester Solness» og sviket mot fellesskapet. – Vinduet 32/1978: 3, 40 – 44.

Sanborn, Torunn Ystaas. Strindberg og Nora, om «Det vidunderlige». – Vinduet 31/1977, 83 – 88.

Sato, Toshihiko. Ibsen and Mayama Seika's The first man (1907). – Proceedings of the 6th Congress of the international comparative literature association. Ed. by M. Cadot, M. V. Dimič, D. Malone, M. Szabolcsi. Stuttgart 1975. S. 131 – 136.

Schödel, Helmut. Ohne Chancen? Ibsen «Nora» in Nürnberg. – Theater heute 18/1977: 12, 58.

Schulerud, Mentz. Ibsen og byen. – Byminner 1978: 2, 3 – 12.

Schulerud. Mentz. Ibsen und die Stadt. – Ausblick (Lübeck) 29/1978: 3/4, 33 – 39.

Schulerud, Mentz, vide *Ibsen, Henrik.* Samlede verker. Tilleggsbind. Ibsen-bilder ved M. S.

Schøyen, Liv, vide *Marowitz, Charles. Schøyen, Liv.* Hedda. Oslo 1978.

Sebald, W. G. Mord an den Vätern: Bemerkungen zu einigen Dramen der spätbürgerlichen Zeit. – Neophilologus 60/1976: 3, 432 – 441.

Seidel, Hans-Dieter. Niels-Peter Rudolph inszeniert «Ein Gespräch im Hause Stein», Alfred Kirchner inszeniert die «Wildente». (Stuttgart). – Theater heute 18/1977: 11, 24 – 25.

Self, David. «Ghosts» by Henrik Ibsen. – Plays and players 26/1978: 3, 22. Anmeldelse av forestillingen på Key Theatre, Peterborough 25/9-1978 med Actors Company.

Serum, Robert William. The evolution of the chorus in the plays of Henrik Ibsen. Diss. Univ. of Alabama 1975. Ann Arbor, Mich. 1977. 209 s.

Sethi, Surjit Singh. The theatre of Ibsenites in Punjab: a critical study. Patiala 1976. 131 s.

Shelton, Frank W. The Wild duck image in Willa Cater and Henrik Ibsen. – American notes and queries 15/1976, 24 – 27.

Silver, Lola, vide *Berke, Jacqueline. Silver, L.* The «awakened» woman in literature and real life.

Simon, John Ivan. Peer Gynt. – Simon, J. I. Singularities: essays on the theater, 1964 – 1974. N. Y. 1976. S. 3 – 16.

Simon, John W. The wild duck. – Simon, J. I. Singularities: essays on the theater, 1964 – 1974. N. Y. 1976. S. 35 – 51.

Sjöbäck, Hans. Psykoanalysen som livslögnsteori: läran om försvaret. Lund 1977. 283 s.

Skien bibliotek. Ibseniana: tillegg 1978. Skien 1978. 39 s. ill.

Skien ønsker seg Ibsen-institutt. – Aftenposten 1978, 10/4, nr. 161, 7. Intervju med Einar Østvedt.

Skipenes, Dagfrid. Ironi og virkelighetsstruktur i Kejser og Galilæer. – Ibsen-årbok 1977, 90 – 106.

Skjønsberg, Simen. Biter ikke Ibsen lenger? – Dagbladet 1978, 22/3, 5.

Slataper, Scipio. Ibsen. «Invito alla lettura» di Ruggero Jacobbi. Firenze 1977. XII, 241 s. (Biblioteca Vallecchi. Collana dir. da Luigi Baldacci.)

Sletbakk, Astrid. Henrik Ibsen uten bremser. – Verdens Gang 1978, 13/4, 31. Anmeldelse av forestillingen på Regionteatret i Sogn og Fjordane.

Smith, Fernanda Sparre. Norsk urpremiere på Operaen. Balletten «Hedda» anmeldt av... – Morgenbladet 1978, 9/10, 10.

Steen, Ellisiv. Det norske nasjonalhistoriske drama 1750 – 1974. Oslo 1976. 159 s.

Stenström, Thure. Ibsen penetrerad i sina drömmars Skien. – Svenska Dagbladet 1978, 12/6, 8. Ibsen-symposiet i Skien, mai 1978.

Stepiņš, Laimonis. Henrik Ibsens latviešu teātri. Riga 1978. 209 s. port.

Stokland, Olav. Hjalmar Ekdal. – Stokland, O., Hjalmar Ekdal og andre essays. Lysaker 1977. S. 77 – 132.

Storeng, Jørn. Ibsen på fransk for fulle hus. – Verdens Gang 1978, 10/1, 31.

Strømberg, Ulla, vide *Den levende Ibsen.* Kbh. 1978.

Svendsen, Paulus. Etterord. – Ibsen, H. Samlede verker. B. 3. Oslo 1978. S. 439 – 454.

Sørensen, Roll. En liten man med fransade byxor. – Gefle Dagblad 1978. 11/7, 6.

Tandberg, Monna. Nye spørsmål bak hvert svar. – Aftenposten 1978, 20/3, nr. 133, 7. Intervju.

They loved to draw Ibsen. (The «Vasari» diary.) – Art news 77/1978: 8, 14 – 18.

Thomsen, Kari. Bravo for Peer ved festivalen i Beograd. Rogaland Teaters forestilling mottatt med begeistring. – Stavanger Aftenblad 1978, 25/9, 1.

Thon, Jahn. Ibsens avsløringskunst. – Tidsskriftet Profil 1977: 4, 13 – 25.

Tredje internasjonale Ibsen-seminar, 22. – 27. mai 1975. Fana folkehøgskole, Store Milde, Bergen. Arr. av Nordisk institutt, Universitetet i Bergen. – Norsk Teaterårbok 1975, 166.

Turco, Alfred. Shaw's pragmatist ethic: A new look at The Quintessence of Ibsenism. – Texas studies in literature and language 17/1975, 855 – 879.

Universitetsbiblioteket i Oslo. «Et dukkehjem». Ibsen-utstilling i Universitetsbiblioteket i Oslo. – Cursus Librorum 1978: 1. Anmeldelse, vide *Ulf Peter Hellstrøm.*

Valency, Maurice Jacques. The flower and the castle. An introd. to modern drama. N. Y. 1975. 460 s. Repr. of 1963 ed. Ibsen, 118 – 237 m.m.

Vanberg, Bent. «Hedda Gabler» nå som opera. – Aftenposten 1978, 20/5, nr. 222, 6.

Vanberg, Bent. Ibsen-jubileet: «Kongsemnerne» i Minneapolis-teater. [Guthrie-teatret.] – Aftenposten 1978, 10/5, nr. 209, 6.

Vindsetmo, Bjørg. «Hedda med bart». Festspillpremiere på Den Nationale Scene anmeldt av ... – Morgenbaldet 1978, 25/5, 1, 10.

Vogelweith, Guy. Ibsen en Angleterre et en Allemagne: Autoritarisme paternel et impérialisme colonial (Jalons pour une étude comparative). – Recherches anglaises et américaines 8/1975, 155 – 162.

Vaagland, Odd, Ibsen i en Ekofisktid. – Norsklæraren 2/1978: 2, 31 – 32.

Waal, Carla. Willian Bloch's The Wild Duck. – Educational theatre journal 30/1978:4, 495 – 512.

Warnken, William P. Kate Chopin and Henrik Ibsen: A study of The Awakening and A Doll's House. – Massachusetts studies in English 1974: 4, 43 – 49.

Webb, Eugene. The ambiguities of secularization: modern transformations of the kingdom in Nietzsche, Ibsen, Beckett, and Stevens. – Webb, E., The dark dove: the sacred and secular in modern literature. Seattle 1975. S. 34 – 87.

Weissert, Elisabeth. Die absolute «Ideale Forderung» – Ibsens «Wildente». – Erziehungskunst 40/1976: 3, 102 – 109.

Whitaker, Thomas R. Fields of play in modern drama. Princeton 1977. 192 s. Kap. 3: Killing ourselves (Rosmersholm), 35 – 57.

Wiik, Steinar. Båten om kvelden. Kroatisk «Peer Gynt». – Aftenposten 1978, 5/5, nr. 201, 6. Anmeldelse av forestillingen på Det kroatiske nasjonalteater, Zagreb.

Wiik, Steinar. En lykkejeger i de lokale forhold. «De unges forbund» på Nationaltheatret. Anmeldt av... – Aftenposten 1978, 6/2, nr. 61, 44.

Wiik, Steinar. Farlig bukkeritt på Amfi. Thesbiteatrets «Peer Gynt». – Aftenposten 1978, 17/3, nr. 129, 7. Anmeldelse.

Wiik, Steinar. Nyskapende og sterk Ibsen. «Peer Gynt» på Rogaland Teater. Anmeldt av ... – Aftenposten 1978, 27/2, nr. 97, 24.

Wiik, Steinar. «Peer Gynt» til Beograd. (Rogaland Teater.) – Aftenposten 1978, 31/5, nr. 240, 6.

Wiik, Steinar. Rogaland Teaters «Peer Gynt»: Blinkende knapp på verdensvesten. – Aftenposten 1978, 17/8, nr. 375, 2.

Wiik, Steinar. Til bunns – og opp igjen. «Vildanden» på Telemark Teater. Anmeldt av ... – Aftenposten 1978, 9/2, nr. 67, 4.

Wiingaard, Jytte. Bygmester Solness. En semantisk analyse. – Ibsenårbok 1977, 180 – 208.

Wiingaard, Jytte, vide *Den levende Ibsen.* Kbh. 1978.

Wiingaard, Jytte, vide *(Ibsen, Henrik).* Henrik Ibsen i scenisk belysning. Kbh. 1978.

Wikborg, Tone. Gustav Vigeland og Henrik Ibsen. Oslo 1978. 40 s. ill. port. (Vigeland-museets skrifter nr. 8). Med katalog over utstilling av skulptur og tegninger i Vigeland-museet 1978.

Winger, Odd. I snoen fra Hedda. – Dagbladet 1978, 4/9, 4. Anmeldelse av Radioteatrets forestilling.

Winger, Odd. Ibsen presenterer Ibsen. – Dagbladet 1978, 14/4, 4. Anm. av forestillingen på Regionteatret i Sogn og Fjordane.

Winger, Odd. Ibsen-feiring. – Dagbladet 1977, 30/12, 5.

Wormdal, Celine. Peer Gynt som dukketeater. – Dagbladet 1978, 25/10, 4. Anmeldelse av Riksteatrets forestilling i Lillehammer.

Wysocki, Alfred. Spotkanie z Ibsenem. [Møte med Ibsen]. – Ciesielski, Zenon. Skandynawia w oczach Polaków. [Skandinavia i polakkenes øyne.] Gdańsk 1974. S. 347 – 348.

Zetkin, Clara. Kunst und Proletariat. Hg. von Hans Koch. Berlin 1977. 340 s. Henrik Ibsen, 259 – 267. Av: Die Gleichheit, 1906: 2, 13.

Ørjasæter, Jo. Nationaltheatret: Om Bolette og Ellida. – Nationen 1977, 27/12, 6. Anmeldelse av «Fruen fra havet».

Ørjasæter, Jo. Peer Gynt, den fotlette fant. – Nationen 1978, 29/4, 6.

Østerud, Erik, vide *Peer Gynt stemnet.* 12. Vinstra 1976.

Østvedt, Einar. Henrik Ibsen og hans barndomsmiljø. Utg. av Ibsenforbundet i samarbeid med Oluf Rasmussens forlag. 2. opplag. Skien 1977. 64 s. ill. port. 4°. O. m. engelsk tekst. 1. opplag 1966.

Østvedt, Einar. Henrik Ibsen, studier og streiftog. Skien 1978. 207 s. ill. port.

Østvedt, Einar, vide *Ibsenårbok 1977.*

Østvedt, Einar, vide *Skien ønsker seg Ibsen-institutt.*

Aalen, Magnhild. Når Nora gikk, hvorfor ble Ellida? – Kirke og Kultur 83/1978: 5, 301 – 311.

Aarseth, Asbjørn. Peer Gynt som tolkningsproblem. – Edda 1978: 6, 371 – 377.

Aarseth, Asbjørn. Scenisk rom og dramatisk erkjennelse i Ibsens «Gengangere». – Drama-analyser fra Holberg til Hoem. Red. av Leif Longum. Oslo 1977. S. 41 – 53.

Contributors

Edvard Beyer, (b. 1920),Ph.D. from the University of Bergen 1956 and Professor of Scandinavian literature at the Unviersity of Oslo 1958. His works include: *Hans E. Kinck* — Livsangst og livstro — I—II (1956-65), *Hamsun og vi* (1959), *Profiler og problemer* (19-6), *Utsyn over nosk litteratur* (1966, third edn. 1978), Harald & Edvard Beyer: *Norsk litterturhistorie* (1979, new edn 1978), *Fra Ibsen til Garborg (= Norges litteraturhistorie,* ed. E. Beyer, vol. 3, 1975). The Ibsen capter of this work has been published as a separate book, *Henrik Ibsen,* (1978), English transl. by Marie Wells, *Henrik Ibsen — The Man and his Work* (Lond. 1978). A number of articles, e.g. Livsgleden som problem i Ibsens diktning *(Edda* 1948), Problemer omkring oversettelsen av Shakespeares dramatikk *(Universitetet i Bergen: Årbok 1956),* Fra bukkerittet til Solvejgs hytte *(Omkring «Peer Gynt»,* ed. O. Hageberg 1967), When We Dead Awaken *(Contemporary Approaches to Ibsen,* 1971), Ibsen today *(Ibsenårboka* 1972), «Slekten fra 1814», Henrik Wergeland (in *Norges litteraturhistorie* vol. 2, 1974), Vilanden og det norske samfunn 1884 *(Nordisk litteraturhistorie,* 1978), postscripts in Henrik Ibsen: *Samlede verker,* vols. 4 and 6, 1978.

Alex Bolckmans, (f. 1923) dr. Ghent University (1949), aggrégé (Ghent University 1960), reader Gent University (1955—1965), full professor (1965—) occupying the only Chair of Scandinavian languages and literature in Belgium. Among his publications are *Henrik Ibsen* (1956), *The Stories of Hans Aanrud* (1960) *Individu en maatschappij in het werk van Knut Hamsun* (1967), *Inleiding tot de moderne literaturen* (1977[4]), *Literature and Reality. Proceedings of the 11 th Study Conference IASS* (1977), and many articles in Scandinavian, Belgian, Dutch, French periodicals.

Cecilie Wiborg Bonafede, f. 1929 i Oslo. Cand. philol. 1956. Førstebibliotekar ved Universitetsbiblioteket i Oslo. Har gitt ut en rekke bibliografiske arbeid, bl.a. Bibliografi til Norges historie siden 1966 og en bibliografi om norsk skjønnliteratur i Italia. Artikler om faglige emner.

John Chamberlain (b. 1938), B.A., M.A., (University of Leeds), Ph.D. (University of London), Canada Council Doctoral Fellowship to study Ibsen in relation to English Literature in London 1967—1970. Visiting Fellow at the University of East Anglia 1973—1974. He has taught in England and Canada and is now Associate Professor of English Literature at the University of Regina. He has published a number of articles including «Tragic Heroism in 'Rosmersholm'» *(Modern Drama,* 1974), «Ibsen's 'Vildanden' in relation to Georg Brandes's 'Gustave Flaubert' and Flaubert's 'Un Cæur Simple'» *(Scandinavica,*

1975) and «'Gengangere' and 'Emigrantlitteraturen'»)*Scandinavica,* 1977). He is at present preparing a book entitled *Ibsen: The Open Vision.*

Derek Russel Davis, (b. 1914), M.D. from Cambridge University 1946. Fellow of The Royal College of Physicians, Fellow of The Royal College of Psyshiatrists. Professor of Mental Health, University of Bristol since 1962, formerly Reader in Medicial Psychology, University of Cambridge and Fellow of Clare College, Cambridge, Emeritus 1979. His academic interests centre on pattern of interaction and crises in families; author of *Pilot Error* (Air Ministtry) and *An Introduction to Psychopathology* (Oxford Unviersity Press) and numerous articles in medical and psychological journals.

Maurice Gravier, Professeur à l'Université de Paris-Sorbonne (langues et litteratures Scandinaves), Directeur de l'Ecole Supérieure d'Interprètes et de Traducteurs, ancien Président de l' Université Internationale du Théatre, Vice-Président de la Société d'Histoire du Théatre, Membre de la Kungliga Vitterhetsakademi (Stockholm) – A publié entre autres, *Tegnér et la France* (1943), Strindberg et le Théatre moderne (1949), *Le féminisme et l'amour dans la littérature norvégienne* (1968), *Ibsen* (1973) et plusieurs articles sur Ibsen, Codirecteur de la Revue *Etudes Germaniques* – Traducteurs de plusieurs pièces de théatre (Strindberg, Soya, Schütt/Lagerkvist).

Otto Hageberg (f. 1936) universitetslektor i nordisk litteratur ved Universitetet i Oslo. Sekretær for det første internasjonale Ibsenseminar, Oslo 1965, med i komitéen for det fjerde, Skien 1978. Har redigert antologien *Omkring «Peer Gynt»* (1967) og skriver etterord til *Vildanden, Rosmersholm, Fruen fra havet* og *Hedda Gabler* i Henrik Ibsen: *Samlede verker,* bd. V (1978-utgave til 150-årsjubileet).

Daniel Haakonsen (b. 1917), Ph.D. at the University of Oslo 1951, Associate Professor of Scandinavian literature at the University of Oslo in 1954, Professor 1966. His works include: *Skabelsen i Henrik Wergelands diktning* (1951), *Henrik Ibsens realisme* (1957), *Arnulf Øverland* (1966), and *Henrik Ibsens «Peer Gynt»* (1967). Various articles including Ethical Implications in Ibsen's Drama *(Ibsenårbok* 1968—69) and Et marxistisk syn på Ibsen *(Ibsenårbok* 1972).

Andrew K. Kennedy (b. 1931), B.A., Ph.D., (University of Bristol), is Senior Lecturer in English Literature at the University of Bergen. He was Visiting Fellow at the University of Edinburgh Institute for Advanced Studies in the Humanities (1977), and he has been elected to a Visiting Fellowship at Clare Hall, Cambridge. His critical studies of drama include *Six Dramatists in Search of a Language,* Cambridge, 1975, and contributions to *Modern Drama, The Yearbook of English Studies,* Theatrical Literature, 1979. He is currently working on a full-scale study of dramatic dialogue.

Charles Leland (b. 1928), priest in the Congregation of St. Basil, was educated at Oberlin College (U.S.A.), Oxford University (England), and St. Michael's College in the University of Toronto, where he is now Associate Professor of English, specializing in Renaissance Literature and Modern Drama. He also conducts a seminar on Ibsen and Strindberg. He has published articles on Ibsen in *The Chesterton Review, Ibsenårboken,* and *Modern Drama.*

Arne Røed (1918), M. A. from the University of Oslo (1948); since 1960 Reader in

English at the Norwegian Naval Academy in Bergen. Various articles, mainly on subjects from English literature. An article on *Little Eyolf, 'The Crutch is Floating'*, was published in the Ibsen-årbok 1974, and a study of *The Master Builder* in the Ibsen Yearbook 1977.

Sandra Saari (b. 1939), B. A. (Arleton College) 1961, M. A. 1964, Ph.D. (Occidental College) 1968, professor of comparative literature and chairman of the humanities division at Eisenhower College in Seneca Falls, N.Y. Among her publications are various articles on Ibsen.

Toshihiko Sato (b. 1929), Ph.D. (University of Washington), 1966. The recipient of Fulbright and Thompson Fellowships, 1954—55; American Philosophical Society Post-Doctoral Reasearch Travel Grant, 1969; American Council of Learned Societies Travel Grant, 1978; The University of Michigan and Northeast Asia Council Research Travel Grants, 1979. Professor of English at Virginia State College, and an author and editor of books, including *Scandinavian Folktales* (in Japanese), 1959. Also published Japanese translations of P. C. Asbjørnsen's *Norske Eventyr,* 1958; Poetry of H. Wergeland and H. Drachmann, 1960. Much of his writings treats Ibsen, particularly his influence in Japan such as «Ibsen and modern Japanese Theater,» *Orient-West,* 1962; «Henrik Ibsen in Japan,» *Edda,* 1962; «Ibsen and Emancipation of Woman in Japan,» *UNESCO Feature,* 1968; «Ibsen and Mayama Seika's *The First Man,»* *Proceedings of the VIth Congress of the International Comparative Literature Association,* 1975.

David Thomas, born 1942. Ph.D. from the University of Cambridge 1970. Since 1966 he has lectured in Drama at the University of Bristol. He has directed productions of operas and plays (including plays by Ibsen) at the Bristol Arts Centre, The Little Theatre, and the University Drama Department. Among his publications are essays on Ibsen, Danish theatre during the 1930s and comedy in Northern Europe. He is currently President of the Bristol Association of University Teachers.

Egil Törnqvist (1932), Swedish lecturer at Harvard University 1957—58, doctor in Comparative Literature at Uppsala University 1969, the same year professor of Scandinavian studies at the University of Amsterdam. Publications: *A Drama of Souls. Studies in O'Neill's Supernaturalistic Technique (diss.), (1968). Svenska dramastrukturer,* (1973). *Bergman och Strindberg.* Spöksonaten – *drama och iscenesättning, Dramaten 1973,* (1973). Articles on drama in various periodicals. Editor of *Drama och teater* (1968), *Ibsens dramatik* (1971). Edits since 1978 a series of Scandinavian literature in Dutch translation entitled Scandinavië/Meulenhoff Editie (Amsterdam).

Asbjørn Aarseth, (f. 1935) universitetslektor i allmenn litteratur, Universitetet i Bergen. Publikasjoner: *Den Nationale Scene 1901—31,* 1969. *Peer Gynt 1867—1970.* En bibliografi, 1970. *Dyret i mennesket, Et bidrag til tolkning av Henrik Ibsens «Peer Gynt»,* 1975, *Episke strukturer. Innføring i anvendt fortellingsteori,* 1976. Sammen med Atle Kittang: *Lyriske strukturer. Innføring i diktanalyse,* 1968 og senere utgaver. Sammen med Eiliv Eide: *Teorier om diktekunsten. Fra Platon til Goldman,* 1970.

Ibsen Society of America

The New York Ibsen Sesquicentennial Symposium met from May 9 through 13, 1978 to celebrate the enduring relevance of Henrik Ibsen's dramatic work in a series of meetings, exhibits, panel discussions, dinners, and performances at the Pratt Institute in Brooklyn and in Manhattan. Organized and directed by Professor Rolf Fjelde – whose father sculpted from life the 1885 bust of Ibsen and whose own recasting of Ibsen into contemporary American idiom issued on 20 March 1978, *Ibsen: The Complete Major Prose Plays* – this assembly focused on current interpretation and performance by scholarly critics and theatre professionals in the United States and Canada. Summarizing the events of the Symposium at its concluding meeting, Professor Emeritus Einar Haugen asserted that such intellectual and insightful exchange as had occurred at these meetings should not cease. He therefore moved the formation of the Ibsen Society of America.

In January 1979, the Ibsen society of America held its organizational meeting. In adopting its by-laws, the Society averred its purpose to be primarily,

> to foster and further an informed understanding of the works of Henrik Ibsen, particularly as they have been and continue to be interpreted textually and produced theatrically in the United States and Canada, through such activities as lectures, readings, performances, discussions, conferences, exhibitions, archives, research projects and publications; and secondarily, to explore the larger context of those works in Ibsen's life and his age, along with the works of those who have influenced his art and those whom in turn he has influenced.

The ISA seeks those scholars, critics, directors, actors, designers, and historians whose interest in Ibsen's work would further these goals. Further information can be obtained from Professor Rolf Fjelde, ISA President, c/o Mellon Programs in Humanities, DeKalb hall 3, Pratt Institute, Brooklyn, N.Y. 11205, or from Professor Sandra Saari, ISA Secretary, Eisenhower College, Seneca Falls, New York 13148.